CLIMATE CHANGE, CATTLE, AND THE INTERNATIONAL LEGAL ORDER

Livestock food systems need to be rapidly rethought to tackle the global climate crisis. This book examines how climate concerns for the livestock sector are governed in international law and addresses the sector's inclusion (or lack thereof) across the international governance of climate change, agriculture, forests and trade.

The book provides a wide-ranging analysis of legal regimes at the international level that affect emissions from cattle (and where relevant, livestock more broadly). On this basis, tensions, interactions, and common themes for livestock emissions mitigation across the international climate change, forestry, agricultural and agri-trade regime are identified. This showcases where productive synergies and damaging tensions have emerged across the cross-cutting nature of livestock governance, enabling goals of fairer and more effective emissions mitigation for the sector to be achieved.

In addition to addressing issues such as food security and public health, the book highlights the problem of affluence in reducing cattle emissions from meat consumption. This key insight is significant in terms of tackling future livestock emissions trajectories, particularly in relation to securing climate justice within the agricultural sector and securing equitable and effective livestock solutions.

The book is a key text for all those with an interest in the legal governance of climate change and agriculture, adding to the timely debate on the future sustainability of the global diet and the relationship between affluence and climate change.

Climate Change, Cattle, and the International Legal Order

Rebecca Williams

• HART •
OXFORD • LONDON • NEW YORK • NEW DELHI • SYDNEY

HART PUBLISHING

Bloomsbury Publishing Plc

Kemp House, Chawley Park, Cumnor Hill, Oxford, OX2 9PH, UK

1385 Broadway, New York, NY 10018, USA

29 Earlsfort Terrace, Dublin 2, Ireland

First published in Great Britain 2024

A catalogue record for this book is available from the British Library.

A catalogue record for this book is available from the Library of Congress.

Library of Congress Control Number: 2024931655

ISBN: HB: 978-1-50996-858-9
ePDF: 978-1-50996-860-2
ePub: 978-1-50996-859-6

Typeset by Compuscript Ltd, Shannon

ACKNOWLEDGEMENTS

Many wonderful people helped in the process of writing this book, which began as PhD research at the European University Institute in 2017. First of all, the biggest thanks must go to my PhD supervisor, Professor Joanne Scott. Joanne provided endless academic and personal support throughout and beyond the PhD process, and I could fill pages of this Acknowledgement to Joanne alone as her mentorship and support will stick with me for the entirety of my academic career and beyond. My thesis examiners, Professor Neha Jain, Professor Maria Lee and Dr Jolene Lin, also provided invaluable feedback and motivation in driving me to develop my PhD research into this book. Special thanks must also go to Professor Michael Cardwell and Tom Robinson of the FAO for their support in developing my thinking in the early stages of my PhD. And last, of course, a thank you to the EUI Environmental Law and Governance Working Group members over the years who provided me with plentiful feedback, numerous enriching exchanges and, of course, coffees in Villa Salviati's gardens over the years.

Since completing my PhD, I have been lucky to work with numerous supportive colleagues at the University of Strathclyde, Edinburgh Napier University, the University of Glasgow and beyond who have helped support me during the book-writing process. An extra big thank you to Dr Stephanie Switzer, Dr Mitchell Lennan and Dr Arpitha Kodiveri for their friendship and feedback on the draft chapters during the writing process. The staff at Hart Publishing have also been wonderful with their support in getting this book published (especially with a cover I love so much!).

Lastly, a big thank you to the family and friends who supported me throughout the PhD and book-writing process in addition to the whirlwinds of early career academic life. From the EUI, Julian, Becky, Justine, Sarah, Matilda and Sophie all made my time at the EUI so memorable, and I feel lucky to have made such wonderful friends. In Glasgow, a big thank you to my friends in my new hometown. As always, thank you to my family for helping and supporting me in every way they can. I always said I would be the first doctor in the family (albeit medical, before realising I was scared of blood) so I hope seeing my first book on your shelf will make you proud.

TABLE OF CONTENTS

ABBREVIATIONS

AoA	Agreement on Agriculture 1994
CBDR(RC)	Common But Differentiated Responsibilities and Respective Capabilities
COP	Conference of the Parties
CRP	United States Conservation Reserve Program
DSU	Dispute Settlement Understanding
DSB	Dispute Settlement Body
FAO	Food and Agriculture Organization
FAST	Food and Agriculture for Sustainable Transformation
FBDG	Food-Based Dietary Guidelines
GASL	Global Agenda on Sustainable Livestock
GATT	General Agreement on Tariffs and Trade
GHG	greenhouse gas
GLEAM	Global Livestock Environmental Assessment Model
I-CAN	Initiative on Climate Action and Nutrition
IPCC	International Panel on Climate Change
KJWA	Koronivia Joint Work on Agriculture
LULUCF	land use, land use change, and forestry
NDC	Nationally Determined Contribution
PPCerrado	Action Plan for the Prevention and Control of Deforestation and Forest Fires in the Cerrado biome
PPCDAm	Action Plan for the Prevention and Control of Deforestation in the Legal Amazon
REDD+	Reducing emissions from deforestation and forest degradation in developing countries

REPS	Ireland Rural Environment Protection Scheme
SBI	Subsidiary Body for Implementation
SBSTA	Subsidiary Body for Scientific and Technological Advice
UN	United Nations
UNFCCC	United Nations Framework Convention on Climate 1992
WHO	World Health Organization
WTO	World Trade Organization
WWF	World Wide Fund for Nature
UNFF	United Nations Forum on Forests
UNEP	United Nations Environment Programme
USDA	United States Department for Agriculture

TABLE OF CASES

TABLE OF CONVENTIONS AND OTHER RELEVANT LEGAL DOCUMENTS

Conventions and International Agreements

International Decisions, Agreements, and Declarations

United Frame Convention on Climate Change (UNFCCC)

World Trade Organisation (WTO)

Other International Institutions

European Union Legal Documents

Introduction

With the International Panel on Climate Change (IPCC) projecting increases of global temperature of between 2.5 and 10°C by 2100, the need for a successful global response to the climate crisis is imperative more than ever before.[1] Climate change has, and will have, catastrophic and widespread impacts on all aspects of daily life, including health, weather conditions, water security, and food and agriculture – particularly in locations that are especially vulnerable to temperature increases and the effects of climate change, most often in developing countries.

Increasingly, the environmental impact of animal agriculture is being recognised. In the past, climate criticism was largely reserved for the fossil fuel sector, or even the transport and aviation sectors. However, now it has been realised that the agricultural sector is also a major contributor to the climate crisis, albeit one that is often overlooked in emissions reduction plans. This is despite the fact that some reports suggest that food emissions alone generate between 21 and 37 percent of all global greenhouse gas (GHG) emissions.[2] Beef and dairy in particular contribute significantly to agricultural emissions, amounting to 40 and 20 percent respectively of all agricultural emissions due to the digestive process of cattle ('enteric fermentation').[3]

At the same time, global hunger is on the increase. Due to agricultural system vulnerability to climate change, global food insecurity is likely to worsen in the future – decreasing yields and the viability of agricultural production. The distribution of climate change impacts on food systems and security is likely to be uneven, particularly exacerbating food insecurity in areas that are already vulnerable to hunger and undernutrition due to their geographical conditions.[4] Beyond this, the world population is projected to increase rapidly, causing significant increases in global food demand if current dietary patterns continue. Some reports suggest that meat consumption is expected to increase up to 60 percent by 2050 from a

[1] IPCC, 'Summary for Policymaker' in TF Stocket et al, *Climate Change 2013: The Physical Science Basis. Contribution of Working Group I to the Fifth Assessment Report of the Intergovernmental Panel on Climate Change* (Cambridge University Press, 2013).

[2] See more in C Mbow et al, *Food Security in Climate Change and Land: An IPCC Special Report on Climate Change, Desertification, Land Degradation, Sustainable Land Management, Food Security, and Greenhouse Gas Fluxes in Terrestrial Ecosystems* (IPCC, 2019).

[3] PJ Gerber and Food and Agriculture Organization of the United Nations (eds), *Tackling Climate Change through Livestock: A Global Assessment of Emissions and Mitigation Opportunities* (FAO, 2013) eg 15–19.

[4] T Wheeler and J von Braun, 'Climate Change Impacts on Global Food Security' (2013) 341 *Science* 508.

2010 baseline.[5] All the while, wealthier countries are seeing rising cases of non-communicable diseases and obesity from poor and excessive dietary choices, and debates over 'plant-based eating' are running riot in public discourse – despite climate concerns.

Regardless of the specifics of the 'ideal global diet' being discussed, a common response to calls for dietary shifts away from resource-intensive livestock products is often seen – reluctance. Whether in the policymaking sphere or around the traditional family dining table, the need for a global sustainable diet often evokes a strong response. The 'uncomfortable knowledge', as Rayner coins, that our dietary choices and agricultural traditions can cause detrimental environmental or public health impacts has led to an unwillingness to address our need for global dietary change.[6] Acknowledging the environmental impacts of livestock reveals a host of substantive epistemological disagreements about the organisational and ethical values of our food systems, thereby disrupting the very foundations of our agricultural systems.

The international legal order is by no means isolated from the proliferation of meat and dairy consumption globally and the distribution of its climate impacts. Despite this, little attention is paid to livestock emissions mitigation in policy or environmental law literature – particularly when compared to other interests relating to agricultural production, such as adaptation, food security or economic interests. With food systems going all the way down to the kitchen table and interwoven with major socioeconomic issues such as global hunger, is the livestock sector a particularly 'untouchable' sector when mandating climate action? This book turns attention to the international legal order and how livestock emissions mitigation can be achieved more fairly through the governance of the global cattle sector.

Given the most significant dietary shifts required for a global sustainable diet are required from wealthier groups in higher-income countries and the effects of climate change are most drastic in poorer global regions,[7] reluctance to undertake dietary changes is also a significant climate justice issue. How does the current international legal order for climate change and cattle contribute to or further embed injustices within the global agricultural system? Is the need for a global sustainable diet acknowledged, or is the 'knowledge' of the link between affluence and meat consumption dismissed, diverted, displaced or even denied?[8]

Overall, the book begins to address the gap that exists in environmental legal literature surrounding livestock. It provides a broad macro-analysis of various legal regimes on the international level that affect emissions from cattle (and

[5] B Revell, 'Meat and Milk Consumption 2050: The Potential for Demand-Side Solutions to Greenhouse Gas Emissions Reduction' (2015) 14 *EuroChoices* 4.

[6] S Rayner, 'Uncomfortable Knowledge: The Social Construction of Ignorance in Science and Environmental Policy Discourses' (2012) 41 *Economy and Society* 107.

[7] More detail on the specifics of these dietary shifts is outlined in ch 1.

[8] Rayner (n 6) from 113.

where relevant, livestock more broadly). On the basis of this, tensions and synergies across these regimes in achieving cattle emissions mitigation can be identified and analysed. Through this analysis, it is possible to strengthen productive synergies and reduce damaging tensions to promote greater emissions reduction for the sector.

The book particularly provides a basis for further research into how better integration of climate concerns into agricultural emissions can be achieved, challenging the narrative of agriculture as the 'evasive' sector in action against climate change. These conclusions provide valuable insight into what climate justice should look like in the agricultural sector, uncovering and reconciling current attributions of responsibility for livestock emissions against a backdrop of human development needs, such as food security. The role of affluence in driving cattle emissions is unveiled, before suggesting approaches to tackle the environmental impacts of affluence and consumption more generally in a rapidly changing global society.

Outline of the Book

The book addresses four key international legal regimes that form the international legal order for the cattle sector and climate change: the international climate regime, the international agricultural regime, the international forest regime and the international agri-trade regime.[9] Through dissecting approaches to cattle emissions in these legal regimes, it is possible to diagnose where the international legal order falls short in addressing livestock emissions. In other words, delineating (1) which interests are promoted or ignored under a particular regime, (2) who (or what) is viewed as responsible for causing cattle emissions and (3) who is viewed as the actor deemed responsible for mitigating emissions.[10] As it stands, the current international legal order legitimises certain solutions, whilst neglecting or devaluing others – in particular, the promotion of dietary change in higher-income groups as a mitigation solution for the agricultural sector.

As alluded to previously, the international legal order for climate change and cattle still has to balance broader socioeconomic interests alongside climate concerns within its international legal frameworks. Through the course of the book, three main approaches to governing livestock within the international legal order for the cattle sector are identified to varying degrees, namely: (1) mitigation, (2) food security and (3) other intersecting interests, such as agricultural industry

[9] Though other regimes such as the animal welfare, biodiversity, or animal health regimes are also relevant, but are not covered in this book.

[10] See more on different 'framing' of approaches to issues generally in RD Benford and DA Snow, 'Framing Processes and Social Movements: An Overview and Assessment' (2000) 26 *Annual Review of Sociology* 611.

interests. Through outlining and analysing the occurrence, legal embeddedness and interrelationships of these different approaches to livestock governance, it is possible to see which cattle emissions solutions are promoted among which global actors – ultimately highlighting the gap that exists within these international legal regimes for recognising the role of developed countries and wealthy groups in addressing livestock emissions.

Figure 1 The three main categorisations of themes identified in the international legal order for the cattle sector and climate change

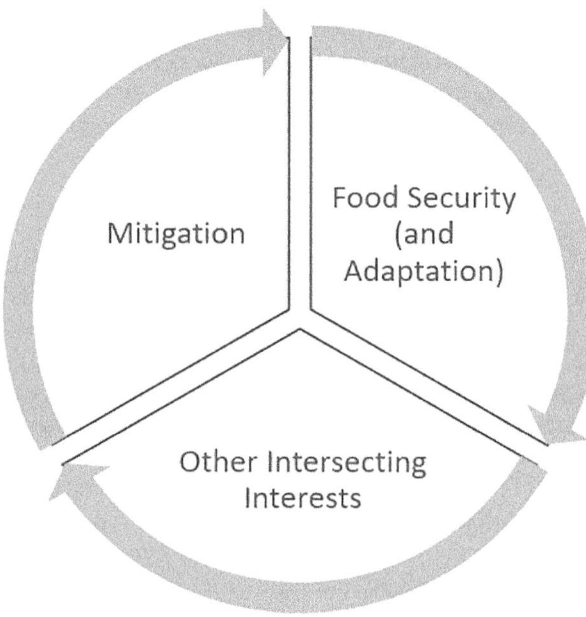

The book consists of six chapters: first, an introduction to the cattle sector and climate change (chapter one), followed by a regime-by-regime analysis of the international climate regime (chapter two), the international agricultural regime (chapter three), the international forest regime (chapter four) and the international agricultural trade regime (chapter five) and their respective approaches to livestock governance for climate change purposes. The final chapter concludes the text (chapter six), highlighting key takeaways from the regime-by-regime analysis of the international legal order for climate change and cattle. The approach, scope and content of each of these chapters will be provided in more detail below to outline the content of the book.

Chapter one provides an introduction to the cattle sector and climate change, outlining the science behind livestock emissions, the history of beef and dairy consumption, and the current emissions picture globally for the sector, both from a production and consumption perspective. Different types of climate solutions for livestock emissions are outlined depending on the actor being targeted. However, the need for more than technical or supply-side solutions to help meet the necessary emissions reduction pathway for the sector is highlighted, particularly emphasising the need for dietary change among wealthier groups and underpinning its environmental and health rationale. This provides context to the rest of the book which often highlights the role of high-consuming nations in reducing their emissions and the mutual public health benefits of doing so.

Following the previous chapter's outlining of the current landscape for beef and dairy production and consumption, chapter two undertakes a mapping exercise of the international climate regime to provide an overview of the historical reluctance to address cattle emissions within the United Nations Framework Convention on Climate Change (UNFCCC) forum. Through analysing provisions of the Paris Agreement 2015, and surrounding legal documents and negotiations up to COP27, gaps in livestock emissions coverage in the international climate regime are unveiled. This begins to reveal the lagging nature of cattle emissions mitigation globally, particularly within high-consuming groups, such as developed countries.

Chapter three builds on these findings, focusing now on the international agricultural regime and particularly work by the Food and Agriculture Organisation (FAO) relating to agricultural emissions. The chapter highlights the FAO's expert role in international agri-climate governance, and its recognition of the socioeconomic importance of the livestock sector alongside its novel promotion of demand-side solutions to tackle livestock emissions, such as dietary change in wealthier groups where public health is being compromised by dietary choices. However, the limits of the FAO's current role in international livestock governance is emphasised. Nonetheless, the technical expertise of the FAO for livestock solutions and its role in informal legal forums are still deemed valuable in encouraging fairer and more effective livestock emissions mitigation.

Chapter four analyses the international forest regime and the extent and manner in which it addresses the climate impacts of livestock production. Firstly, the fragmented and decentralised nature of international forest governance is outlined, noting the contentious nature of Global North/South political relations with respect to managing forests. Then, initiatives tackling the climate impacts of forest degradation are analysed to determine their coverage of livestock emissions. Ultimately, this coverage is seen to be weak – even in 'hot spot' regions such as Brazil which has been labelled as a 'poster-child' for initiatives such as the 'Reducing emissions from deforestation and forest degradation in developing countries' Programme (REDD+) in the past. Lastly, the predominantly production-based nature of addressing forest emissions under REDD+ is highlighted as problematic because agricultural emissions driven by consumption (especially from developed countries) are not a focus of the initiative.

Chapter five focuses on the international agri-trade regime, namely World Trade Organisation (WTO) law and its specific Agreement on Agriculture 1994 (AoA). A strong agricultural trade liberalisation mandate is identified from the Agreement's provisions, and the impact of this liberalisation is extensively outlined from an agri-economic perspective. A high threshold for WTO-compliant domestic livestock emissions mitigation measures from members is established, in addition to a discussion of food security 'safety nets' and provisions under the AoA and their potential environmental impacts. However ultimately, the main takeaway of the chapter is that the agri-trade regime's focus on agricultural trade liberalisation is seen to dominate other opportunities for members to create WTO-compliant livestock emissions mitigation measures – at odds with the general goal of cattle emissions reduction being addressed in this book.

Chapter six concludes the book, pulling together common themes and tensions from across the chapters to help shed light on the current institutional approaches to cattle emissions mitigation and avenues for further livestock emissions reduction in the future. Common themes across the book are identified. These include: (1) agriculture being an 'evasive' sector for climate change mitigation; (2) a preference for policymakers to refer to agri-climate issues in terms of adaptation or food security rather than mitigation; and (3) a common emerging trend of synergies between agri-climate goals and public health being utilised for further livestock emission reductions goals. A key common tension identified from the analysis is also provided, namely, a tension between agricultural industry interests and agricultural emissions reduction.

The last part of the conclusion is dedicated to one key lesson of the book – highlighting affluence as the evasive issue in reducing cattle emissions. The importance of this key insight in terms of tackling future livestock emissions trajectories is outlined, particularly in relation to the climate justice dimension of climate mitigation. The responsibility of both affluent countries and affluent groups within poorer countries to reduce excessive consumption of beef and dairy is emphasised in light of the established principle of Common but Differentiated Responsibilities and Respective Capabilities in light of different national circumstances (CBDRRC). From this, a better understanding of responsibility attribution between wealthier and poorer actors can be derived and future directions for fairer and more effective livestock solutions can be delineated. Moreover, this understanding provides additional insight for tackling broader consumption-driven environmental issues that are pervasive in our current global society.

Overall, a vast amount of substantive content is covered in the book to help provide a basis and inspiration for further research into the agri-climate sector and the role livestock plays in reducing global GHG emissions. It is hoped that following the completion of this initial groundwork, further academic legal study can be undertaken for the sector.

Methodology, Scope and Use of Terms

A brief outlining of the methodology used in the book's analysis is beneficial for understanding the approach of the author in addressing the largely unexplored international legal order for climate change and cattle. Firstly, the book's methodological approach is summarised, explaining the 'nexus approach' used to delineate the scope of the analysis. Then the use of terms, such as regime, is expanded upon before outlining the importance of utilising this methodology to ensure better coherence of livestock emissions goals across the international legal order for climate change and cattle.

The Nexus Approach to Climate Change and Cattle

There are various drivers of the climate impacts of the cattle sector. Many different regimes play a role in the functioning of the cattle sector – whether they be economic, such as the agricultural trade regime; environmental, such as the forest regime; or regimes with more social goals, such as food security or ending hunger. Due to the diversity of goals and objectives of each of these regimes, their parallel functioning may not always be coherent and synergistic. To address this heterogeneity and divergence, the book uses a nexus approach to map the relevant regimes at play when considering cattle sector emissions mitigation. This approach also helped to direct the scope of the text's analysis and to inform a broad, macrolevel approach to the issue of livestock emissions – rather than a more problem-specific analysis (such as solely the deforestation impact of livestock). This better aligns with the book's overall goal of providing an initial assessment and overview of the international laws and policies currently in place that help (and hinder) an overall objective of livestock emissions mitigation.

The nexus approach itself is seen as a way to understand and systematise the interdependences of different regimes, by 'balanc[ing] conflicting sectoral objectives', 'enhanc[ing] resource efficiency' and 'promot[ing] policy coherence and integration'.[11] Equal importance is given to each of the regimes included in the nexus, and to the objectives that they pursue, thereby requiring 'conscious efforts' by sectoral actors to 'enhance synergies' and 'minimise trade-offs' across different policy domains.[12] The end goal of using a nexus approach is to achieve overall 'system efficiency' with the emergence of integrated and mutually beneficial solutions, rather than the prioritisation of the goal(s) pursued by any individual sectoral regime within the nexus. This is particularly important where non-negotiable

[11] C Soto Golcher and IJ Visseren-Hamakers, 'Framing and Integration in the Global Forest, Agriculture and Climate Change Nexus' (2018) 36 *Environment and Planning C: Politics and Space* 1415.

[12] ibid; G Rasul and B Sharma, 'The Nexus Approach to Water–Energy–Food Security: An Option for Adaptation to Climate Change' (2016) 16 *Climate Policy* 682.

human development goals, such as food security or ending global hunger, exist within the nexus and require balancing against environmental goals.

Soto Golcher and Visseren Hamaker identify the existence of the global forest–agriculture–climate change nexus as these regimes are closely interconnected, with action (or lack thereof) in each individual regime causing knock-on effects for the rest of the regimes in the nexus.[13] For example, agriculture and forestry are reported to account for almost 25 percent of all anthropogenic GHG emissions, while agriculture has been found to be a leading cause of deforestation globally.[14] Agricultural production uses scarce natural resources such as land and forests for both cattle rearing and feed production, thereby removing potential carbon sinks from the planet. By-products of agricultural production, such as methane emissions from enteric fermentation or manure, also directly produce GHG emissions.

Figure 2 The nexus for climate change and cattle (including main sources and aspects of production)

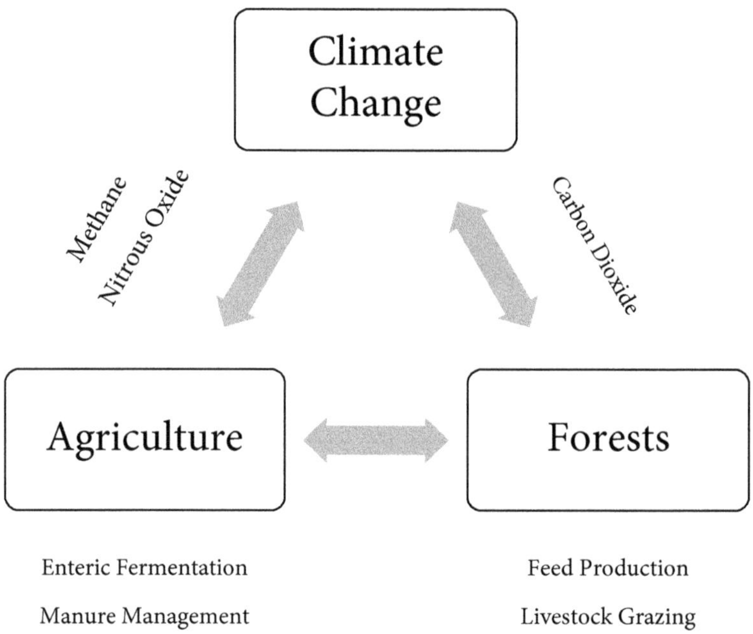

[13] Soto Golcher and Visseren-Hamakers (n 12).

[14] G Kissinger, 'Linking Forests and Food Production in the REDD+ Context' in M Behnassi, O Pollmann and G Kissinger (eds), *Sustainable Food Security in the Era of Local and Global Environmental Change* (Springer Netherlands, 2013) http://link.springer.com/10.1007/978-94-007-6719-5_4, accessed 20 January 2020; Soto Golcher and Visseren-Hamakers (n 12).

Figure 2 presents the nexus of sectoral regimes that exists when exploring the climate impact of the cattle sector. The boxes show the different regimes that exist within the nexus explored in the book – agriculture, climate change, forests – although other regimes, such as the biodiversity, animal welfare or animal health regimes, may also be relevant but are not included in the book's analysis. As this book focuses particularly on climate change mitigation, the figure's text identifies the drivers of GHG emissions from cattle farming that each regime may be expected to address. For example, the forest regime may be expected to regulate the production of animal feed on previously forested land. The text also outlines the types of emissions that each of these drivers affects; for example, methane emissions stemming from the digestive process of cattle herds. On a practical note, the identification of this nexus resulted in the analytical scope of the book including key international institutions and documents from each of these regimes on the international level, including any trade-offs or synergies caused by their interdependence.

With regard to conceptualising the meaning of a 'regime', the International Law Commission Study Report of the Fragmentation of International Law suggests a regime can be defined in many terms: 'In a narrow sense, the term is used to denote a special set of secondary rules under the law of State responsibility that claims primacy to the general rules concerning consequences of a violation.'[15] In a broader sense, the term is used to refer to 'interrelated wholes of primary and secondary rules, sometimes also referred to as 'systems or subsystems of rules that cover some particular problem differently from the way it would be covered under general law. … Sometimes whole fields of functional specialization, of diplomatic and academic expertise, are described as self-contained (whether or not that word is used) in the sense that special rules and techniques of interpretation and administration are thought to apply.'[16]

Due to the largely unexplored nature of livestock emissions as an area of academic study, the concept of regime in this book takes a largely institutional approach in the first instance. Nevertheless, it also encapsulates relevant stakeholder or national interests and systems where institutional responses to livestock emissions and its surrounding issues are lacking, undeveloped or unclear. Language of 'governance' is also used to refer to both traditional forms of regulation as well as soft-law approaches to livestock emissions mitigation.[17]

In light of these approaches, analysis of the international climate regime particularly looks at the United Framework Convention on Climate Change (UNFCCC)

[15] See more Study Group of the International Law Commission, *Fragmentation of International Law: Difficulties Arising from the Diversification and Expansion of International Law* (ILC, 2006) A/CN.4/L.682, from 32.

[16] ibid.

[17] See more on this generally throughout the book, but also in KW Abbott and D Snidal, 'Hard and Soft Law in International Governance' (2000) 54 *International Organization* 421.

and the Paris Agreement 2015 (including its broader governance architecture). In terms of agricultural regimes, both the FAO's work on livestock is analysed, in addition to agricultural trade law, such as the AoA 1994. International forest law is also analysed, looking at international mechanisms such as the REDD(+) programmes, though prominent non-state initiatives, such as the Forest Stewardship Council labelling scheme, are also included.

The benefit of this nexus approach in the international legal order for climate change is that it can help to systematise the conflicting sectoral objectives and improve overall policy coherence in the regimes analysed. The approaches of these different regimes to livestock may not always be compatible, and different regimes may be working at odds with each other depending on their priorities and perspectives. For example, as will be shown in the subsequent chapter, the high consumption of livestock products in many wealthy regions of the world is contrasted with the existence of significant global hunger statistics. As a result, it is plausible that certain agricultural regimes may have an objective of increasing access to food for the hungry through increased agricultural production. Equally, it is also plausible that public health and environmental regimes may want to decrease high dietary climate footprints and encourage 'healthier' diets for public health reasons. Unless these regimes are well integrated, there is the potential for unproductive, or 'stalemate' tensions to arise between different regimes' objectives.[18]

Analysing institutional approaches (particularly in light of new contentious or 'disruptive' information, such as agricultural emissions science or the role of sustainable diets in climate change mitigation[19]) can reveal underlying biases or assumptions of actors that have may so far gone unchallenged.[20] Sometimes, it can reveal that stakeholders engage in certain behaviours to avoid confronting or fully acknowledging this disruptive knowledge in their strategies or organisations – such as denial, dismissal, diversion (or decoy) and displacement.[21]

The identification of instances of inter-regime objective conflicts can be important in developing and creating new, improved livestock emissions approaches which involve a dynamic and, ideally, a deliberative process of engagement, negotiation and debate across relevant international forums.[22] This is particularly important because, as the rest of this book will demonstrate, a multitude of

[18] For more on these stalemate situations, see AJ Hoffman, 'Talking Past Each Other? Cultural Framing of Skeptical and Convinced Logics in the Climate Change Debate' (2011) 24(1) *Organisation & Environment* 3–33.

[19] Rayner (n 6) 113–14.

[20] ibid.

[21] ibid.

[22] See more in C Jonathan, 'Four Stages of Social Movements' in *Sociology Reference Guide: Theories of Social Movements*, 2nd edn (Salem Press, 2016).

(socially, environmentally and economically) important objectives exist within the cattle sector and climate change mitigation nexus, such as agricultural emissions mitigation, food security and farmer livelihood protection. However, first, the subsequent chapter will outline the emissions landscape of cattle emissions to provide context to the rest of the book.

1

Introduction to Climate Change and the Cattle Sector

Climate change is caused predominantly by human activities that increase atmospheric concentrations of GHGs, such as carbon dioxide (CO_2), methane (CH_4), nitrous oxide (N_2O) and certain fluorinated gases. Climate change has, and will continue to have, catastrophic and widespread impacts on all facets of society, including water, energy, transportation, wildlife, agriculture, ecosystems and human health – particularly in locations that are especially vulnerable to temperature increases and the effects of climate change, most often in developing countries. The IPCC predicts that a global response to the climate crisis is imperative more than ever before.[1] Yet, current mitigation pathways are not enough to prevent the devastating impacts of climate change on the planet, its ecosystems and humans.[2]

Historically in environmental campaigns, the act of burning fossil fuels is presented as the primary human activity that contributes to global GHG emissions, whether it be through energy production or the transport sector. However, following the publication of seminal reports, such as the FAO's *Livestock's Long Shadow*, it has become more apparent that the global agricultural sector, and particularly the livestock sector, contributes significantly to global GHG emissions.[3] Conservative estimates report that livestock supply chains account for nearly 14.5 percent of global GHG emissions.[4] The supply of beef and milk is reported to account for 40 and 20 percent of these emissions, respectively.[5] As a result, pursuing global 'sustainable diets' (commonly classified as those including fewer livestock products) and reducing the emissions impact of the agricultural

[1] IPCC, 'Summary for Policymaker' in TF Stocket et al, *Climate Change 2013: The Physical Science Basis. Contribution of Working Group I to the Fifth Assessment Report of the Intergovernmental Panel on Climate Change* (Cambridge University Press, 2013).

[2] See here 'Climate Action Tracker', https://climateactiontracker.org/, accessed 24 August 2021.

[3] H Steinfeld et al, *Livestock's Long Shadow: Environmental Issues and Options* (FAO, 2006) www.fao.org/publications/card/en/c/9655af93-7f88-58fc-84e8-d70a9a4d8bec/, accessed 6 October 2020.

[4] PJ Gerber and Food and Agriculture Organization of the United Nations (eds), *Tackling Climate Change through Livestock: A Global Assessment of Emissions and Mitigation Opportunities* (FAO, 2013) 115–19 or xiii.

[5] ibid.

sector has been highlighted by the IPCC as imperative in stabilising atmospheric concentrations of GHGs.[6]

However, climate change is not the only issue impacting the global agricultural sector. Global hunger continues to rise, and global food security is further vulnerable to the impacts of climate change on agriculture – likely worsening future yields and the viability of agricultural production.[7] The distribution of climate change impacts on the agricultural sector and food security is likely to be uneven, particularly intensifying food insecurity in areas that are already susceptible to hunger and malnutrition due to their geographical conditions.[8] Alongside this, the world population continues to grow rapidly, likely requiring significant increases in global food supply if current dietary patterns continue.[9] Meanwhile, wealthier countries are facing increasing public health concerns stemming from poor and excessive dietary choices, with contention surrounding 'plant-based diets' continually frequenting public discourse.

This initial chapter will set out some key initial tensions that surround the debate about sustainable diets, including environmental concerns, global hunger and public health considerations that stem from the inclusion of animal products, particularly beef and dairy, in the human diet.

The Environmental Impact of the Cattle Sector

Enteric Fermentation

Livestock production has wide-ranging environmental impacts, particularly on large and commercial scales. Beef and dairy production is particularly detrimental to the climate, with a large proportion of emissions from this production stemming from methane emissions from enteric fermentation. Enteric fermentation is part of the natural digestive process of ruminant animals (such as cattle, sheep, goats and buffalo). Microbes in the digestive tract (or rumen) decompose and ferment food, thereby causing large amounts of methane as a by-product. The FAO reports that 39 percent of all GHG emissions caused by livestock production stem from enteric fermentation.[10]

Methane is a unique GHG because it has a short atmospheric lifetime in addition to a high warming potential. The atmospheric lifetime of a GHG refers to the

[6] See more in C Mbow, et al. *Food Security in Climate Change and Land: An IPCC Special Report on Climate Change, Desertification, Land Degradation, Sustainable Land Management, Food Security, and Greenhouse Gas Fluxes in Terrestrial Ecosystems* (IPCC, 2019).

[7] See the most recent Global Hunger Index: 'Global Hunger Index 2023: Food Systems Transformation and Local Governance', www.globalhungerindex.org/, accessed 2 August 2023.

[8] T Wheeler and J von Braun, 'Climate Change Impacts on Global Food Security' (2013) 341 *Science* 508.

[9] ibid.

[10] Gerber et al (n 4) xiii.

length of time it takes for an atmospheric increase in a gas to return to a normal level – in other words, the length of time a gas remains in the atmosphere. The warming potential of a GHG is its ability to absorb and trap heat energy in the atmosphere and cause global warming effects. Methane is a short-lived pollutant in comparison to other GHG emissions. It has an atmospheric lifetime of only 12 years, whereas carbon dioxide has an atmospheric lifetime of up to 200 years.[11] Methane also has 86 times the global warming potential of carbon dioxide over a 20-year time frame.[12] As a result, cutting methane emissions could allow for more immediate emissions reductions than tackling solely carbon emissions.

Land-Use Impacts

Livestock rearing also contributes to the worsening of climate change through the land-use impacts of feed production and grazing. This is because the carbon-converting potential of forests is also destroyed during the process of land conversion or usage for livestock and their feed. Livestock require vast amounts of feed to meet the demand for animal products, making feed production the largest source of emissions from livestock production.[13] A single beef cow can require up to 6 kg of feed per day depending on their age, feed and gender.[14] It is reported that up to 34 percent of crops that are suitable for human consumption are fed to livestock instead.[15] On a global scale, the World Wide Fund for Nature (WWF) estimates that to grow the soy and maize required to feed livestock by 2030 on our current demand growth trajectory, agricultural land would need to expand by 280 million hectares.[16] This is equivalent to the land areas of Austria, Belgium, the Czech Republic, France, Germany, Italy, Ireland, the Netherlands, Poland, Portugal, Slovakia, Spain and the United Kingdom combined.[17]

There are particular global hotspots for agricultural expansion, often in biodiversity-sensitive regions. For example, animal agriculture has been reported to be responsible for up to 91 percent of the Amazon's destruction to date – around 1.4 million hectares of land per year between 2001 and 2012, resulting in a total

[11] DT Shindell et al, 'Improved Attribution of Climate Forcing to Emissions' (2009) 326 *Science* 716.

[12] S Solomon and Intergovernmental Panel on Climate Change (eds), '2.10.2 Direct Global Warming Potentials', *Climate Change 2007: The Physical Science Basis: Contribution of Working Group I to the Fourth Assessment Report of the Intergovernmental Panel on Climate Change* (Cambridge, Cambridge University Press, 2007).

[13] Gerber et al (n 4) 17.

[14] 'Agriculture, Forestry and Rural Economic Development', www.alberta.ca/agriculture-forestry-and-rural-economic-development.aspx, accessed 7 December 2021.

[15] M Berners-Lee et al, 'Current Global Food Production Is Sufficient to Meet Human Nutritional Needs in 2050 Provided There Is Radical Societal Adaptation' (2018) 6 *Elementa* 52.

[16] WWF, *Appetite for Destruction* (WWF, 2017) www.wwf.org.uk/updates/appetite-for-destruction, accessed 6 November 2018.

[17] ibid.

loss of 17.7 million hectares of land.[18] If current trends continue, the WWF reports that land-use change in the Amazon rainforest alone could double to 48 million hectares before 2030, meaning that more than a quarter of the Amazon would be without trees.[19] It is perhaps unsurprising then that the FAO reports feed production as the largest emissions source of livestock production, totalling 45 percent of all global livestock emissions.[20]

Manure Management

Other aspects of livestock production are also emissions intensive, both for cattle and other types of livestock. Manure itself contains carbon and nitrogen, and when it is stored in vast pools, breaks down anaerobically (without oxygen) to produce methane. Worryingly, one report suggests that a farm with 2,500 dairy cows can produce the same amount of waste as a city of 411,000 people.[21] Depending on the type of manure storage system adopted by cattle farms, these high levels of waste contribute to the significant methane emission levels of beef and dairy production processes. Nitrous oxide also has 100 times the global warming potential of carbon dioxide,[22] making it another potent gas that is often overlooked in favour of carbon emission reductions.

On top of this, manure is also often used as a fertiliser in agriculture, which can cause problems with nitrogen run-off and 'ocean dead zones'. It has been reported that 'ocean dead zones with zero oxygen have quadrupled in size since 1950 … while the number of very low oxygen sites near coasts have multiplied tenfold'.[23] Ocean 'dead zones' can occur as a result of eutrophication caused by livestock and feed crop farming. Eutrophication is a process where a water source gains too many nutrients, particularly phosphorus and nitrogen.[24] Rearing livestock can cause eutrophication, as poor manure management and fertiliser used in farming can cause 'run-off' into coastal waters and the ocean.[25] This is harmful as it causes an excessive growth of blue-green algae in a water system and shortages of oxygen, which in turn limits the normal functioning of ecosystems in these

[18] S Margulis, *Causes of Deforestation of the Brazilian Amazon* (World Bank, 2004) https://openknowledge.worldbank.org/handle/10986/15060, accessed 7 December 2021.

[19] WWF, *Deforestation* (WWF, undated) wwf.panda.org/our_work/forests/deforestation_fronts/deforestation_in_the_amazon, accessed 6 November 2017.

[20] Gerber et al (n 4) xiii.

[21] EF Barth et al, *Risk Management Evaluation for Concentrated Animal Feeding Operations* (Office of Research & Development, 2004) EPA/600/R-04/042, https://cfpub.epa.gov/si/si_public_record_report.cfm?Lab=NRMRL&dirEntryId=85107, accessed 7 December 2021.

[22] Solomon and IPCC Intergovernmental Panel on Climate Change (n 12).

[23] D Carrington, 'Oceans Suffocating as Huge Dead Zones Quadruple since 1950, Scientists Warn', *The Guardian*, 4 January 2018, www.theguardian.com/environment/2018/jan/04/oceans-suffocating-dead-zones-oxygen-starved, accessed 7 November 2019.

[24] National Geographic, 'Dead Zone' (National Geographic, undated) www.nationalgeographic.org/encyclopedia/dead-zone/, accessed 7 November 2011.

[25] ibid.

areas.[26] In particular, biodiversity in these ecosystems is negatively impacted, as many aquatic species cannot survive in the lower levels of oxygen stemming from the overpopulation of blue-green algae.[27]

Broader Environmental Impacts

The FAO reports that feed production and processing (including land-use change) and enteric fermentation from ruminants are the two main sources of GHG emissions, representing 45 and 39 percent of total emissions respectively, with manure storage and processing representing 10 percent.[28] The small remainder is attributable to the processing and transportation of animal products. However, livestock production has further environmental impacts beyond its climate impacts, including biodiversity loss and water usage issues.

Biodiversity

Biodiversity issues also arise when land-use change or deforestation occurs due to an expansion of pasture and feed croplands. Ecosystems and natural habitats are destroyed or altered during this expansion, thereby impacting the number and variety of species inhabiting these areas. The FAO itself has reported that livestock currently covers 30 percent of the Earth's land surface which was once the habitat for naturally occurring wildlife.[29] Furthermore, analysis of the World Conservation Union's Red List of Threatened Species also reports that most of the world's most threatened species are affected by habitat loss where livestock is a contributing factor.[30] It is therefore unsurprising that some studies report that animal agriculture is the leading cause of species extinction, ocean dead zones and habitat destruction globally.[31]

Water Usage

Industrial beef and dairy farming also contribute to issues with water resource management, including potential water shortages. One study reports that approximately 1,000 litres of water are required to produce 1 kg of cereal grain for

[26] ibid.

[27] See Carrington (n 23); also D Breitburg et al, 'Declining Oxygen in the Global Ocean and Coastal Waters' [2018] *Science* 359(6371).

[28] Gerber et al (n 4) xiii.

[29] ibid.

[30] ibid.

[31] TG Benton et al, *Food System Impacts on Biodiversity Loss* (Chatham House 2021) www.chathamhouse.org/sites/default/files/2021-02/2021-02-03-food-system-biodiversity-loss-benton-et-al_0.pdf.

livestock, and 43,000 litres to produce 1 kg of beef.[32] Milk production is reported to be equally water-intensive, with some reports suggesting up to 11,000 litres of water being needed to produce 1 litre of milk.[33] The FAO's AQUASTAT data suggest that over 70 percent of freshwater is used for agriculture, with a further 15 percent increase anticipated by 2050 as global demand for agricultural goods grows.[34] A large share of this consumption is due to watering feed crops for livestock.[35] Some view this as inefficient (particularly in regions with water shortage problems), as limited water supplies used for feed production could be used for human consumption or other critical uses.[36] Particularly considering the impact of climate change on drought occurrences, water management is increasingly a concern when seeking to achieve global food security and a global sustainable diet.

History of the Global Meat and Dairy Industry

But how did we get here? The current landscape for livestock production has been sculpted by various cultural, economic and technological developments over the years. The livestock sector is reported to be valued at US$1.4 trillion, equal to 40 percent of agricultural gross domestic product (GDP) worldwide.[37] Understanding the historical pathway of today's livestock industrial powerhouse provides important context to understanding how the international legal order has facilitated (and in some cases, sustained) the wide-reaching environmental impacts of the sector. The account often takes a European-focused approach to the historical development of the consumption of milk and dairy in the first instance – largely due to the focus of the book on 'developed' countries' consumption and its impact on livestock emissions. However, more global examples are provided where appropriate, in particular, where European eating habits and colonial control have impacted other meat and dairy markets globally.[38]

[32] D Pimentel et al, 'Water Resources: Agricultural and Environmental Issues' (2004) 54 *BioScience* 909.

[33] MK Joy et al, 'The Grey Water Footprint of Milk Due to Nitrate Leaching from Dairy Farms in Canterbury, New Zealand' (2022) 29 *Australasian Journal of Environmental Management* 177.

[34] FAO, 'AQUASTAT – FAO's Global Information System on Water and Agriculture', www.fao.org/aquastat/en/, accessed 6 December 2022.

[35] ibid.

[36] For more details on 'Water Footprints' see A Hoekstra, 'The Water Footprint of Food' (Water for Food) https://waterfootprint.org/media/downloads/Hoekstra-2008-WaterfootprintFood.pdf, accessed 8 November 2021, 4.

[37] R Jevinger, 'Growing the Good: Growing the Good: The Case for Low-Carbon Transition in the Food Sector' (Changing Markets, 2018) https://changingmarkets.org/portfolio/growing-the-good/, accessed 10 September 2020) 14.

[38] This can also provide useful context to understand how Western capitalist industrialisation norms have had global impacts of dietary and production trends for the sector.

A (Brief) History of Meat Consumption

Historically, trade in meat products was largely Anglo-centric (stemming from the British Empire) and relatively minimal, making meat a luxury item afforded only by the wealthiest in society.[39] Beef, in particular, is documented as a prestigious and expensive meat only eaten in any significant quantity by the elite.[40] However, the Industrial Revolution enabled a number of technological innovations that made trading greater quantities of meat more feasible and thus more accessible for consumption beyond the elite.[41] In particular, industrialisation enabled improvements in transport technologies, food preservation and agricultural farming that resulted in an increase in the production and trade of meat products (and increased scope for Anglo beef-eating tendencies to be spread worldwide).[42]

When a shortage of meat products was experienced in Western Europe in the mid-nineteenth century,[43] a food regime began to emerge that tied suppliers in North and South America, as well as Australia and New Zealand, to supply the growing European market demand for meat.[44] European colonists had implanted commercial meat production in these countries in the eighteenth century, as their soils were more suitable for rearing greater numbers of livestock than domestic soils during this shortage.[45]

On the other side of the globe at this time, Eastern countries had similar lower levels of meat consumption.[46] For example, in China moral norms at the time made beef-eating a 'taboo'[47] in society[48] and any market for beef was largely reserved for the increasing numbers of foreigners in the Western culinary culture in Shanghai at the time (who arrived after the forced opening of international trade routes).[49] China at that time largely only reared cattle to help plough agricultural crops. However, due to an influx of Western culture and particularly evangelising missionaries, beef propaganda led to a change in the perception of beef consumption from a taboo to a more fashionable and nutritious lifestyle choice.[50]

[39] R Perren, *Taste Trade and Technology* (Ashgate, 2006) 1–30.
[40] N Fiddes, *Meat: A Natural Symbol* (Routledge, 1991) 22.
[41] Perren (n 39).
[42] ibid 30–51.
[43] ibid.
[44] W Warren, *Meat Makes People Powerful* (University of Iowa Press, 2018) 18.
[45] ibid.
[46] ibid 27; V Smil, *Should We Eat Meat?* (Wiley Blackwell, 2013) 64.
[47] However, Chinese Muslims were allowed by the government to slaughter cows and sell beef.
[48] At times, this taboo even amounted to criminality. Wei notes, in particular, 'the imperial court of the Tang dynasty (AD 618–907) and its successor states introduced strict protections for oxen used in plowing, making their killing a serious criminal offense on par with counterfeiting or homicide'. See H Wei, 'It's the Year of the Ox, So Where's the Beef?', *#SixthTone*, 11 February 2021, www.sixthtone.com/news/1006796, accessed 9 August 2023.
[49] V Goossaert, 'The Beef Taboo and the Sacrificial Structure of Late Imperial Chinese Society' in R Sterckx (ed), *Of Tripod and Palate: Food, Politics, and Religion in Traditional China* (Palgrave Macmillan, 2005) https://doi.org/10.1057/9781403979278_12, accessed 9 August 2023.
[50] Wei (n 48).

By the late twentieth century, production trends continued to shift and increase significantly. For example, in the United States and Western Europe, there was a change in consumption habits. Whereas meat was previously sold exclusively by butchers with expensive cuts only available to the wealthier in the population, the 'rise of the supermarket' led the way for cheap, easy prepackaged food that made previously expensive cuts more readily available to all household budgets.[51] The consumption of meat consequently increased and farming processes became more intensive to meet the high demand for supermarket meats (and their low costs).[52]

Meanwhile, industrialisation continued to take its course on the other side of the globe, such as in China and India. Household incomes, particularly around the more industrial cities, were rising, which continued to increase demand for meat products in their growing middle classes.[53] As a consequence meat consumption was beginning to increase in these new markets as incomes increased, although, in the case of India,[54] levels of beef consumption often still remained contingent on religious demographics.[55] However, generally, increasing demand has continued on into the twenty-first century, with meat and dairy consumption continuing to increase across both developed and developing countries alongside increases in household income.[56]

As has been alluded to so far, the consumption of meat has not been isolated from cultural and social narratives over the years. The rise in vegetarianism and concern about animal welfare arguably has been taking its course throughout Western countries in the twentieth century – providing a counternarrative to general trends in increasing meat consumption. Religious factors have also played into historical consumption patterns globally depending on dominant national religions.[57] For example, the Quran defines for Muslims what is *halal* (lawful) and what is *haram* (prohibited) food and meat. Other religions, including Hinduism, Buddhism and Jainism, also generally support a meatless lifestyle of non-violence.

Equally, food safety concerns (such as the bovine spongiform encephalopathy (BSE) or 'mad cow' crisis) have caused ebbs and flows in trends of meat eating.[58] Nonetheless, national health authorities consistently label meat as one of the main protein sources in our diets, thereby encouraging and seemingly necessitating its consumption.[59] Meat has been conditioned to become a mainstay of the family

[51] Perren (n 39) 208–13.

[52] ibid.

[53] Smil (n 46) 85–88.

[54] S Mohana Devi et al, 'An Outline of Meat Consumption in the Indian Population – A Pilot Review' (2014) 34 *Korean Journal for Food Science of Animal Resources* 507.

[55] See more detail on this in K-C Nam et al, 'Meat Products and Culture in the East' [2010] *Meat Science* 86(1).

[56] More detail in the next section. It is worth noting anomalies in this trend, such as with India and beef due to its heavily Hindu population. See Smil (n 46) 75-78 and Warren (n 44) 28–46 for more detail on religious taboos surrounding meat consumption.

[57] L Kemmerer, *Animals and World Religions* (Oxford University Press, 2012).

[58] C Ansell, *What's the Beef?: The Contested Governance of European Food Safety* (MIT Press, 2006).

[59] Warren (n 44) 180.

diet, with a family meal often not felt as 'complete' without some kind of animal protein source. This has been written on extensively through a variety of lenses, particularly of the masculinity of meat eating and the traditional role of women feeding the 'working man'.[60] As a result, meat consumption patterns can be said to be impacted substantially by growths in global income, although additional societal narratives, events and phenomena have also played a role in the embeddedness of meat consumption (or lack thereof) across different social groups.

A (Brief) History of Dairy Consumption

The consumption and trade of dairy followed a similar trajectory to meat although with some slight nuances, wonderfully outlined by Valenze in her book *Milk: A Local and Global History*.[61] In the Middle Ages, milk was in sparser supply, and, beyond subsistence farming, its consumption was often reserved for sacred religious occasions, or linked to spiritual or divine powers (due to the symbolism of mammalian breast milk for potency, vitality and providing life).[62] Many regions in the world were (and still are) naturally lactase non-persistent (unable to digest raw milk), meaning its consumption again was rarer or socially unacceptable.[63]

In Europe, Valenze described how during the Italian Renaissance, the health benefits of dairy and cheese were promoted.[64] The Dutch similarly promoted the consumption of dairy products from the seventeenth century, gaining the reputation as being skilled in animal husbandry and therefore capable of securing a plentiful and consistent supply of milk.[65] As a result of their successful dairy production methods, Valenze suggests that increasing consumption of dairy products by the Dutch helped make cheese and milk a fashionable foodstuff among the European elite.[66] This was also reinforced through 'countryside' imagery, with dairy being popularised in art at this time.

Other European countries were envious of Dutch skilled production and high yields and sought to learn from their experience to gain stakes in the lucrative dairy market of the time – eventually leading to the modernisation of European dairy production more generally.[67] At the time, milk, due to its shorter shelf-life, was viewed as a more expensive commodity. However, as cheese has a longer shelf-life

[60] CJ Adams, *The Sexual Politics of Meat: A Feminist-Vegetarian Critical Theory*, 10th anniversary edn (Continuum, 2000).
[61] D Valenze, *Milk: A Local and Global History* (Yale University Press, 2011).
[62] ibid 13–34.
[63] ibid, 31.
[64] With milk being viewed as 'twice cooked' blood, so perfect for 'balancing' levels of different of bodily fluids for optimal health, as was medical best practice at the time. See ibid 58–83.
[65] ibid 83.
[66] ibid 100–18.
[67] ibid.

(due to the removal of its perishable components) it became a core component of the diets of both the wealthy and the poorer in society. In contrast to meat, Valenze suggests this made cheese an accessible protein alternative for the poorer in society as milk production improved and scaled up in size across Europe.[68] This help to embed dairy into food cultures across European society, from cheese to chocolate and beyond. In a trend similar to meat production at the time, European colonists (and particularly the British) imposed production of dairy products on their colonies and indigenous peoples, especially in North America where conditions were more amenable to rearing dairy cattle.[69]

The dairy industry continued to thrive, with technology and preservation techniques continuing to improve (including the popularisation of pasteurisation).[70] At the end of the nineteenth century, the creation of condensed canned milk[71] again allowed the dairy industry to thrive due to the long life of the product.[72] This spurred mass production of canned milk, in Europe but also especially in North America.[73] By this point, condensed canned milk factories also began to emerge in East Asia.[74] For example, in 1868, following the Meiji Restoration,[75] Japan began to be influenced by Western diets and culture, spurring the creation of a native dairy industry (also in their occupied territories, such as Taiwan, with customers spreading beyond to China and other South Sea islands after World War One).[76] Into the early twentieth century, prices continued to fall, technology advanced and competition between international companies increased, bringing with it new global favourite dietary staples such as mass-produced chocolate, ice cream and so on.[77]

The world wars disrupted global milk production and supply considerably, but narratives surrounding the health benefits of milk (particularly for children) proliferated in the twentieth century.[78] Public health became fixated with the health benefits of milk for children's growth and development, and the dairy industry propagated this narrative further – investing heavily in 'educational publicity' for milk consumption, placing milk on the same moral pedestal as other public goods, such as water.[79]

[68] ibid 118–38.
[69] ibid, eg 140.
[70] ibid 210–35.
[71] Particularly by producers, such as modern-day Nestlé before they diversified their production. See more ibid 187–89.
[72] ibid.
[73] ibid.
[74] ibid.
[75] This saw the removal of the feudal system and created the Meiji constitution, establishing a centralised government. Universal education and industrialisation helped build a more educated population with improved transportation and communication technology.
[76] ibid, eg 192.
[77] ibid 196.
[78] ibid, eg from 235.
[79] ibid 263.

This health narrative of milk consumption has been maintained even until the present day, often underpinning the rationale for 'school milk' programmes in place in many nations.[80] For a further regional narrative of the national importance dairy at this time, postcolonial India (one of few regions outside of Europe that also had a strong historical milk culture) was also seeking to scale up its domestic smaller-scale production in a programme called 'Operation Flood' in order to reduce dependency on Western powdered milk supplies and to tackle food shortages.[81] 'Dairy aid' imports were still initially required to address India's hunger and poverty levels, although by the time Operation Flood was complete India became and continues to be one of the world's greatest producers of milk, further demonstrating the importance of the dairy industry to a multitude of nations.[82]

The role of globalisation of commodity markets, including that of national dishes and cuisines, should also not be underestimated in explaining the growth in popularity in dairy consumption during the twentieth and twenty-first centuries, particularly in East Asia. It is argued that this globalisation influenced the incorporation of dairy products such as cheese into traditionally dairy-free diets.[83]

The growth of the dairy market in China is an example of this,[84] with a similar so-called 'wheyvolution' also seen in Latin America.[85] This 'wheyvolution' is still predicted to continue across the globe, with investment from Western food corporations into milk sales in East Asia, with easily digestible options such as yoghurt becoming particularly popular in regions more predisposed to lactose intolerance.[86] As Wiley has said, milk is undergoing a 'radical transformation from a marginal or disliked food to one positively associated with modernity, wealth, health and strength' in East Asia.[87] While perhaps the unwavering health benefits of milk are beginning to be challenged in Western regions such as North America or Europe (particularly in cases of lactose intolerance[88]), consumption levels are still high. Moreover, growth of the dairy industry is anticipated outside of Europe – although even there the trajectory of its consumption can be directly linked to European influence.[89]

[80] ibid eg from 259.
[81] ibid from 270.
[82] ibid 279.
[83] US Dairy Export Council, 'Six Growth Drivers for US Dairy In South East Asia' (USDEC, 2015) http://blog.usdec.org/usdairyexporter/dairy-innovation-opportunities-in-southeast-asia, accessed 8 November 2018; J Beghin, 'Dairy Markets in Asia: An Overview if Recent Findings and Implications' (CARD Reports and Working Papers, 2005) and Smil (n 46) 97–100.
[84] See L Cozza, 'Dairy Sector in China: A Challenging and Dynamic Market' (2017) http://dspace.unive.it/handle/10579/11958, accessed 13 November 2011; for more context to this, see Felicity Lawrence, 'Can the World Quench China's Bottomless Thirst for Milk', *The Guardian*, 29 March 2019, www.theguardian.com/environment/2019/mar/29/can-the-world-quench-chinas-bottomless-thirst-for-milk, accessed 5 April 2019.
[85] Valenze (n 61).
[86] ibid 288.
[87] ibid.
[88] ibid 290.
[89] See statistics in upcoming section on consumption and trajectories.

Factors Contributing to the Growth of the Global Meat and Dairy Industry

Through recalling this history in the development of the milk and dairy industries historically, a number of key factors that have contributed to the growth of these sectors can be identified, namely: wealth, technology, globalization and colonisation, and social and cultural narratives.

Figure 3 Factors contributing to the growth of the global meat and dairy industry

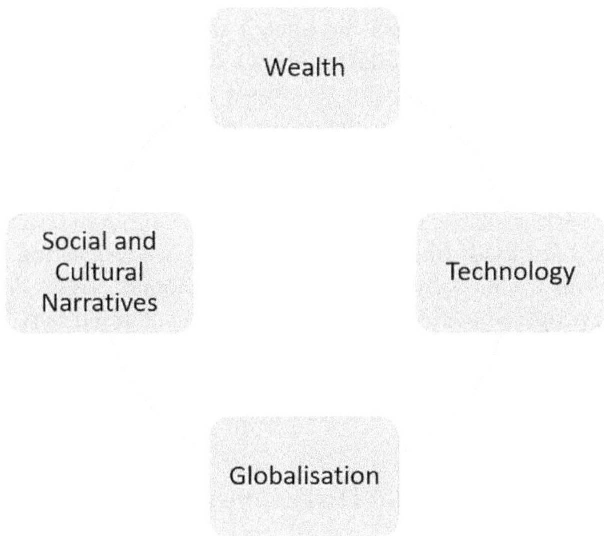

Wealth

A country's level of economic development plays a key role in its demand for meat products. Whereas red meat and dairy products are generally only available to the more wealthy, global demand for meat is shifting to include more countries, such as transition economies that are becoming wealthier, like China or India. This preference for a meat-based, rather than grain-based, diet in countries with increased income is a recognised economic phenomenon. Bennett's law suggests that as income increases, demand for meat products also increases.[90] Some statistics suggest that rice consumption (the alternative to a meat diet in many countries) falls by one-third with every doubling of income.[91] Today, as many developing countries continue to pursue

[90] M Bennett, 'Wheat in National Diets' [1941] *Food Research Institute Studies* 18, 37–76.
[91] For further statistics on this, see Smil (n 46).

economic growth, their demand for meat products is projected to increase further as their middle classes grow.[92]

Globalisation and Colonisation

Globalisation (defined as growing interdependence between different economies through cross-border processes such as trade) also played a role in increasing meat and dairy consumption. The first food trading patterns imposed between Europe and European colonists in North and South America, New Zealand and Australia established a process of international food trade favourable to colonisers. As further international governance emerged throughout the twentieth century (including through the creation of international trade law), the size of the global food regime increased further as more countries developed economically[93] and entered the global agricultural market.[94] This globalisation led to an increased number of businesses operating internationally, thereby enabling a greater choice of food goods on the global market, such as different national dishes, cuisines and brands that were not previously available in other regions of the world. As a result of this, meat and dairy-based fast foods (that arguably stem from Western eating culture) have gained ground in traditionally grain-based diets amongst certain demographics, such as young people who are influenced by Western cultural trends.[95] As a consequence, globalisation can be seen as a key factor for the current size of the beef and dairy market, due to its impact in spreading different national tastes across borders in addition to the legacy of colonial control on global food trade dynamics.[96]

Social Narratives of Meat and Dairy Consumption

Alongside national and international factors, social and consumer narratives also played a role in increasing the size of beef and dairy markets.[97] It was previously mentioned that meat was often (and perhaps still is) viewed as a prestigious food

[92] R Bailey et al, 'Breaking the Vicious Circle: Food, Climate & Nutrition' (Chatham House, 2018) https://hoffmanncentre.chathamhouse.org/article/breaking-the-vicious-cycle-food-climate-nutrition/, accessed 8 November 2018.

[93] Agricultural markets often are very important for the development of developing countries, as it is an industry where natural resource endowment can be utilised.

[94] Perren (n 39) 167–71.

[95] See China and the Western fast food cultural influence in T Del Guidice et al, 'New Trends in the Chinese Diet: Cultural Influences on Consumer Behaviour' (2016) 5(2) *Italian Journal of Food Safety* 5273; G Ma, 'Food, Eating Behaviour and Culture in Chinese Society' [2015] *Journal of Ethnic Foods* 195–99.

[96] Though natural resource endowment can play a role as to where certain industries are based. See, for example, the forestry chapter of this book, which demonstrates that the majority of forest-related industry occurs in the Global South due to the large natural endowment of natural forests there.

[97] Further interesting narratives have been raised in the literature, including in relation to gender and meat consumption – though significant investigation into these narratives is beyond the scope of this book, though may be relevant in more prognostic research into agri-environmental issues. See eg feminist-vegetarian critical theory, including C Adams, *The Sexual Politics of Meat* (Bloomsbury, 2015).

in society, eaten by the elite. Therefore, as incomes increased, this coupling of meat with prestige played a role in influencing consumers to purchase more meat products and eat more 'wealthily'.[98] Other consumption narratives have been created over the years in addition to this. Encouraging meat and dairy consumption for health reasons is a key example of this. Many national health authorities labelled meat as one of the only adequate protein sources in our diets, thereby encouraging and seemingly necessitating its consumption.[99] Free milk has also been provided in schools as it was marketed as a key source of protein and calcium for children.[100] Both of these narratives impacted entire generations' perceptions of these products as being staple dietary components.[101] Other social narratives were also outlined in the prior analysis, such as religious restrictions on meat consumption, food safety concerns, and the gender politics surrounding meat eating.

Technology

Finally, it is important not to underestimate the significance technological developments have played in increasing the size of the beef and dairy market. Not only were improvements in the early nineteenth century in transport technologies, food preservation and agricultural farming key to making an international beef and dairy market, but the rise of intensive industrial farming in the twentieth century, such as automated machinery, to produce cheaper cuts of meat or dairy products, also drove the consumption of these products globally.[102] Generally, cheaper production through technological developments has enabled greater access to these goods for lower-income groups, further driving consumption and international trade.

Each of these factors has paved the way for current 'overconsumption' of livestock goods, predominantly in high-income developed countries (that will be outlined in more detail in subsequent sections). Reports suggest that the world now produces more than four times the quantity of meat and double the amount of milk it did fifty years ago.[103] With this, the climate impacts of the sector have soared, though the production landscape of meat and dairy is varied.

[98] ibid.

[99] Warren (n 44) 180.

[100] These schemes may have been necessary post-World War 2 when children were undernourished and economies needed to prosper, but the marketing of milk during this period has influenced, even today, how consumers view milk. See more in P Atkins, 'The Milk in Schools Scheme, 1934–45: Nationalization and Resistance' (2005) 34(1) *Journal of the History of Education Society*. For examples of current milk schemes that are still in place today, see the 'European School Milk Scheme – A Subsidy for Dairy Products for School Children', https://ec.europa.eu/agriculture/milk/school-milk-scheme_en, accessed 9 November 2018.

[101] See Atkins (n 100).

[102] See section above.

[103] H Ritchie and M Roser, 'Meat and Dairy Production' (Our World in Data, 2017) https://ourworldindata.org/meat-production, accessed 11 September 2020.

The Current Landscape for Global Beef and Dairy Production

There is a great disparity in the emissions intensity of beef and dairy production globally. The biggest beef and dairy producers, namely the United States and the European Union, have relatively low emissions intensity per kilogram of product produced.[104] Some of the areas where the highest emissions intensity of production occurs are those simultaneously producing lower yields of beef and dairy products – such as in some Sub-Saharan African countries.[105] Overall, the highest cumulative level of emissions from livestock comes from Latin America and the Caribbean, with East and South East Asia and South Asia following behind.[106]

This being said, meat consumption is at its highest in high-income countries with the average European and North American reported to consume almost 80 and over 110 kilograms of meat per year, respectively.[107] A similar trend exists with regards to milk, with the European Union, North America and other high-income countries such as Australia stated as the biggest consumers.[108] Consumption per capita of these goods is rising in transition economies, particularly countries in the initial food trading routes created between Western Europe and sites of early European colonisation with natural resource endowment, such as Brazil and Argentina.

Perhaps surprisingly, international trade in beef and dairy does not underpin the majority of this consumption. For example, it is suggested that the United States only exports just over 10 percent of the beef products it produces, and Brazil exports around 20 percent of its beef products (though, of course, these amounts are not negligible).[109] However, the situation is different when it comes to animal feed production that contributes to the production of livestock. It is reported that Argentina exports close to 94 percent of its soybean meal produced and Brazil exports around 45 percent of its soybean meal – around 50 million tonnes of soybean meal in total.[110] The European Union is the largest importer of soybean meal in the world, with some studies suggesting that 63 percent of the total soybean meal used in the European Union is imported.[111] As a result, certain regions such as the European Union are, to a considerable degree, externalising the environmental impacts of feed production to countries such as Brazil and Argentina, rather than experiencing the land-use impacts associated with feed production within their own borders.[112]

[104] Gerber and FAO (n 4) see figure 6 and OL Ortigue, 'Greenhouse Gas Emissions from Agrifood Systems' (2022) FAOSTAT Analytical Brief 50, pp 7-12.

[105] Ortigue (n 104) eg at 8.

[106] Gerber and FAO (n 4) eg pp 15-21.

[107] Ritchie and Roser (n 103).

[108] ibid.

[109] USDA Foreign Agricultural Service, 'Livestock and Poultry: World Markets and Trade' (USDA, 2018); and USDA Foreign Agricultural Service, 'Dairy: World Markets and Trade' (USDA, 2018).'

[110] ibid.

[111] ibid.

[112] See EU chapter or forests chapter for more details on this.

The Coexistence of Global Hunger, Increasing Population and Overconsumption

Whilst wealthier countries and groups are highly consuming livestock goods or feedstock, global hunger is still rife. Approximately 821 million people worldwide were reported in 2020 to be undernourished (up from 785 million in 2015).[113] South Asia and Sub-Saharan Africa have the highest level of hunger globally (as per the Global Hunger Index) particularly due to their levels of child undernutrition.[114] Global food insecurity is likely to increase in the future due to agricultural system vulnerability to climate change decreasing yields and the viability of agricultural production.[115] However, the distribution of the impacts of climate change on food systems and security will be unbalanced.[116] This is because climate change is most likely to worsen food insecurity in areas that are even now vulnerable to hunger and undernutrition due to their geographical location and characteristics.[117]

Despite this, increasing pressure will be put on global agricultural systems as the global population increases. The world population is projected to increase by 3 billion, primarily in developing countries, resulting in a reported 60–120 percent increase in global crop demand.[118] As developing countries secure further economic growth, their middle classes will increase demand for resource-intensive, luxury agricultural goods.[119] As mentioned previously, increased beef consumption is particularly strongly correlated with increased income. It is suggested that by 2050 40 percent of the world's population will have undergone this 'livestock revolution' with their plant-based diets shifting towards more intensive demand for livestock products.[120] Addressing the overconsumption of livestock goods – starting in historically high emitting countries with low food insecurity – will be key to engaging with and understanding climate solutions that can tackle consumption driven by increasing affluence.

[113] FAO, *The State of Food Security and Nutrition in the World 2020* (FAO, 2020) www.fao.org/publications/sofi/2020/en/, accessed 8 September 2020.

[114] Global Hunger Index, '2019 Global Hunger Index Results – Global, Regional, and National Trends', www.globalhungerindex.org/results.html, accessed 11 July 2020.

[115] W Scott et al, *Great Power Resource Competition in a Changing Climate: New America's Natural Security Index* (New America, 2019) www.newamerica.org/resource-security/reports/great-power-resource-competition-changing-climate/.

[116] M Parry, C Rosenzweig and M Livermore, 'Climate Change, Global Food Supply and Risk of Hunger' (2005) 360 *Philosophical Transactions of the Royal Society B: Biological Sciences* 2125.

[117] Wheeler and von Braun (n 8).

[118] G Fischer, MM Shah and HT van Velthuizen, 'Climate Change and Agricultural Vulnerability' (2002) http://pure.iiasa.ac.at/id/eprint/6670/, accessed 7 September 2020; ES Cassidy et al, 'Redefining Agricultural Yields: From Tonnes to People Nourished per Hectare' (2013) 8 *Environmental Research Letters* 034015.

[119] M van der Veen, 'When Is Food a Luxury?' (2003) 34 *World Archaeology* 405. It is worth noting that this trend is not unique to only current developing economies, but also was a historical trend also for currently developed countries. In this sense, this analysis is not finding culpability in this trend in transitional economies, but rather highlighting the common trajectories seen in the agricultural sector correlated with income growth.

[120] Cassidy et al (n 120).

But what is a global sustainable diet? And how do we address livestock emissions fairly given the distribution of consumption and production of beef and dairy historically, presently and in the future? Is the current international legal order for climate change and cattle fit for achieving this purpose?

Solutions for Livestock Emissions Mitigation

The current international legal order for tackling livestock emissions has promoted and neglected different livestock emissions mitigation solutions depending on the interests of the actors involved. This book seeks to delineate these interests and their consequent realisation in the current international legal order for cattle and climate change, agriculture, agri-trade and forests. However, at this stage, it is useful to outline the potential options for livestock emissions that exist, regardless of their current utilisation within the international legal landscape. These can broadly be categorised into two types of livestock emissions measures: supply-side measures and demand-side measures.

Supply-side emissions mitigation measures seek to improve the environmental efficiency of livestock production. In other words, they strive to use fewer natural resources to produce a greater quantity of agricultural output, such as beef or dairy. Sometimes these supply-side measures are also referred to as 'technical solutions' – although this is often also commonly referred to as the 'sustainable intensification pathway' by policymakers.

Whilst not clearly defined in the international sphere, the sustainable intensification pathway recognises that supply-side measures can be implemented to improve the environmental efficiency of agricultural production.[121] However, it also recognises the need for better food security, encouraging an improvement in supply-side efficiency to enable an increase in overall agricultural output. This is a particularly appealing strategy for countries where there is high emissions intensity of production paired with low production levels. For example, using the sustainable intensification approach in countries in Sub-Saharan Africa would enable their emissions intensity of production to improve while also increasing livestock production levels. This increase in output levels may help address any food security issues in the region or meet increasing demand from growing populations or middle classes.

For the cattle sector, supply-side measures could include:

- Using more efficient herd breeds or dual utilisation breeds so that fewer cattle are needed to produce the same or more beef and dairy products, thereby reducing overall emissions through reducing cattle herd sizes and the methane and manure they produce;

[121] M Cardwell and F Smith, 'Renegotiation of the WTO Agreement on Agriculture: Accommodating the New Big Issues' (2013) 62 *ICLQ* 865.

- Altering cattle feed composition so that less methane is produced by the cattle's digestive process, including adding feed additives, such as seaweed,[122] to reduce the amount of methane produced;
- More effective manure storage to minimise the amount of methane produced whilst manure is being stored; and
- Carbon sequestration, removing CO_2 from the atmosphere to slow climate change.[123]

As mentioned previously, the concept of 'sustainable intensification' is often ill-defined. In some cases, it may involve trade-offs with other environmental costs if not implemented with due consideration of all impacts of livestock production. For example, if a farm is trying to reduce the amount of land deforested for grazing, they may opt for more concentrated feed lots for cattle. Whilst reducing the amount of land being deforested, this may cause a more concentrated accumulation of the environmental impacts of livestock manure on the farm lot. Whilst not the focus of this book, concentrated feed lots can also raise animal welfare issues, including well-being concerns and the risk of the spread of animal disease.[124] Overall, these 'technical' solutions need to be implemented with extensive due diligence of the general environmental impact – which is often not the case.

Solutions Beyond the Supply Side?

More generally, it has been reported that supply-side efficiency improvements alone will not mitigate agricultural emissions to the extent required to meet global climate targets.[125] As current agronomic and policy interventions are reported to only achieve 21–40 percent of the needed mitigation for the sector,[126] if dietary trends continue to grow based on GDP, improvements in efficiency are unlikely to prevent the environmental burden of agricultural production.[127] In fact, global agricultural non-CO_2 emissions are reported to be on track to increase significantly

[122] S Vijn et al, 'Key Considerations for the Use of Seaweed to Reduce Enteric Methane Emissions From Cattle' (2020) 7 *Frontiers in Veterinary Science*, www.frontiersin.org/articles/10.3389/fvets.2020.597430, accessed 12 September 2023.

[123] Steinfeld et al (n 3) eg from 115.

[124] D Fraser, 'Animal Welfare and the Intensification of Animal Production' in PB Thompson (ed), *The Ethics of Intensification*, vol 16 (Springer Netherlands, 2008) http://link.springer.com/10.1007/978-1-4020-8722-6_12, accessed 12 May 2022.

[125] KF Davis et al, 'Meeting Future Food Demand with Current Agricultural Resources' (2016) 39 *Global Environmental Change* 125.

[126] To determine the emissions budget necessary to limit warming in 2100 to no more than 2°C above pre-industrial levels, Wollenberg et al used a scenario prepared for the IPCC known as Representative Concentration Pathway (RCP) 2.6: E Wollenberg et al, 'Reducing Emissions from Agriculture to Meet the 2°C Target' (2016) 22 *Global Change Biology* 3859 (see van Vuuren et al 2011 in the article). The RCP 2.6 scenario represents 2.6 W/m^2 radiative forcing in 2100, or ~450 ppm CO_2e in 2100, which results in a 66 percent or 'likely' chance of staying below the 2°C warming limit (van Vuuren et al 2011). The RCP 2.6 is one of four reference scenarios used to model concentration pathways for the IPCC.

[127] Davis et al (n 125); Wollenberg et al (n 126).

until 2055 if food energy consumption and dietary preferences remain at 1995 levels of wealth–diet correlation.[128] While not denying the possibility of this changing, Wollenberg et al have found that neither the dissemination of existing and potential technological agri-climate solutions (considered in Smith et al[129]) or large-scale transformation of crop and livestock production (analysed by Havlik et al[130]) contribute to the necessary mitigation reductions at low costs.[131] Moreover, for many agricultural subsectors, current technologies only secure a fraction of the mitigation required.[132]

Transitioning to alternative and less resource-intensive diets among certain global demographics would allow the world to keep pace with the growth in demand for food without resorting to increasing overall resource usage, including increasing emissions. Under scenarios of decreased meat consumption, some studies suggest that non-CO_2 GHG emissions may even decrease from 1995 levels.[133] Also under these scenarios, the reductions also have the ability to require less financial investment into technological solutions than those based solely upon supply-side measures.[134] It is reported that the highest reduction potential arises from a combination of both supply-side efficiency improvements and demand-side measures designed to reduce consumption.[135] However, currently these demand-side measures are neglected in climate policy.

Demand-side policies are policies that may be able to encourage changes in consumer behaviour and consumption patterns. Examples include:

- Fiscal controls, such as border carbon adjustment or taxes for resource-intensive livestock goods such as beef and dairy products, to make consumption of these goods more costly;
- Subsidies, such as a removal of farming subsidies for meat and dairy farming to discourage their production; or subsidisation of fruits and vegetables or other foods to encourage consumption of alternatives to beef and dairy; and

[128] A Popp, H Lotze-Campen and B Bodirsky, 'Food Consumption, Diet Shifts and Associated Non-CO_2 Greenhouse Gases from Agricultural Production' (2010) 20 *Global Environmental Change* 451.

[129] P Smith et al, 'Greenhouse Gas Mitigation in Agriculture' (2008) 363 *Philosophical Transactions of the Royal Society of London B: Biological Sciences* 789–813; P Smith et al. 'How Much Land-Based Greenhouse Gas Mitigation Can Be Achieved without Compromising Food Security and Environmental Goals?' (2013) 19 *Global Change Biology* 2285–2302.'

[130] P Havlik et al, 'Climate Change Mitigation through Livestock System Transitions' (2014) 111(10) *Proceedings of the National Academy of Sciences of the United States of America* 3709.

[131] Wollenberg and others (n 126).

[132] ibid.

[133] Popp, Lotze-Campen and Bodirsky (n 130); E Stehfest et al, 'Climate Benefits of Changing Diet' (2009) 95 *Climatic Change* 83; Wollenberg et al (n 126).

[134] Eg Wollenberg et al (n 126) at 3862.

[135] Popp, Lotze-Campen and Bodirsky (n 128).

- Information and education, such as labelling and campaigns to raise awareness about the issues surrounding agricultural emissions and the health impacts of excessive livestock consumption, enabling consumers to alter their consumption behaviours in light of this.[136]

These demand-side policies do not seek to 'sustainably intensify' agricultural production but rather readjust market demand for specific environmentally unfriendly goods. Food shortage issues and socioeconomic risk assessment will be needed alongside these policies. Risk mitigation strategies, such as support for diversification, may need to be created alongside these measures to protect farmer livelihoods – even in developed countries. Moreover, there may be a desire to support more environmentally friendly production rather than 'penalise' environmentally unfriendly production, again to minimise unnecessary hardship on producers. Without risk-aware strategies, such as these, there may be unwanted impacts on vulnerable producers and consumers.

Nonetheless, for actors whose domestic livestock emissions are driven by high consumption of livestock goods rather than production inefficiency (such as higher-income countries), using these demand-side strategies to alter market conditions may be more appropriate to aspire to in conjunction with other more technical solutions.

Many of these demand-side measures allude to the creation of conditions conducive to a sustainable global diet, but what is specifically meant by a sustainable global diet? The rationale and current conceptualisation of the 'ideal' global diet is outlined in more detail below.

'Ideal Diets'

The 'Food Choice' Rationale

It may not be obviously clear to most what our dietary choices have to do with climate change. One of the key underlying rationales for utilising dietary change as a climate solution is described as the 'food choice argument'.[137]

Livestock products, and particularly beef and dairy, are very resource-intensive dietary components. One study estimates feeding 9 billion people a Western diet with Western technologies would require almost double the amount of cropland under cultivation presently.[138] It is reported that average dietary footprint

[136] See more in Felix Creutzig et al, 'Demand-Side Solutions to Climate Change Mitigation Consistent with High Levels of Well-being' (2022) 12 *Nature Climate Change* 36.
[137] R Oppenlander, *Food Choice and Sustainability: Eating Less Meat, and Taking Baby Steps Won't Work* (Langdon Street Press, 2013).
[138] Cassidy et al (n 120).

intensities will have to be substantially improved to prevent increases in environmental burdens from agricultural production beyond current levels.[139] According to Davis et al, the average dietary footprint emissions intensity will need to decrease by 72 percent, its land footprint intensity by 97 percent and its nitrogen footprint intensity by 85 percent by mid-century to maintain current levels of resource use and emissions as global demand for food increases.[140] They report the predicted increase in demand for animal products alone before 2050 would lead to a temperature increase of 1.5°C.[141] Taking the most ambitious target established by the Paris Agreement, this would leave little or no room for any other source of increase in anthropogenic GHG emissions.[142] Moreover, other studies report that agricultural emissions will contribute the largest share of excess emissions of any sector in the future given current mitigation trajectories and plans.[143]

The food choice argument argues that livestock production is an inefficient way to feed the global population. This is because reports suggest that currently 36 percent of the calories produced by the world's crops are used for animal feed.[144] This translates to only 12 percent of those feed calories being used for human consumption (often in high-income countries with high meat consumption levels).[145] Moreover, of all plant protein produced, it is suggested that only 49 percent is delivered to the human food system.[146] The reported protein efficiency of beef is particularly low, with only a 3.8 percent protein efficiency conversion rate – compared to a 25 percent conversion rate for other animal products, such as eggs.[147] In Brazil – a hotspot for feed production – it is reported that 79 percent of all produced plant protein is directed to animal feed and only 16 percent for direct human consumption.[148]

By shifting the current mix of crop uses and growing food solely for human consumption where agriculturally viable, Cassidy et al report that available food calories could increase by 70 percent.[149] This reported increase could feed an additional 4 billion people, surpassing the predicted increase in global population of 2–3 billion people.[150] Naturally, these are only statistics and dietary patterns are interwoven with a variety of socioeconomic and cultural factors. However, they report that reducing consumption of grain-fed animal products by even 50 percent could increase calorie availability enough to feed a further 2 billion people.[151]

[139] Davis et al (n 127).
[140] ibid.
[141] ibid.
[142] R Jevinger, 'Growing the Good' (Changing Markets, 2018) https://changingmarkets.org/portfolio/growing-the-good/, accessed 10 September 2020.
[143] Wollenberg et al (n 126).
[144] Cassidy et al (n 120).
[145] ibid.
[146] ibid.
[147] Ritchie and Roser (n 103).
[148] ibid.
[149] Cassidy et al (n 120).
[150] ibid.
[151] ibid.

'Ideal Diet' Modelling

So, what dietary shifts would be required to make human diets sustainable? As was previously stated, meat consumption is higher in high-income groups and countries. Consequently, these groups arguably require a greater dietary shift to ensure adequate emissions reductions will occur in the global agricultural sector. 'Ideal diet' modelling studies rely heavily on aligning the sustainability of the human diet with the positive human health impacts of increasing the consumption of plant-based foods and reducing the consumption of products such as red meat.

There are reported associated health impacts of consuming high and unbalanced levels of livestock goods. Red and processed meat, such as beef, have been deemed carcinogenic by the World Health Organization (WHO) as its consumption is significantly linked to contracting colorectal cancer.[152] Scientific reports on meat consumption also investigate meat eating with regard to an increased risk of type 2 diabetes and cardiovascular disease, in addition to higher levels of inflammation in the body (which is particularly to the detriment of those with chronic illnesses).[153] Dairy consumption has also been investigated in relation to the risk of development of certain cancers, such as prostate cancer.[154] More broadly, meat and dairy products can often be high in fat which may contribute to negative impacts on human health if not consumed in a balanced manner.[155]

[152] IARC, *Red Meat and Processed Meat* (WHO, 2018) https://publications.iarc.fr/Book-And-Report-Series/Iarc-Monographs-On-The-Identification-Of-Carcinogenic-Hazards-To-Humans/Red-Meat-And-Processed-Meat-2018, accessed 17 August 2023; V Bouvard et al, 'Carcinogenicity of Consumption of Red and Processed Meat' (2015) 16 *Lancet Oncology* 1599; CK Roberts et al, 'Effect of a Diet and Exercise Intervention on Oxidative Stress, Inflammation and Monocyte Adhesion in Diabetic Men' (2006) 73 *Diabetes Research and Clinical Practice* 249; SC Larsson and A Wolk, 'Meat Consumption and Risk of Colorectal Cancer: A Meta-analysis of Prospective Studies' (2006) 119 *International Journal of Cancer* 2657.

[153] 'Prevention of Cardiovascular Diseases: Role of Exercise, Dietary Interventions, Obesity and Smoking Cessation', www.ncbi.nlm.nih.gov/pmc/articles/PMC2716237/, accessed 30 September 2020; PW Siri-Tarino et al, 'Meta-analysis of Prospective Cohort Studies Evaluating the Association of Saturated Fat with Cardiovascular Disease' (2010) 91 *American Journal of Clinical Nutrition* 535; N Barnard, S Levin and C Trapp, 'Meat Consumption as a Risk Factor for Type 2 Diabetes' (2014) 6 *Nutrients* 897; R Micha, G Michas and D Mozaffarian, 'Unprocessed Red and Processed Meats and Risk of Coronary Artery Disease and Type 2 Diabetes – An Updated Review of the Evidence' (2012) 14 *Current Atherosclerosis Reports* 515; L Qi et al, 'Genetic Predisposition, Western Dietary Pattern, and the Risk of Type 2 Diabetes in Men' (2009) 89 *American Journal of Clinical Nutrition* 1453; W Chai et al, 'Dietary Red and Processed Meat Intake and Markers of Adiposity and Inflammation: The Multiethnic Cohort Study' (2017) 36 *Journal of the American College of Nutrition* 378; J Montonen et al, 'Consumption of Red Meat and Whole-Grain Bread in Relation to Biomarkers of Obesity, Inflammation, Glucose Metabolism and Oxidative Stress' (2013) 52 *European Journal of Nutrition* 337; A Pan et al, 'Red Meat Consumption and Risk of Type 2 Diabetes: 3 Cohorts of US Adults and an Updated Meta-Analysis' (2011) 94 *American Journal of Clinical Nutrition* 1088.

[154] JM Chan et al, 'Dairy Products, Calcium, and Prostate Cancer Risk in the Physicians' Health Study' (2001) 74 *American Journal of Clinical Nutrition* 549.

[155] Siri-Tarino et al (n 155); CH Kroenke et al, 'High- and Low-Fat Dairy Intake, Recurrence, and Mortality After Breast Cancer Diagnosis' (2013) 105 *Journal of the National Cancer Institute* 616.

A healthy diet containing more plant-based foods has been linked to improved health outcomes when compared to the typical Western diet that is higher in meat and dairy.[156] However, as with any diet, balance and knowledge of micronutrients are needed to ensure that no nutritional deficiencies occur.[157] Moreover, barriers to accessing these healthier foods may exist for marginalised communities, such as lower-income groups or those living in food deserts.[158] Nonetheless, scientists have tried to model 'ideal diets' to combine these sustainability and health considerations to begin to sculpt the dietary considerations that should be taken going forward.

The common trend in 'ideal diet' modelling is that higher-income groups (more prone to health risks associated with high consumption of processed meat or poor dietary choices) are required to reduce their consumption of red and processed meat, and increase consumption of healthier plant-based foods, such as legumes, wholegrains, and fruits and vegetables. One of the landmark (and at times, controversial) studies completed was by the EAT-Lancet Commission – an initiative led by *The Lancet* as part of an ongoing series on nutrition.

The EAT-Lancet Commission launched a report in 2019 that presented an integrated global framework and quantitative scientific targets for healthy diets and sustainable food production.[159] The 'Planetary Health Diet' presented by the Commission was designed to avoid severe environmental degradation and save 11 million human deaths annually.[160] The 'Planetary Health Diet' recommendations include a more than doubling of the consumption of healthy foods such as fruits, vegetables, legumes and nuts, and a greater than 50% reduction in global consumption of less healthy foods such as added sugars and red meat (primarily by reducing excessive consumption in wealthier countries).[161] The EAT-Lancet

[156] ND Barnard et al, 'A Low-Fat Vegan Diet and a Conventional Diabetes Diet in the Treatment of Type 2 Diabetes: A Randomized, Controlled, 74-Wk Clinical Trial' (2009) 89 *American Journal of Clinical Nutrition* 1588S; M Dinu et al, 'Vegetarian, Vegan Diets and Multiple Health Outcomes: A Systematic Review with Meta-Analysis of Observational Studies' (2017) 57 *Critical Reviews in Food Science and Nutrition* 3640; CT McEvoy, N Temple and JV Woodside, 'Vegetarian Diets, Low-Meat Diets and Health: A Review' (2012) 15 *Public Health Nutrition* 2287; ND Barnard et al, 'A Low-Fat Vegan Diet Elicits Greater Macronutrient Changes, but Is Comparable in Adherence and Acceptability, Compared with a More Conventional Diabetes Diet among Individuals with Type 2 Diabetes' (2009) 109 *Journal of the American Dietetic Association* 263; NS Rizzo et al, 'Nutrient Profiles of Vegetarian and Non Vegetarian Dietary Patterns' (2013) 113 *Journal of the Academy of Nutrition and Dietetics* 1610; H Kahleova et al, 'A Plant-Based Diet in Overweight Individuals in a 16-Week Randomized Clinical Trial: Metabolic Benefits of Plant Protein' (2018) 8 *Nutrition & Diabetes* 1; JI Mann, 'Optimizing the Plant-Based Diet' (2000) 9 *Asia Pacific Journal of Clinical Nutrition* S60; M McMacken and S Shah, 'A Plant-Based Diet for the Prevention and Treatment of Type 2 Diabetes' (2017) 14 *Journal of Geriatric Cardiology* 342.

[157] McEvoy, Temple and Woodside (n 156).

[158] See more in J Beaulac, E Kristjansson and S Cummins, 'A Systematic Review of Food Deserts, 1966–2007' (2009) 6 *Preventing Chronic Disease* A105.

[159] W Willett et al, 'Food in the Anthropocene: The EAT–Lancet Commission on Healthy Diets from Sustainable Food Systems' (2019) 393 *The Lancet* 447.

[160] ibid.

[161] EAT Lancet Commission, 'EAT Lancet Commission Summary Report' (EAT Lancet Commission, undated) https://eatforum.org/content/uploads/2019/01/EAT-Lancet_Commission_Summary_Report.pdf, accessed 7 November 2019.

Commission also recommend limiting dairy intake to one serving a day, based on the absence of a clear positive correlation between milk intake, bone health and reduced risk of non-communicable diseases, contrary to historical narratives on the 'healthiness' of consuming dairy products.[162]

Subsequent studies, such as those by Springmann et al, report that government (and even WHO) dietary recommendations fall significantly short of the EAT-Lancet's 'Planetary Health Diet' recommendations.[163] Springmann et al created a graded coding method to extract qualitative recommendations from 85 different Food-Based Dietary Guidelines (FBDGs).[164] The health and environmental impact (as compared with international targets[165]) of these FBDGs were assessed using (1) comparative risk assessment of deaths from chronic diseases and (2) country-specific environmental footprints for GHGs, freshwater use, cropland use and fertiliser application.[166] These impacts were then compared with dietary recommendations of the WHO and the EAT-Lancet Commission's 'Planetary Health Diet'.[167] The emissions budget utilised was allocated to food production under a climate stabilisation pathway that is in line with fulfilling Paris Agreement targets (as determined by Wollenberg et al).[168]

It was found that adopting FBDGs was associated with reductions in premature mortality of 15 percent on average, with mixed changes in environmental resource demand, such as an average reduction in GHGs of 13 percent.[169] However, when universally adopted globally, 98 percent of the national guidelines were deemed incompatible with at least one of the global health and environmental targets.[170] Moreover, 67–87 percent were deemed incompatible with the Paris Agreement and other environmental targets.[171] This does not take into consideration that the

[162] ibid; Chan et al (n 156); K Michaëlsson et al, 'Milk Intake and Risk of Mortality and Fractures in Women and Men: Cohort Studies' (2014) 349 *BMJ*, www.bmj.com/content/349/bmj.g6015, accessed 30 September 2020; SA Bondi and K Lieuw, 'Excessive Cow's Milk Consumption and Iron Deficiency in Toddlers: Two Unusual Presentations and Review' (2009) 1 *Infant, Child, & Adolescent Nutrition* 133; D Feskanich, WC Willett and GA Colditz, 'Calcium, Vitamin D, Milk Consumption, and Hip Fractures: A Prospective Study among Postmenopausal Women' (2003) 77 *American Journal of Clinical Nutrition* 504; EF Villagrán-García et al, 'Introduction of Pasteurized/Raw Cow's Milk During the Second Semester of Life as a Risk Factor of Type 1 Diabetes Mellitus in School Children and Adolescents' (2015) 32 *Nutricion Hospitalaria* 634; H zur Hausen and E-M de Villiers, 'Dairy Cattle Serum and Milk Factors Contributing to the Risk of Colon and Breast Cancers' (2015) 137 *International Journal of Cancer*, www.readcube.com/articles/10.1002%2Fijc.29466, accessed 2 October 2020.

[163] M Springmann et al, 'The Healthiness and Sustainability of National and Global Food Based Dietary Guidelines: Modelling Study' [2020] *BMJ* m2322.

[164] ibid.

[165] Includes the Sustainable Development Goal of reducing premature mortality from non-communicable diseases (NCDs by a third), the Paris Agreement's 2°C target, the Aichi biodiversity target of land-use change (cropland), and the sustainable development goals and planetary boundaries related to freshwater use, and nitrogen and phosphorus pollution.

[166] Springmann et al (n 166).

[167] ibid.

[168] Wollenberg et al (n 126).

[169] Springmann et al (n 166).

[170] ibid.

[171] ibid.

actual consumption of goods such as red and processed meat is reported to be on average 44 percent and 51 percent more than is recommended in FBDGs, respectively (with even higher percentages in wealthier regions such as Europe and North America).[172] Moreover, the consumption of healthier foods was on average lower than recommended in FBDGs (reported as up to 166 percent lower on average than recommended in the FBDGs for legumes).[173] Consequently, actual global diets are even further away from international environmental and health targets than existing national guidelines.

By comparison, adoption of the EAT-Lancet Commission's 'Planetary Health Diet' was associated with 34 percent greater reductions in premature mortality and more than three times greater reductions in GHGs and achievement of global health and environmental targets.[174] As a consequence, Springmann et al reported that national guidelines could be healthier and more sustainable with clear advice in most contexts limiting the consumption of animal source foods.[175] In particular, reductions in beef and dairy consumption were found to have the greatest potential for increasing the environmental sustainability of dietary guidelines.[176] It was reported that more whole grains, fruits and vegetables, and legumes, and reducing the intake of red and processed meat, were associated with most additional health benefits (in addition to ensuring balanced energy and calorie intake).[177]

Nevertheless, the EAT-Lancet report was deemed controversial, rattling public bodies, scientists and the general public alike. The controversy was grounded in a number of concerns about the 'Planetary Health Diet', including the micronutrient quality of the recommendations[178] and the cultural acceptability[179] or affordability of such a diet.[180] Other studies have attempted to model their own 'sustainable and healthy diets' that they perceive to be more nutritionally complete and acceptable to consumers than the EAT-Lancet 'Planetary Health Diet'.

For example, Chaudhary and Krishna created country-specific sustainable diets using an optimisation algorithm.[181] They were able to identify diets for 152 countries that meet four culturally acceptability constraints, five food-related per-capita environmental planetary boundaries (carbon emissions, and water, land,

[172] ibid.

[173] ibid.

[174] ibid.

[175] ibid; C Gonzalez Fischer and T Garnett, *Plates, Pyramids, Planet: Developments in National Healthy and Sustainable Dietary Guidelines: A State of Play Assessment* (FAO 2016) www.fao.org/documents/card/en/c/d8dfeaf1-f859-4191-954f-e8e1388cd0b7/, accessed 7 October 2020.

[176] Springmann et al (n 166).

[177] ibid.

[178] 'The EAT Lancet Diet: New Findings' (Friedman School of Nutrition Science and Policy, 2019) https://nutrition.tufts.edu/news/eat-lancet-diet-new-findings, accessed 14 June 2021.

[179] A Chaudhary and V Krishna, 'Country-Specific Sustainable Diets Using Optimization Algorithm' (2019) 53 *Environmental Science & Technology* 7694.

[180] K Hirvonen et al, 'Affordability of the EAT–Lancet Reference Diet: A Global Analysis' (2020) 8 *Lancet Global Health* e59.

[181] Chaudhary and Krishna, (n 179).

nitrogen and phosphorus use), and the daily recommended levels for 29 nutrients (as some reports[182] had called into the question the micronutritional completeness of the EAT-Lancet diet).[183] These cultural acceptability constraints included alcohol/tea/spice amounts, goods not consumed in a country because of religious, cultural or availability reasons, avoiding unrealistic consumption of certain items, and no excessive reductions of food currently consumed.[184] In this study, reductions in the consumption of animal products were also deemed as necessary to achieve a healthy and sustainable diet.[185] In particular, European, North American and Latin American diets were found to need to reduce their consumption of these goods.[186]

Numerous other studies echo the finding that a sustainable and healthy global diet involves reductions in the consumption of animal products, and particularly red and processed meat in high-income countries.[187] Alongside food waste and loss reduction and production efficiency improvements, determining policy interventions to alter consumer behaviour may be key to ensure a sustainable agricultural system that achieves global nutrition and health goals.[188]

Regardless of the specific formulations of the dietary shifts being modelled, calls for reducing meat consumption are often met with unwillingness from policymakers. Given the most significant dietary shifts required are for wealthy people in higher-income countries and the effects of climate change are most drastic in poorer global regions, this unwillingness to address the sustainability

[182] GT Hanley-Cook et al, 'EAT-Lancet Diet Score Requires Minimum Intake Values to Predict Higher Micronutrient Adequacy of Diets in Rural Women of Reproductive Age from Five Low- and Middle-Income Countries' (2021) 126 *British Journal of Nutrition* 92.

[183] Chaudhary and Krishna (n 179).

[184] ibid.

[185] ibid.

[186] ibid.

[187] Stehfest et al (n 135); L Wellesley, C Happer and A Froggatt, *Changing Climate, Changing Diets: Pathways to Lower Meat Consumption* (Chatham House, 2015); L Vranken et al, 'Curbing Global Meat Consumption: Emerging Evidence of a Second Nutrition Transition' (2014) 39 *Environmental Science & Policy* 95; JL Capper, 'Is the Grass Always Greener? Comparing the Environmental Impact of Conventional, Natural and Grass-Fed Beef Production Systems' (2012) 2 *Animals* 127; S McLaren, 'Sustainable Diets: Eating Within Planetary Boundaries' [2017] *New Zealand Land and Food Annual* 9; JJ Hyland et al, 'The Role of Meat in Strategies to Achieve a Sustainable Diet Lower in Greenhouse Gas Emissions: A Review' (2017) 132 *Meat Science* 189; E Röös et al, 'Greedy or Needy? Land Use and Climate Impacts of Food in 2050 under Different Livestock Futures' (2017) 47 *Global Environmental Change* 1; Davis et al (n 118); HHE Van Zanten et al, 'Defining a Land Boundary for Sustainable Livestock Consumption' (2018) 24 *Global Change Biology* 4185; H Harwatt, 'Including Animal to Plant Protein Shifts in Climate Change Mitigation Policy: A Proposed Three-Step Strategy' (2019) 19 *Climate Policy* 533; Oppenlander (n 139); Cassidy et al (n 113); HC J Godfray et al, 'Meat Consumption, Health, and the Environment' (2018) 361 *Science* eaam5324; Popp, Lotze-Campen and Bodirsky (n 121); S Frank et al, 'Reducing Greenhouse Gas Emissions in Agriculture without Compromising Food Security?' (2017) 12 *Environmental Research Letters* 105004; MN Hayek and RD Garrett, 'Nationwide Shift to Grass-Fed Beef Requires Larger Cattle Population' (2018) 13 *Environmental Research Letters* 084005.

[188] P Alexander et al, 'Losses, Inefficiencies and Waste in the Global Food System' (2017) 153 *Agricultural Systems* 190; Berners-Lee (n 15); Wollenberg et al (n 128).

of the global diet is also an unwillingness to reconcile climate justice in the livestock sector. As stated in the Introduction, this book is dedicated to understanding how the current international legal order contributes to or further embeds these unjust dynamics in the livestock sector, delineating the extent to which the need for a global sustainable diet is appropriately acknowledged and addressed in these regimes – starting with the international climate regime in the following chapter.

2

Climate Change and Cattle in the International Climate Regime

The role of the agricultural sector within international climate governance has gained traction over the years, but active recognition of the role of livestock emissions mitigation (and particularly dietary change) in reaching global targets has lagged. The core legal instruments at the heart of much of the international climate regime stem from the UNFCCC agreed in 1992. This framework treaty paved the way for subsequent climate treaties, including the Kyoto Protocol 1997 and the current Paris Agreement on Climate Change 2015 (Paris Agreement). Throughout the international negotiations of these treaties, both agriculture and food systems have often taken a back seat on the negotiation agenda. However, in recent negotiation rounds at COPs to the UNFCCC and the Paris Agreement, the agricultural sector has been more present in the UNFCCC process, both in the periphery of the COP fanfare at 'Blue Zone' side events organised by stakeholders, but also in the COP negotiations themselves.

Following the previous chapter's outlining of the landscape for beef and dairy production and consumption, this chapter maps the historical reluctance to address cattle emissions within the UNFCCC forum that persists even in recent COPs, such as COP27 in Sharm El Sheikh in 2022. Specifically, it reveals how the issue of livestock emissions has (or has not) been addressed within the UN Climate Regime, referring to key climate objectives under the Paris Agreement of climate mitigation, adaptation and finance, but also broader global priorities such as food security. Through this, gaps in livestock emissions mitigation in the international legal order begin to be unveiled, revealing the lagging nature of cattle emissions reductions globally, particularly for high-consuming groups such as developed countries.

Firstly, key instruments and 'pillars' of the international climate regime are outlined to provide context to the rest of the analysis in the chapter. Then, the reluctant coverage of cattle emissions mitigation under the Paris Agreement is compared with the more willing coverage of adaptation in the cattle sector in its legal instruments. Developments at the agri-climate intersection in the international climate regime are then outlined in more detail, including the KJWA and developments on livestock emissions at more recent COPs, such as COP27. The overall takeaways from the chapter are then outlined, providing key conclusions on the international climate regime's coverage of livestock emissions that contribute to the overall macrolevel analysis that the book provides across the international legal order for climate change and cattle.

Key Instruments

In general, the international climate regime focalises on the UNFCCC, which was agreed in 1992 following the Rio Summit. The UNFCCC was the first[1] international environmental treaty that expressly attempted to govern climate change.[2] There is near-universal membership for the treaty, ratified in 1992 with 197 signatories. The UNFCCC's objective is to 'stabilise GHGs concentrating in the atmosphere at a level that would prevent dangerous anthropogenic interference with the climate system'.[3] Although the treaty did not set binding limits on GHGs or establish any enforcement mechanisms, it did establish a framework for negotiating further treaties, protocols or decisions at annual COP meetings that can be binding.[4]

The current and most recent international climate change treaty is the Paris Agreement,[5] often cited as addressing the shortcomings of the Kyoto Protocol 1997.[6] While the creation of the Kyoto Protocol – as the first international climate change treaty to impose GHG emission reduction obligations upon developed states – is often described as a milestone in climate change governance, by the end of its first commitment period it was already deemed to have a number of fundamental flaws.[7] Although a second commitment period for the Protocol was agreed upon in 2012, only 95 of the required 144 parties to the Protocol ratified the Doha Amendment which was intended to commence this second commitment period. As a result, this means that although the Protocol is still in force and binding on the parties, and the parties still meet every year at COPs, the Protocol does not place mitigation obligations on these parties due to the failure of the commencement of the second commitment period.

[1] Although arguably the Montreal Protocol 1987 may have implicitly achieved some climate change mitigation.

[2] United Nations Framework Convention on Climate Change 1992.

[3] ibid.

[4] COP Decisions under the Paris Agreement are generally seen as binding on parties, in the words of Daniel Bodanksy, 'Although ordinarily COP decisions are not legally binding, the article 4 provisions on the information necessary to facilitate clarity, transparency and understanding (ICTU) and accounting provide that parties are to act "in accordance with" relevant COP decisions (technically, decisions of the Conference of the Parties serving as the Meeting of the Parties to the Paris Agreement, or CMA), making the Paris Rulebook decisions on ICTU (the information necessary to facilitate clarity, transparency and understanding) and accounting binding on parties.' See, Climate Action Network International Ad Hoc Legal Working Group, 'COP Decisions: Binding or Not?' (CAN International, 2009).

[5] Paris Agreement on Climate Change 2015.

[6] R Clémençon, 'The Two Sides of the Paris Climate Agreement: Dismal Failure or Historic Breakthrough?' (2016) 25 *Journal of Environment & Development* 3.

[7] ibid.

Following years of fraught negotiations, on 12 December 2015 the new Paris Agreement text was agreed upon at COP21. The Agreement entered into force on 4 November 2016 after reaching the required number of ratifications. Under Article 2(1), the core aim of the Paris Agreement is to '[hold] the increase in the global average temperature to well below 2°C above pre-industrial levels and pursu[e] efforts to limit the temperature increase to 1.5°C above pre-industrial levels, recognizing that this would significantly reduce the risks and impacts of climate change'.[8] To meet this target, parties aim to peak global emissions by 2050 (Article 4.1).[9] The Agreement also mandated numerous other provisions, including: increased transparency and reporting requirements (Article 13[10]) (including a peer scrutiny process in the form of the Talanoa Dialogue[11]); regular Global Stocktakes (Article 14); climate finance (Article 9[12]); market (and non-market) measures (Article 6[13]); adaptation measures (eg Article 7[14]); and re-embedding and adjusting the principle of common-but-differentiated-responsibilities and respective capabilities (CBDRRC), adding the phrase 'in light of different national circumstances'[15] to the Agreement's Preamble and throughout the Agreement.[16]

The Paris Agreement is largely operationalised through national action plans for climate change called NDCs. Under Article 4 of the Agreement, parties are required to submit an NDC every five years that reflects their highest possible ambition and represents a progression over time.[17] The format and content of these NDCs is somewhat flexible in that their contents are determined on the national level via a bottom-up approach – differentiated on different national circumstances, such as socioeconomic development.[18] Nonetheless parties are required to properly account for their NDCs and follow the 'Paris rulebook' created across COP negotiations.[19] In preparing their NDCs, parties shall 'promote environmental integrity, transparency, accuracy, completeness, comparability and consistency, and ensure the avoidance of double counting' and implementation

[8] Paris Agreement on Climate Change 2015, Art 2(2).

[9] ibid Art 4.1.

[10] ibid Art 13.

[11] = Paragraphs 10-11 and Annex II, Decision 1/CP.23, Fiji momentum for implementation, Report of the Conference of the Parties on its twenty-third session, held in Bonn from 6 to 18 November 2017, FCCC/CP/2017/11/Add.1.

[12] Paris Agreement (n 6) Art 9.

[13] ibid Art 6.

[14] ibid Art 7.

[15] This principle will be expanded up and discussed further in the Conclusion, linking the concept of common but differentiated responsibilities and respective capabilities (CBDRRC) in light of different national circumstances to the context of cattle-sector emissions mitigation and the findings of this book.

[16] Paris Agreement (n 6) Art 2.2.

[17] ibid Art 4.

[18] L Rajamani, 'Ambition and Differentiation in the 2015 Paris Agreement: Interpretative Possibilities and Underlying Politics Shorter Articles and Notes' (2016) 65 *ICLQ* 493.

[19] See more in L Rajamani and D Bodansky, 'The Paris Rulebook: Balancing International Prescriptiveness with National Discretion' (2019) 68 *ICLQ* 1023.

progress is monitored regularly at Global Stocktakes.[20] National climate priorities can often be identified when looking at NDCs due to their high-profile status and subsequent scrutiny from civil society, other interested parties, and inclusion in NDC Synthesis Reports produced ahead of COP Meetings by the UNFCCC Secretariat.[21] However, ultimately the content of NDCs remains in the control of the states signed up to the Agreement.

Core Pillars of the Paris Agreement

As time has gone on, the Paris Agreement framework has increasingly been fleshed out and its provisions operationalised during COP meetings in Poland, Madrid, Scotland and Egypt. Whereas 'big' COPs were a rarity prior to the Paris Agreement's ratification, each subsequent COP has been deemed as critical in halting the climate crisis, perhaps in part due to increased media attention, and pressure from civil society groups and those experiencing the realities of climate change. As a result, the core pillars of the Agreement – mitigation, adaptation and climate finance – have been further clarified, with expectations of increased state action and responsibility in tow.

Mitigation

Whether this be the UNFCCC's objective to 'stabilise GHGs concentrating in the atmosphere at a level that would prevent dangerous anthropogenic interference with the climate system', or the Paris Agreement's temperature-limiting goal under Article 2 alongside its requirement for parties to submit and aim to work towards this goal in their NDCs, mitigation is a high priority within the international climate regime.[22] There is a broad range of sectors that can be included within this mitigation focus, including agriculture. Although it created no obligation to achieve results, the Paris Agreement does create binding NDC reporting requirements for its parties.[23] In combination with a principle of non-retrogression to drive ambition,[24] and enforcement mechanisms, such as the enhanced transparency framework,[25] there is an expectation that mitigation will take a central role in state climate action.

[20] Paris Agreement (n 6).
[21] See, for example, the popular Climate Action Tracker that utilises NDCs to assess states' efforts in relation to climate action. More at www.climateactiontracker.org. See also an example of the most recent NDC Synthesis Report produced by the UNFCCC Secretariat: https://unfccc.int/ndc-synthesis-report-2022. These reports are produced ahead of each COP to help inform negotiations.
[22] Paris Agreement (n 6) Arts 3 and 4.
[23] See more in L Rajamani, 'The 2015 Paris Agreement: Interplay Between Hard, Soft and Non-obligations' (2016) 28 *Journal of Environmental Law* 22.
[24] Paris Agreement (n 6) Art 4(3).
[25] ibid Art 13.

Adaptation

Adaptation provisions, by comparison, have progressed more slowly, despite the UNFCCC's original objectives under Article 2 referring to both mitigation and adaptation.[26] In the first years following the UNFCCC agreement, mitigation was arguably the primary focus of climate action, such as mitigation targets and timetables up to 2001 for developed countries under the Kyoto Protocol.[27] However, following the 2001 third assessment report from the IPCC, 'it became clear that mitigation alone would not be sufficient, and Parties began planning and implementing adaptation measures in earnest'.[28] This catalysed adaptation considerations at subsequent COPs, such as at Cancun at COP16 in 2010, where the milestone Cancun Adaptation Framework was agreed upon by UNFCCC parties.[29] Following this increased prioritisation, unsurprisingly adaptation provisions are significantly strengthened under the Paris Agreement, and they are now considered to be of virtually equal importance to mitigation – particularly as the impacts of climate change are becoming a reality globally rather than a hypothetical future risk.[30]

A long-term adaptation goal is established under Article 7 of the Agreement, entrenching adaptation's importance in the global climate regime, whilst signifying an urgency to reduce vulnerability to climate change.[31] Article 7 calls on all parties to engage in assessments of impacts and vulnerability, to adopt national adaptation plans, to determine national priority actions, and to monitor and evaluate their implementation of these measures.[32] Developed countries are required under Article 9 to support and mobilise scaled-up climate finance to assist with adaptation (though it also exists for mitigation), including a biennial reporting requirement to monitor climate finance provisions.[33] The scope of adaptation is equally broad; it is not specified which anthropogenic sources must be included and how they should be included (eg in NDCs), although again adaptation efforts are included in the Global Stocktake – entrenching the deemed importance of addressing adaptation within the international climate regime.[34]

[26] UNFCCC (n 2) Art 2.

[27] See Kyoto Protocol 1997, Annex B.

[28] UNFCCC Adaptation Committee, *25 Years of Adaptation under the UNFCCC* (UNFCCC, 2019).

[29] Decision 1/CP.16 'The Cancun Agreements: Outcome of the work of the Ad Hoc Working Group on Long-term Cooperative Action under the Convention', FCCC/CP/2010/7/Add.1. See more in L Di Pietro Paolo, 'From the Cancun Adaptation Framework to the Paris Agreement' in M del Pilar Bueno Rubial and L Siegele (eds), *Negotiating Climate Change Adaptation: The Common Position of the Group of 77 and China* (Springer, 2020) https://doi.org/10.1007/978-3-030-41021-6_8, accessed 18 August 2023.

[30] A Lesnikowski et al, 'What Does the Paris Agreement Mean for Adaptation?' (2017) 17 *Climate Policy* 825.

[31] ibid.

[32] Paris Agreement (n 6) Art 7.

[33] ibid Art 9.

[34] ibid Art 7(14).

Climate Finance

Article 9 of the Paris Agreement stipulates that developed-country parties shall provide financial resources to assist developing-country parties with respect to both mitigation and adaptation in continuation of their existing obligations under the Convention.[35] Climate finance measures are often a contentious part of COP negotiations. Great sums are needed to finance necessary mitigation and adaptation measures, particularly in terms of financial flows from the Global North to South as part of the former's responsibility for historic levels of GHG emissions and the relative capabilities of these regions.[36] As a result, developed countries are supposed to provide financial resources to assist developing countries to implement the Paris Agreement.[37] Financial mechanisms were developed prior to the Paris Agreement, with international entities such as the Global Environment Facility (GEF) and the Green Climate Fund (GCF) being entrusted to operate the financial mechanisms of the UNFCCC.[38] At COP15 in Copenhagen, developed countries pledged to mobilise US$100 billion in climate finance annually by 2020 to help vulnerable nations deal with climate change – although, in 2023, this target has still not been met.[39]

One aspect of climate finance that has received particular attention during recent COP negotiations was establishing and operationalising a Loss and Damage Fund for nations most vulnerable to the effects of the climate crisis. Progress arguably fell short in negotiations at COP26 in the Glasgow Pact, although the following year at COP27 some further details of the Loss and Damage Fund were decided upon.[40] Governments made a decision to establish new funding arrangements, and a specific fund, to provide finance for developing countries in response to loss and damage. A Transitional Committee was agreed to be established to make recommendations on how to operationalise the new funding arrangements and funds at COP28.[41] The institutional arrangements of the Santiago Network for Loss and Damage were also agreed upon to help catalyse technical assistance to

[35] ibid.

[36] An estimated US$1.2–1.7 trillion of climate finance per year by 2030 is reported to be needed. See more Independent High-Level Expert Group on Climate Finance, *Finance for Climate Action: Scaling Up Investment for Climate and Development* (IHELG, 2022).

[37] For more on climate finance provision in reality, see P Pauw and K Mbeva, *Self-differentiation of Countries' Responsibilities: Addressing Climate Change through Intended Nationally Determined Contributions* (Deutsches Institut für Entwicklungspolitik, 2016) from 24.

[38] eg see UNFCCC (n 2) Art 21(3).

[39] 'COP27 Reaches Breakthrough Agreement on New "Loss and Damage" Fund for Vulnerable Countries | UNFCCC' (UN Press Release, 2022) https://unfccc.int/news/cop27-reaches-breakthrough-agreement-on-new-loss-and-damage-fund-for-vulnerable-countries, accessed 11 August 2023.

[40] Decision 2/CP.27, Funding Arrangements for Responding to Loss and Damage Associated with the Adverse Effects of Climate Change, Including a Focus on Addressing Loss and Damage, FCCC/CP/2022/10/Add.1.

[41] ibid.

developing countries.[42] The high-level status of these negotiations in recent COPs again highlights the importance attributed to climate finance provisions under the Agreement and for developing and least-developed countries globally.

Reluctant Coverage of Cattle Emissions Mitigation in the International Climate Regime

Despite these core pillars of the Agreement underpinning state action and collective progress towards the 2°C temperature goal, agricultural emissions, and more specifically livestock emissions, are essentially non-existent as a sectoral priority under the Agreement. There is a divergence in the willingness to address cattle emissions across the three core pillars of the Paris Agreement – with a clear tendency to swerve the issue of livestock emissions mitigation, instead limiting climate action in the livestock sector to measures focusing on adaptation and food security, particularly for developing regions. This section outlines the historical divergence of agri-climate law-making across these core pillars, particularly in relation to livestock emissions mitigation.

Mitigation for the Agricultural Sector under the International Climate Regime

Under the initial UNFCCC, agriculture is only considered a 'relevant sector' under Article 4(c) and Article 4(e) of the initial UNFCCC in reference to technology transfer and adaptation, not mitigation.[43] In fact, in the initial UNFCCC text, protecting food production was put on an equal (or perhaps even greater) pedestal as the need for climate change mitigation. For example, Article 2 of the UNFCCC states that:

> The ultimate objective of this Convention and any related legal instruments that the Conference of the Parties may adopt is to achieve, in accordance with the relevant provisions of the Convention, stabilization of greenhouse gas concentrations in the atmosphere at a level that would prevent dangerous anthropogenic interference with the climate system. Such a level should be achieved within a time-frame sufficient to allow ecosystems to adapt naturally to climate change, *to ensure that food production is not threatened* [emphasis added] and to enable economic development to proceed in a sustainable manner.[44]

[42] Decision 11/CP.27, Santiago Network for Averting, Minimizing and Addressing Loss and Damage Associated with the Adverse Effects of Climate Change under the Warsaw International Mechanism for Loss and Damage Associated with Climate Change Impacts, FCCC/CP/2022/10/Add.1.
[43] UNFCCC (n 2) Art 4(c) and (e).
[44] ibid Art 2(b).

This provision identifies the perceived trade-off that can exist between food production and climate change mitigation, thereby limiting any mitigation action under the Convention to the extent it compromises food production.

Under the Paris Agreement, there are no specific mitigation requirements relating to agriculture or livestock in the text itself. Despite the lack of concrete provisions relating to agriculture in the Agreement, some NDCs have included mitigation provisions for their agricultural sector – whether merely in a party's emission logs[45] or in relation to more concrete provisions.[46] In the Enhanced Transparency Framework, the provision of qualitative and quantitative agricultural emissions information is also listed as a possible 'mitigation co-benefit' when expanding on NDC plans for economic diversification or adaptation projects.[47] However, an expectation of all parties to include agriculture in their NDC's mitigation plans is not strongly embedded in the Agreement – particularly in relation to livestock emissions.

This is best reflected in the first round of NDCs following ratification of the Paris Agreement. The FAO reported that 148 of the 165 Paris parties actually included agriculture in their mitigation contributions under their initial NDCs (71 percent, 88 percent and 98 percent of developing countries, economies in transition and developed countries, respectively).[48] Of the 69 countries that mentioned livestock, 19 countries highlighted concrete measures[49] referring to 'feed management' (10 countries), 'breeding management' (5 countries) and 'manure management' (15 countries).[50] The FAO stated that 54 percent of countries did not elaborate beyond simply including agriculture in their economy-wide emissions target to create more targeted mitigation policies, such as those for their domestic cattle sectors.[51] Moreover, none of the largest global agricultural emitters included

[45] For example, see the EU's NDC on page 13, Council of the EU, 'Submission to the UNFCCC on behalf of the European Union and its Member States on the update of the nationally determined contribution of the European Union and its Member States' [2023] 14222/1/20.

[46] See, for example, Uruguay's NDC, República Oriental del Uruguay, 'Segunda Contribución Determinada a nivel Nacional al Acuerdo de París' (2022). Or more in n 49 on Uruguay's first NDC.

[47] See UNFCCC, 'ETF Reference Manual', https://unfccc.int/sites/default/files/resource/ETFReferenceManual.pdf, accessed 27 August 2021.

[48] R Strohmaier et al, 'The Agriculture Sectors in the Intended Nationally Determined Contributions – Analysis' (FAO, 2016) Environment and Natural Resources Working Paper No 62, 5.

[49] Uruguay provides a good example of concrete measures for dealing with livestock in an NDC. Uruguay's first NDC contains quantitative agricultural mitigation targets that targets both methane and N_2O from cattle stocks and their manure. The NDC records an unconditional target intensity reduction of 32 percent in methane emissions per kg of beef cattle by 2025 (from a base year 1990). Manure emissions are also covered, with an unconditional 34 percent intensity reduction target in N_2O per kg of beef cattle. Specificity is also provided in how these objectives may be achieved, such as: Climate Smart Agriculture policy and the use of zero discharge technologies for rivers and streams; and/or applications of good practices of nutrient minimisation/recovery for at least 40 percent of dairy farms. See Oriental Republic of Uruguay, 'First Nationally Determined Contribution to the Paris Agreement' (2017).

[50] Strohmaier et al (n 41) 13.

[51] ibid.

agricultural-sector-specific contributions in their first NDCs, and no developed-country party referred to livestock in their first NDC.[52]

Arguably as momentum gathered and awareness increased of the impact of the livestock sector on the climate, the coverage of livestock in updated NDCs improved. The WWF analysed updated NDCs following a similar methodology to the FAO, reporting that 63 updated NDCs have mitigation measures that explicitly consider livestock, a 133 percent increase from 27 of the previous NDCs that did so.[53] Beyond this, increased consideration of post-harvest demand-side mitigation policies was identified, such as reducing food waste, or even dietary change. For example, 36 updated NDCs consider post-harvest food measures, a 71 percent increase compared to 21 previous NDCs reported.[54] Nineteen updated NDCs consider food waste reduction, compared to only three parties in their previous NDCs.[55] Dietary shift measures were also found in five NDCs, compared to only one of the previous NDCs.[56]

An interesting example of a diet-related measure in an NDC comes from Costa Rica. In its updated NDC in 2020, 'Adapted Food Guides' were to be developed for two of the country's territories and included measures to encourage the consumption of 'Indigenous, traditional, and seasonal agricultural and food products',[57] highlighting their 'nutritional value, and their contribution to the protection of cultural heritage, the reduction of emissions, and food security'.[58] In particular, plants, animals and fungi that are native to the environment in which they are grown were promoted, as they require less external and economic inputs than 'conventional' crops – thereby producing fewer GHG emissions.

This being said, none of the five NDCs including diet-related measures were from developed countries, despite their higher consumption of meat and dairy products.[59] Instead, developing countries such as Eswatini were most often the ones including dietary shifts in their NDCs – motivated from food security concerns rather than necessarily because their dietary choices are driving global agricultural emissions.[60] The United Kingdom had referred to changes in diets and sustainable food systems in previous NDCs. However, now these diet-related

[52] ibid.

[53] WWF, *Unlocking and Scaling Climate Solutions in Food Systems: An Assessment of Nationally Determined Contributions* (WWF, 2022) wwfint.awsassets.panda.org/downloads/unlocking_and_scaling_climate_solutions_in_food_systems___wwf_analysis_of_ndcs_2022.pdf, accessed 10 January 2023, 5–6.

[54] ibid 5.

[55] ibid.

[56] ibid 6.

[57] ibid 8.

[58] 'Contribución Nacionalmente Determinada de Costa Rica 2020' (2020) https://cop23.unfccc.int/sites/default/files/NDC/2022-06/Contribucio%CC%81n%20Nacionalmente%20Determinada%20de%20Costa%20Rica%202020%20-%20Versio%CC%81n%20Completa.pdf, accessed 10 August 2023.

[59] WWF (n 46) 21.

[60] ibid.

measures were not included – despite food waste loss reductions making the cut for inclusion in their updated NDC.[61]

Generally, food waste was more willingly addressed than dietary change in NDCs by states. For example, China – a rapidly developing country – listed a joint mitigation and adaptation programme called the 'empty-plate' public awareness campaign in their NDC.[62] This is essentially an awareness campaign about food waste that notably was not included in any of its previous NDC submissions.[63] Whilst food waste is not as commonplace in NDCs as measures related to other sectors, it is interesting to note the political willingness to include food waste in NDCs, but not to reduce overall levels of consumption of emissions-intensive livestock products at the root of the problem.

Food Security and Adaptation under the International Climate Regime

Much of the momentum surrounding the livestock sector and climate change actually focuses on the issue of food security or adaptation. Food security, for the author's purpose,[64] refers to the Rome Declaration on World Food Security 1996 definition, where food security is seen as when 'all people, at all times, have physical and economic access to sufficient, safe and nutritious food that meets their dietary needs and food preferences for an active and healthy life'.[65] In this sense, it appears that the state *is* willing to undertake climate action within the food or livestock sector, but only where food supply or security is threatened or vulnerable to the impacts of climate change. When a change – or even a reduction – in meat consumption is discussed in climate negotiations, the issue is quickly brushed under the (dinner) table.

Adaptation and Food Security under the International Climate Regime

This section focuses on the development of food production, agricultural adaptation and food security provisions under the regime – particularly in comparison to the lack of mitigation provisions. Agricultural sector adaptation

[61] ibid 66.

[62] ibid 21.

[63] See more generally '"Operation Empty Plate": Xi Jinping Makes Food Waste his Next Target', *The Guardian*, 13 August 2020, www.theguardian.com/world/2020/aug/13/operation-empty-plate-xi-jinping-makes-food-waste-his-next-target, accessed 10 August 2023.

[64] No clear working definition of food security is provided by the UNFCCC, or in the climate treaties. Instead, the author opts for the FAO's generally accepted definition – as another UN-level body.

[65] Rome Declaration on World Food Security 1996.

and food security often go hand-in-hand in climate governance. This is because adaptation measures are required for agricultural systems that are vulnerable to the impacts of climate change, as this vulnerability threatens food security and farmer livelihood – particularly in typically poorer and heavily agrarian economies.[66]

The importance of food security and the need for adaptation in the agricultural sector was recognised even in early international climate governance. It was explicitly referred to in the initial UNFCCC framework treaty under Article 4(e), which required that all parties shall '[c]ooperate in preparing for adaptation to the impacts of climate change; develop and elaborate appropriate and integrated plans for coastal zone management, water resources and *agriculture*, and for the protection and rehabilitation of areas, particularly in Africa, affected by drought and desertification, as well as floods' (emphasis added).[67] Additionally, as per the aforementioned Article 2(b) of the UNFCCC, any mitigation action under the Convention should not compromise food production.[68]

Adaptation and food security are equally held in high importance under the Paris Agreement. For example, Article 2(1)(b) of the Agreement similarly seeks to limit climate measures to the extent they compromise food security, 'seek[ing] to increase the ability to adapt to the adverse impacts of climate change and foster climate resilience and low greenhouse gas emissions development, in a manner that *does not threaten food production*' (emphasis added).[69] It is not entirely clear why the language of 'food production' is used over 'agriculture' more generally again.[70] The negotiation texts are not of much assistance in understanding this,[71] although Zahar suggests this may simply be to reflect the language used in the original UNFCCC treaty that referred to 'food production'.[72]

Under the Paris Agreement, references to food systems are additionally expressed in terms of food security and adaptation, rather than solely in the language of 'food production' as under the UNFCCC – though echoing the UNFCCC's recognition of the importance of food production's role in this. For example, the preamble to the Agreement recognises 'the fundamental priority of safeguarding food security and ending hunger and the particular

[66] FAO, *The Role of Agriculture in the Development of Least-Developed Countries and their Integration into the World Economy* (FAO, 2002) www.fao.org/3/y3997e/y3997e.pdf, accessed 12 July 2023.

[67] UNFCCC (n 2) Art 4(3).

[68] ibid Art. 2(b).

[69] Paris Agreement (n 6) Art 2(1)(b).

[70] Especially considering the increased use of terminology related to climate change and agriculture, such as the 'AFOLU' sector (agriculture, forestry and other land use).

[71] J Verschuuren, 'The Paris Agreement on Climate Change: Agriculture and Food Security Mini-Symposium on the Paris Agreement on Climate Change' (2016) 7 *European Journal of Risk Regulation* 54.

[72] A Zahar, 'Agricultural Exceptionalism in the Climate Change Treaties' (2023) 12 *Transnational Environmental Law* 42.

vulnerabilities of food production systems to the adverse impacts of climate change'.[73] This expansion in language surrounding food security provides the additional socioeconomic context to the agricultural sector's importance for human development given current global hunger levels – rather than solely 'food production' references.

From this analysis, it can be said that food security and adaptation also have more explicit prioritisation in the key climate treaty instruments than agricultural emissions mitigation. This explicit prioritisation may have also translated into better inclusion of adaptation measures for food security in NDC submissions by state parties. For example, 97 percent of countries that included the agriculture sector in an adaptation context in their initial NDCs (127 out of 131) referred to either the agriculture sector generally or more specifically in the context of crops and livestock.[74] Of these 127 countries, 114 outlined specific adaptation policies and/or measures for agriculture, 25 percent of which refer to food security specifically.[75] In total 71 countries referred to livestock and pastoral systems, 66 of which mentioned specific actions from rehabilitation of degraded rangeland to improved management of transhumance and agro-pastoralism.[76] Sub-Saharan African states especially denoted livestock and pasture management as a significant element of their adaptation strategies.[77]

Whilst a similar number of countries mentioned livestock in adaptation and mitigation language in their initial NDCs, nearly 3.5 times more countries highlighted concrete measures relating to livestock under adaptation compared with under mitigation – again, most often coming from developing countries.[78] This makes the comparative neglect of developed countries' livestock emissions mitigation measures in NDCs starker.

As evidenced by the prevalence of livestock and adaptation measures in even the initial rounds of NDCs, food systems do not exist in a silo from the international climate regime. Yet, livestock emissions mitigation measures appear to be actively neglected despite the contribution the sector makes to global GHG emissions levels. This does not undermine the co-benefits for mitigation that agricultural adaptation measures can bring – nor does it undermine the importance of adaptation measures in vulnerable agricultural systems. However, a predominant focus on adaptation measures (or only the mitigation co-benefits of adaptation) neglects the role of developed-country consumption patterns of agricultural and livestock emissions. Instead, developing countries are the only regions undertaking commitments for their food systems.

[73] Paris Agreement (n 6) Preamble.
[74] Strohmaier et al (n 41) 27.
[75] ibid 28.
[76] ibid.
[77] ibid 29.
[78] Author's own calculations from statistics in Strohmaier et al (n 41).

Agricultural Climate Finance under the International Climate Regime

Agricultural climate finance flows from developed to developing countries could somewhat plug this gap in coverage. However, issues surrounding the consistency of definitions of agriculture and climate finance globally (despite the aforementioned developments in research at COPs) can make it difficult to track climate finance flows for livestock over the years compared to other (even non-agricultural) sectors.

Despite this, the FAO has nevertheless identified a generally stagnated trend in agricultural climate finance in comparison to other sectors.[79] The FAO reported that, between 2000 and 2018, the share of global climate finance in the agriculture and land-use sector has decreased, passing from an average of 45 percent of the total flows at the beginning of the century to 24 percent in 2013, where it has since stayed.[80] The total of the contributions to the agriculture and land-use sector between 2000 and 2018 was reported to amount to US$122 billion, which represented only 26 percent of the global climate finance flows to all sectors.[81]

Therefore, whereas it is not possible from the existing data to make any conclusion on what these agricultural finance flows were for (namely, adaptation or mitigation), there is evidence that suggests the agricultural sector as a whole is a neglected sector for climate finance. This contributes to the narrative of general neglect of agri-climate issues that will be identified in this book. However, it may also serve as another example of where developed countries and wealthy global actors are falling short in the contributions they can make to support agri-climate measures globally.

Agri-climate-Specific Work Programmes in the International Climate Regime

Despite the lack of agriculture-specific provisions in the core treaties in the international climate regime, other work programmes have emerged out of COP Meetings and Decisions. One important initiative under the international climate regime, which at one time one would have been labelled promising, that has not been mentioned in this chapter so far is the KJWA (and its more recent successor, the Sharm El Sheikh Joint Work on implementation of climate action on agriculture and food security[82]).

[79] FAO, *Climate Finance in the Agriculture and Land Use Sector – Global and Regional Trends between 2000 and 2018* (FAO, 2021) www.fao.org/documents/card/en/c/cb6056en, accessed 17 January 2023, 8.

[80] ibid.

[81] ibid.

[82] Decision 3.CP/27, Sharm El-Sheikh Joint Work on Implementation of Climate Action on Agriculture and Food Security Decision 3.CP/27, FCCC/CP/2022/10/Add.1.

The KJWA was the first substantive COP outcome on agriculture, and the Joint Work was the first substantive COP decision that brought both the international agricultural and climate regimes together to work on agri-climate issues. A 'dedicated' agenda item on issues related to agriculture under the Subsidiary Body for Scientific and Technological Advice[83] (SBSTA) was first formalised in 2011 (under section D Decision 2/CP.17[84]), followed by five in-session workshops on the status of scientific knowledge concerning agriculture and climate change. The interactions among countries led to a specific decision on agriculture, the KJWA, which was passed at COP23 in 2017.[85]

The joint work called for collaboration between the SBSTA and the Subsidiary Body for Implementation (SBI), extending the scope of the discussions from merely scientific and technical details towards implementation. Decision 4/CP.23 itself requests the two Subsidiary Bodies under the UNFCCC – the SBSTA and SBI – to jointly address issues related to agriculture, taking into account the vulnerabilities of agriculture to climate change and approaches to addressing food security. It was a key decision for agri-climate measures, as it 'it emphasiz[ed] the key role of agriculture and food security in the international climate change agenda', as well as solidifying the FAO's work to support the UNFCCC in the development and implementation of agri-climate work. Although the COP Decision does not place binding action on signatories to the Agreement, the Decision represents a recognition of the increasing importance of agriculture and climate change in recent years, as well as an intention to provide material for parties to draw on with regard to their agri-climate provisions.

The baseline of topics covered by the KJWA were: (a) modalities for implementation of the outcomes of the five in-session workshops on issues related to agriculture and other future topics that may arise from this work; (b) methods and approaches for assessing adaptation, adaptation co-benefits and resilience; (c) improved soil carbon, soil health and soil fertility under grassland and cropland as well as integrated systems, including water management; (d) improved nutrient use and manure management towards sustainable and resilient agricultural systems; (e) improved livestock management systems; and (f) socioeconomic and food security dimensions of climate change in the agricultural sector.[86]

Prior to COP27, the scope setting of the Joint Work was often broad, with workshop groups and submissions covering a vast array of agriculture-related

[83] The SBSTA carries out methodological work under the Convention, the Kyoto Protocol and the Paris Agreement, and promotes collaboration in the field of research and systematic observation of the climate system.

[84] Decision 2/CP.17, Report of the Conference of the Parties on Its Seventeenth Session, Held in Durban from 28 November to 11 December 2011, FCCC/CP/2011/9/Add.1.

[85] Decision 4/CP.23, Koronivia Joint Work on Agriculture, FCCC/CP/2017/11/Add.1.

[86] ibid.

climate action loosely linked to the modalities above. The support for a food security focus in the KJWA workshops from state participants was widespread. Given the greater willingness of states to include food security or adaptation measures in their climate plans, perhaps this is unsurprising.

More reluctance was met when demand-side mitigation measures were raised, such as dietary change. For example, at the workshop at COP25 in Madrid on Topic 2(d) manure management, the promotion of a diet where meat consumption was reduced by 50 percent in developed countries to free up land for crop production was discussed but was not necessarily well-received.[87] Workshop participants thought it would not be successful or viable due to (1) implementation issues with trying to change dietary systems; (2) a lack of comparability of the suitability of land for changing from livestock to crop production; (3) needing protein as a health source, particularly in children; (4) improving livestock production efficiency actually reducing meat prices and therefore increasing meat production; and (5) consequential potential increased production of meat and grain for export, minimising any gross environmental benefits on a global scale.[88] In the reporting of these workshops, the participants who raised specific arguments are omitted. Therefore, due to this lack of knowledge of the participants who raised these particular arguments in the workshop report, it is hard to understand the underlying interests at play when making these arguments and how they played into the development of the Joint Work.

This being said, at the Topic 2(f) workshop on socioeconomic and food security dimensions of climate change in the agricultural sector, it was recognised that 'food waste, food loss and unbalanced diets are a *preventable* source of GHG emissions' (emphasis added).[89] This statement demonstrates recognition of the role dietary choices play in adding to GHG emissions within the Joint Work development. In light of this, a 'point of entry' for the KJWA to take action was delineated – namely, 'advocating for policy reform in relation to food loss and food waste, dietary changes, agricultural subsidies and inclusion of the private sector and trade [in agri-environmental policies]'.[90]

[87] See para 50 in UNFCCC Secretariat, 'Improved Nutrient Use and Manure Management towards Sustainable and Resilient Agricultural Systems Workshop Report by the Secretariat' (UNFCCC 2020) FCCC/SB/2020/1, https://unfccc.int/sites/default/files/resource/sb2020_01E.pdf, accessed 18 August 2023.

[88] ibid.

[89] See summary of discussions in this Workshop here: FAO, *Koronivia Joint Work on Agriculture – Summary of Workshop on Topic 2(f): Socio-economic and Food Security Dimensions of Climate Change in the Agricultural Sector* (FAO, 2021) www.fao.org/documents/card/en/c/cb5018en/, accessed 7 December 2021. See the full Workshop report here: UNFCCC Secretariat, 'Socioeconomic and Food Security Dimensions of Climate Change in the Agricultural Sector Workshop Report by the Secretariat' (UNFCCC, 2021) FCCC/SB/2021/2, https://unfccc.int/sites/default/files/resource/sb2021_02E.pdf, accessed 18 August 2023.

[90] FAO (n 83).

COP 27 Developments

Although consensus on the need for more mitigation and demand-side livestock solutions, such as dietary change, was not solidified in the agenda-setting workshops for the KJWA as food security or adaptation measures, there is evidence suggesting that demand-side measures, such as dietary choice, are increasingly being raised in the UNFCCC forum. At COP27 the prioritisation of addressing agriculture in the international climate regime was further solidified. The first 'food-systems pavilion' at a COP was hosted, despite the significant presence of animal livestock industry giants at the COP meeting.[91] In terms of COP decisions negotiated, a four-year plan on agriculture and food security was agreed upon – the Sharm El Sheikh Joint Work on the Implementation on Agriculture of Food Security.[92] This Decision includes implementation of the outcomes of the KJWA[93] and previous activities addressing issues related to agriculture,[94] including future topics as they arise recognising that solutions are context-specific and take into account national circumstances.[95]

A number of objectives were outlined for this work plan, although mitigation was only mentioned three times in the Decision, always paired alongside adaptation co-benefits.[96] The majority of references to agricultural climate action to be addressed by the work path are paired with food security concerns.[97] Naturally, adaptation is important in protecting the well-being of these groups. For vulnerable groups, adaptation is the priority but even the IPCC endorses the need for differentiated livestock solutions for diverse production systems and national contexts.[98] Without a strong parallel effort being invested into the mitigation of agricultural emissions from wealthier and high-consuming groups, a gap in livestock emissions mitigation in these parties exists. The Sharm El Sheikh Joint Work is in its earlier stages of implementation so the future direction of efforts may expand to include these concerns. However, given the past reluctance of the KJWA to address demand-side strategies for mitigation in wealthier groups, any optimism for this shift must be taken with a grain of salt.

[91] A So, 'Power, Access & Influence: Which Food Organisations Participated at COP27?' (Food Research Collaboration, 2022) https://foodresearch.org.uk/blogs/power-access-influence-which-food-organisations-participated-at-cop27/, accessed 22 June 2023.

[92] 'Sharm El-Sheikh Joint Work' (n 75).

[93] The mandate of which has now ended.

[94] See eg ibid paras 2, 3, 4, 6, 8, 14.

[95] ibid para 14.

[96] Ibid, para 14(a), (o) and (t).

[97] Food security is actually mentioned 22 times throughout the Decision, compared to mitigation only being mentioned three times.

[98] See more in C Mbow et al, 'Food Security' in PR Shukla et al (eds), *Climate Change and Land: An IPCC special Report on Climate Change, Desertification, Land Degradation, Sustainable Land Management, Food Security, and Greenhouse Gas Fluxes in Terrestrial Ecosystems* (IPCC, 2019), ch 5, eg 440.

Here, the context of the lengthy negotiations of the Joint Work provides valuable insight on its provisions. Carbon Brief reported that negotiations of the Joint Work agenda were fraught with political tensions, and that the Joint Work agenda item at COP27 required more hours of negotiation in the first week than any item on the negotiating agenda.[99] Part way through negotiations, the 'whole food systems approach' – which also considers elements such as the consumption of livestock goods – was deleted from the text, with more language on implementation, support and vulnerability added.[100] Carbon Brief noted that 'whole food systems approaches' were a key dividing element between countries that already have language around food systems in policies, such as the EU's Farm to Fork Strategy, versus countries that were either unclear or reluctant to talk about aspects such as consumption and diets.[101] Other notable tensions included India objecting to the words 'climate action' (over simply, 'action') in the title of earlier drafts of the Decision for the Joint Work, although this ultimately remained in the title as 'climate action'.[102]

Despite these tensions in formal negotiations, the consideration of livestock emissions mitigation in more informal avenues in the international climate regime may be increasing. For those avidly watching agri-climate developments in the COP process, the non-binding Global Methane Pledge launched during COP26 piqued interest and optimism.[103] The initiative was led by Joe Biden and Ursula von der Leyen and participants joining the Pledge agreed to take voluntary actions to contribute to a collective effort to reduce global methane emissions by at least 30 percent from 2020 levels by 2030, which could eliminate over 0.2°C warming by 2050.[104] The Pledge has grown to over 100 countries, though notably missing India and China. While initial planning for the Pledge focused heavily on oil and gas infrastructure to reduce methane emissions, as the Pledge has developed, a Food and Agriculture Pathway was created.[105]

The GMP Food and Agriculture Pathway largely focuses on advancing climate and food security goals through new actions that increase agricultural productivity, reduce food loss and waste, and improve the viability of future agriculture.[106] Initial elements of the Pathway include boosting financial support for smallholder farmers, particularly in developing countries such as Kenya, Rwanda or Uganda.[107]

[99] Carbon Brief Staff, 'COP27: Key Outcomes for Food, Forests, Land and Nature at the UN Climate Talks in Egypt', *Carbon Brief*, 24 November 2022, www.carbonbrief.org/cop27-key-outcomes-for-food-forests-land-and-nature-at-the-un-climate-talks-in-egypt/, accessed 10 January 2023.
[100] ibid.
[101] ibid.
[102] ibid.
[103] See more CCA Coalition, *Global Methane Pledge* (CCA Coalition, 2021).
[104] ibid.
[105] Office of the Spokesperson, 'Global Methane Pledge: From Moment to Momentum – United States Department of State' (Global Methane Pledge, 2022) www.state.gov/global-methane-pledge-from-moment-to-momentum/.
[106] ibid.
[107] ibid.

A new Enteric Methane Research and Development Accelerator is supported by the Global Methane Hub to advance technical research on potential methane solutions.[108] It is interesting here again to see the linking of agriculture with food security, and supply-side technical solutions.

Demand-side strategies are arguably being considered in some form within the work surrounding the Pledge. There is an explicit reference to the role of reducing food loss and waste in meeting global methane targets on a factsheet on the Pledge released by the United States and European Union. For example, as part of both the GMP Waste Pathway and the GMP Food and Agriculture Pathway, a Food Waste Management Accelerator is set to develop methane mitigation projects in ten countries in Latin America and the Caribbean.[109] However, the issue of dietary change is circumvented in the examples of work undertaken and is planned to be undertaken as part of the Pledge.

Ultimately, the Pledge remains a separate venture that, while complementing the Paris Agreement, does not require any active participation or contribution from state signatories to the Agreement. With many states signed up to the Pledge, awareness of the need to tackle methane emissions (as well as carbon emissions) may increase. However, against the backdrop of the piecemeal coverage of the livestock sector in the international climate regime identified (and the path dependency of livestock production that will be identified across the entirety of this book) there is concern about how far band-aid solutions, such as the Pledge, may fill the gaps left in formal negotiations.

Other more informal livestock emissions solutions have arisen around recent COP negotiations (rather than in COP decisions), particularly at COP27 in Egypt. One example of this relates to agricultural climate finance. A new initiative, – Food and Agriculture for Sustainable Transformation (FAST) was launched at COP27 by more than twenty agriculture ministers and the Egyptian COP27 presidency.[110] FAST is a multi-stakeholder programme that aims to increase finance to transform the agricultural sector through (1) enhancing country capacities to identify and access climate finance, (2) providing analysis and developing voluntary guidelines to support capacity development across stakeholders, and (3) improving the embedding of agri-food systems in climate change policies.[111] This is still in its early stages, making calls for interest for participation and with only provisory lists of relevant initiatives, networks and coalitions listed on the COP27 website page for the initiative. The FAST initiative may offer some potential to better address livestock emissions –on both the demand and supply sides.

[108] ibid.

[109] ibid.

[110] See more on FAST here: 'FAST Initiative', http://example.com/index.htm, accessed 14 July 2023.

[111] ibid.

Another relevant informal initiative launched at COP27 was the Initiative on Climate Action and Nutrition (I-CAN).[112] This was launched jointly with the WHO with the goal of integrating the global delivery of climate change adaptation and mitigation policy and nutrition and sustainable food outcomes. To achieve these goals, the I-CAN has established a number of pathways to help Member States to accelerate progress in connecting climate and nutrition actions, including: (1) building nutrition into NDCs; (2) including climate in national nutrition plans; and (3) encouraging more countries to include climate considerations in their dietary guidelines.[113]

While the menus at COP27 included a range of resource-intensive animal-based foods,[114] more direct linking of diet and climate is seen in these informal ventures from the meeting. However, there again is no requirement for parties to the Paris Agreement to be involved in their development or implementation. It may spur momentum to consider the role of consumption (and particularly the public health impacts of high consumption of certain resource-intensive dietary components) more fully in the UNFCCC forum, possibly at COP side events. However, the extent of its impact will be reliant upon the national will of motivated states and delegates to develop alongside other COP decisions that are part of the formal process of negotiations under the UNFCCC, such as the new Sharm El Sheikh Joint Work that builds upon the previous work of the KJWA.

Conclusion

This chapter began this book's investigation of livestock emissions coverage (or lack thereof) in the international legal order for climate change and cattle. Through its analysis, the historical reluctance to formally address livestock emissions within the international climate regime has been demonstrated. This reluctance has persisted across multiple COP negotiations, revealing how the issue of livestock emissions mitigation is less willingly addressed in formal international climate governance, despite livestock being far more readily addressed in relation to issues of adaptation or food security. While livestock does play a key role in achieving food security and adaptation goals under the international climate regime, failing to address the role of livestock in driving emissions – predominantly from wealthier, high-consuming groups – excludes key actors from

[112] 'Initiative on Climate and Nutrition (I-CAN) Launched at COP27' (Nutrition Connect, 2022) https://nutritionconnect.org/news-events/initiative-climate-and-nutrition-i-can-launched-cop27, accessed 18 August 2023.

[113] WHO, 'Initiative on Climate Action And Nutrition (WHO, undated) =https://.gainhealth.org/sites/default/files/publications/documents/Initiative-on-climate-action-and-nutrition-I-CAN.pdf, accessed 23 November 2023.

[114] A Buxton, 'COP27, World's Largest Climate Crisis Conference, Sparks Controversy After Serving Meat', *Plant Based News*, 12 November 2022, https://plantbasednews.org/news/environment/cop27-climate-crisis-conference-serving-meat/, accessed 14 August 2023.

their responsibility to address their unsustainable consumption of luxury dietary components, such as beef.

Firstly, overviews of key instruments under the international climate regime were provided to provide context to the analysis that followed. The core pillars of the Paris Agreement – mitigation, adaptation and climate finance – were outlined to demonstrate the generally high priority placed on the role of mitigation (and even climate finance) in the broader climate regime, even if this does not extend to the issue of livestock emissions. The historical consideration of the agricultural sector, and specifically the livestock sector, was outlined over the course of international climate negotiations from the UNFCCC's agreement to the Paris Agreement. Despite an increasing trend to consider livestock and agriculture in mitigation under NDCs, dietary change remained a lagging area of mandated action. Most current analysis of NDCs notes that of the five references made in NDCs to dietary change as a policy action, none are NDCs from developed countries with higher levels of wealthier groups consuming resource-intensive dietary components, such as beef.[115] When compared to the willingness of parties to include considerations of the livestock sector in relation to other aspects of the international climate regime, such as adaptation or food security, there appears to be a clear preference to avoid the issue of consumption or demand-side strategies within the UNFCCC forum.

More agriculture-focused initiatives and their inclusion of livestock and the consumption of livestock were also outlined. In particular, the KJWA offered some initial promise of the climate impact agricultural sector becoming fully integrated into the international climate regime with the assistance of the FAO. However, the progress of this initiative did not make significant ground in relation to the issue of consumption. The initial work of the KJWA is picked up by the Sharm El Sheikh Joint Work Decision agreed upon at COP27 – with various non-formal initiatives also more recently arising, such as I-CAN which attempts to bring nutrition concerns (such as public-health concerns relating to livestock products) into the climate arena. However, these initiatives are only informal in comparison to the Sharm El Sheikh decision which appears to be strongly food security and adaptation focused once again.

Overall, while the issue is perhaps becoming increasingly considered in climate discourse, the formal avenues requiring developed-country state parties to the Paris Agreement to consider the impact of their livestock consumption are lacking under the international climate regime. Instead, adaptation and food-security-focused initiatives dominate the regime, largely mandating systemic changes in developing countries' production systems (with or without the financial support of developed countries). Food security is an important issue that plagues vulnerable agricultural systems in many developing regions as the impacts of climate change increase. However, the willingness to discuss and address this issue is more of a

[115] WWF (n 46).

given under the international climate regime – with references to protecting food production systems even appearing in the original UNFCCC in the early 1990s. The recognition that wealthier, developed groups play a role in driving agricultural emissions through their consumption is largely avoided – a trend that is also recognised across the range of international legal regimes analysed in the rest of the chapters in this book. The following chapter explores this finding further in the context of the international agricultural regime, looking particularly at the FAO regime and its work.

3

Climate Change and Cattle in the International Agricultural Regime

The work of the FAO was briefly touched on already when examining the international climate regime in the previous chapter. In particular, the chapter looked at the institutional intersection between the international climate and agricultural regimes in the form of Joint Work COP Decisions, such as the KJWA, in addition to other informal climate governance initiatives, such as the FAST Initiative. This chapter instead focuses more specifically on the FAO's wider work on the environmental impact of livestock. The FAO is a key international actor with regard to agricultural policymaking direction and information provision, with its seminal 2006 report, *Livestock's Long Shadow*,[1] spurring increased interest in international environmental law and policymaking with regards to the environmental impact of the livestock sector, such as methane emissions from cattle. The FAO has played a key role in raising awareness of the environmental effects of livestock production, but how does it approach the issue of livestock production, and how far does their work on livestock contribute to roadblocks or pursuance of livestock emissions mitigation in the international legal order for climate change and cattle?

First, the historical development of the FAO's agenda will be introduced to provide context to their prioritisation of different issues relating to livestock emissions. In particular, the historical background of the FAO's development will be linked to their promotion of livestock production as a solution for poverty and food insecurity eradication. However, the more recent climate-focused work of the FAO is then delineated – including their focus on technical, production-side solutions, in addition to their consumption-side, health-focused solutions. The FAO's role as an international environmental institution is then considered, and the extent to which its mandate and information-provision role can influence formal law-making procedures is evaluated. Overall, the chapter provides an additional perspective on how livestock emissions are addressed (and what types of emissions are neglected) by different legal regimes within the international legal order for climate change and cattle, and the consequences this can have for addressing livestock emissions fairly and comprehensively on the international level.

[1] H Steinfeld et al, *Livestock's Long Shadow: Environmental Issues and Options* (FAO, 2006) www.fao.org/publications/card/en/c/9655af93-7f88-58fc-84e8-d70a9a4d8bec/, accessed 6 October 2020.

The Historical Development of the FAO

The FAO is a specialised agency of the United Nations (UN) that leads international efforts to end hunger. With 194 Member States, its aim is to achieve food security[2] for all and ensure that people have access to food that enables them to lead healthy lives. The FAO was founded during the Second World War, although ongoing efforts to form an international agricultural institution began before then.[3] Allied governments engaged in collaborative agricultural and nutritional planning due to the need for wartime food rationing and carefully managed agricultural output.[4] This cross-border agricultural cooperation laid the groundwork for postwar international agricultural governance. In the words of Pernet and Forclas,[5] the creation of the FAO was 'steeped in the hopes of the Allies' to bring about nothing less than the ending of hunger, global improvement of nutritional standards through modernising production, and a universal improvement in living standards.[6]

These intentions are reflected in the preamble of the FAO's Constitution signed in 1945, which sets out the FAO's objectives of 'raising levels of nutrition and standards of living'; 'securing improvements in the efficiency of the production and distribution of all food and agricultural products'; 'bettering the condition of rural populations'; and 'contributing toward an expanding world economy and ensuring humanity's freedom from hunger'.[7] Such goals have persisted through the years, including through the FAO's more recent commitment to achieving the UN's Sustainable Development Goals (SDGs),[8] which include ending poverty and hunger.[9]

Over time, concerns about the impact of agriculture on the environment have also been added to the FAO agenda. Arguably, UN bodies began to recognise the importance of preserving the environment in 1972 at the UN Conference on the Human Environment.[10] However, as concerns about climate change accelerated in

[2] The 1996 World Food Summit in Rome defined food security as existing 'when all people, at all times, have physical and economic access to sufficient, safe and nutritious food to meet their dietary needs and food preferences for an active and healthy life'.

[3] S O'Broin et al, *70 Years of FAO (1945–2015)* (FAO, 2015) www.fao.org/3/i5142e/I5142E.pdf, accessed 26 October 2020.

[4] CA Pernet and AR Forclaz, 'Revisiting the Food and Agriculture Organization (FAO): International Histories of Agriculture, Nutrition, and Development' (2018) 41(2) *International History Review* 346.

[5] Who also highlight the difficulty of historical analysis of the FAO as an institution due to the lack of accessibility to their archival resources. Ibid 347.

[6] Pernet and Forclaz (n 4) 347.

[7] Preamble, FAO Constitution 1945.

[8] Of particular importance here is Sustainable Development Goal 2: Zero Hunger; and Sustainable Development Goal 1: No Poverty, although the FAO has committed to all 17 SDGs in its work plans.

[9] See timelines since 1945 of the different FAO agendas to date, in 'About FAO' (FAO, undated) www.fao.org/about/en/, accessed 8 October 2020 and also O'Broin et al (n 3) 95.

[10] Though TWAIL literature provides a valuable counternarrative to Western environmentalist narratives of the growth of environmental considerations globally; see U Natarajan and J Dehm, *Locating Nature: Making and Unmaking International Law* (Cambridge University Press 2022).

the 2000s,[11] the FAO increasingly recognised the importance of the interlinkages between climate change and agriculture. For example, they published their seminal report, *Livestock's Long Shadow*, in 2006 which has since been a staple reference in the climate and agriculture field, with some sources suggesting it has been cited around 6,500 times in other academic works.[12] Popular culture has relied upon the report in several leading documentaries, such as the popular *Cowspiracy* which is on the Netflix streaming platform.[13] Beyond the impact of this seminal report, the FAO has also held a specific conference on climate change in 2008[14] and committed to achieving SDG 13 on climate action in 2015, in addition to joining global climate negotiations as a key stakeholder in relation to the climate.[15] Other information provision pursuits – such as its leading Global Livestock Environmental Assessment Model (GLEAM) for data provision on the agri-environmental impacts of livestock systems – will be outlined below. Though, generally, it can be said the FAO has cemented itself in the international discourse relating to livestock and the environment.

Livestock Emissions Mitigation under the FAO

The FAO's interest in promoting livestock emissions mitigation is clear in its work path and outputs. In many ways, the FAO has been a leader in recognising and beginning to tackle the environmental footprint of agriculture. As mentioned above, the FAO's ground-breaking report, *Livestock's Long Shadow*, truly rocked the environmental world and is often viewed as the seminal document addressing the environmental footprint (including climate) of the global agricultural sector.[16]

The FAO's creation and ongoing development of the Global Livestock Environmental Assessment Model (GLEAM) framework is also evidence of its work to actualise environmental improvements in the agricultural sector through technical capacity building and information provision.[17] GLEAM is a 'modelling framework that simulates the interaction of activities and processes involved

[11] For example, after the 'failure' of the Kyoto Protocol and the long process of agreeing the Paris Agreement, see A Savaresi, 'The Paris Agreement: A New Beginning?' (2016) 34 *Journal of Energy & Natural Resources Law* 16.

[12] According to Google Scholar, as of August 2023, the report has been cited 6,777 times.

[13] 'COWSPIRACY: The Sustainability Secret', *COWSPIRACY*, www.cowspiracy.com, accessed 28 February 2023.

[14] See more on the Conference here: 'High Level Conference: Home', www.fao.org/foodclimate/hlc-home/en/, accessed 15 August 2023.

[15] See the previous chapter's discussion of the KJWA.

[16] Steinfeld et al (n 1).

[17] For more on the GLEAM model, see the FAO's website. 'Global Livestock Environmental Assessment Model (GLEAM) (FAO, undated) www.fao.org/gleam/en/, accessed 26 October 2020.

in livestock production and the environment'.[18] It operates on a (sub)national, regional and global scale, and enables estimates of lifecycle GHG emissions from different livestock products, different stages of livestock production, different livestock species, etc, to help facilitate improvements in agri-environmental practices. In essence, GLEAM provides a global assessment of livestock emissions, and it can also be applied using country-specific data to estimate national baselines and scenarios to help with agricultural emissions accounting and planning.[19] It was developed to both diagnose areas of improvement in livestock sustainability and inform intervention where action is necessary.

The impact of GLEAM has been widespread: the FAO is already working through GLEAM with 25 countries (often in key hotspots for livestock sector emissions, such as South America and Sub-Saharan Africa[20]), and GLEAM is also being used by many prominent organizations, research institutes and universities, including the World Bank, Global Environment Facility (GEF), Green Climate Fund (GCF), Commonwealth Scientific & Industrial Research Organisation (CSIRO), International Livestock Research Institute (ILRI), Wageningen University and the University of Central Asia.[21]

Significantly, FAO GLEAM outputs are also used by the IPCC to 'inform the development of guidelines relevant to livestock emissions'.[22] Under Article 21(2) of the UNFCCC, the UNFCCC secretariat 'cooperate[s] closely with the Intergovernmental Panel on Climate Change to ensure that the Panel can respond to the [Secretariat's] need for objective scientific and technical advice'.[23] This thereby embeds the FAO's role in international agri-climate governance, as its information provision underpins the climate accounting and guidelines used by the IPCC.[24] As a consequence, GLEAM feeds directly into the international climate regime and its coverage of the agricultural sector.

Beyond this, the FAO has published significantly over the years on its research to promote improvement of the sustainability of agriculture, including mitigating livestock emissions.[25] Within this research, there are two approaches endorsed by the FAO to address livestock emissions, each offering different potential solutions.

[18] ibid.

[19] FAO, *Five Practical Actions towards Low-Carbon Livestock* (FAO, 2019) 40, 18.

[20] FAO, *GLEAM in Practice* (FAO, undated) www.fao.org/gleam/in-practice/en/,accessed 17 May 2021.

[21] FAO (n 19) 18.

[22] ibid. For more in the role on the IPCC's relationship to the UNFCCC, see NS Ghaleigh, 'Science and Climate Change Law – The Role of the IPCC in International Decision-Making' (Oxford Handbook of International Climate Change Law, 24 March 2016) www.oxfordhandbooks.com/view/10.1093/law/9780199684601.001.0001/oxfordhb-9780199684601-e-3, accessed 19 March 2021.

[23] United Nations Framework Convention on Climate Change 1992, Art 21(2).

[24] Ghaleigh (n 22); M Hulme and M Mahony, *Progress Report Climate Change: What Do We Know about the IPCC?* (2010) 34(5) *Progress in Physical Geography: Earth and Environment* 705–18; E Vasileiadou, G Heimeriks and C Petersen, 'Exploring the Impact of the IPCC Assessment Reports on Science' (2011) 14 *Environmental Science & Policy* 1052.

[25] For just one example, see FAO, *Livestock Solutions for Climate Change* (FAO, 2017).

The first approach focuses on the production side of the livestock sector, and the second approach focuses on the consumption side of the livestock sector and wider food systems. Both of these approaches promote livestock emissions mitigation, but each presents the issue of livestock emission from a different perspective, thereby offering a different mitigation solution. The production-side approach refers to policies that target the production of livestock production (such as farm-side technical methods and techniques), whereas the consumption side refers to policies that target the consumption of livestock (such as heavy subsidisation of agricultural production or dietary guidelines).

Production-Side Livestock Emissions Mitigation under the FAO

One of the ways the FAO presents the issue of livestock emissions is as a matter of production inefficiency. In other words, the production of livestock products is seen to be environmentally inefficient, producing a number of unnecessary negative environmental impacts, such as methane emissions. The FAO thus identifies numerous technical supply-side efficiency improvements as mitigation solutions in their published works.[26] In particular, these include encouraging 'climate smart agriculture' (agricultural processes that minimise the emissions intensity of production), including changes to cattle breeds, feeds, etc, to make livestock production more efficient.[27] As a result of this focus on 'inefficient' production systems, it is more often than not the case that developing countries or lower-income countries are targeted by the FAO in putting forward policy recommendations under this approach.[28] In fact, the majority of the FAO's country- or region-specific reports or case studies on sustainable dairy and livestock were focused on developing (or in the case of Ukraine, comparatively lower-income[29]) countries characterised by more inefficient production.[30]

By comparison, there has been only one FAO case study or report on livestock sustainability in developed countries or regions.[31] Even while focusing on

[26] See FAO (n 19) eg 144–22.

[27] See eg FAO, *Climate-Smart Agriculture Sourcebook* (FAO, 2017)www.fao.org/climate-smart-agriculture-sourcebook/en/.

[28] In line with emissions data for agriculture, which shows high emissions intensity of production in developing or low-income regions (see ch 1 for more statistics on this).

[29] FAO, *Ukraine: Improving Milk Supply in Northern Ukraine: Technical Assistance to Ukraine's Dairy Sector.* (FAO, 2013).

[30] See eg the Dairy Development for the Resource Poor series by FAO Regional Offices, eg FAO, *Dairy Development for the Resource Poor Part 1: A Comparison of Dairy Policies and Development in South Asia and East Africa* (FAO, 2008).

[31] See M Halderman and M Nelson, 'EU Policy Making: Reform of the CAP and EU Trade in Beef and Dairy with Developing Countries' (Pro Poor Livestock Policy Initiative, undated) Working Paper No 18.

EU agricultural policies, the report still focused on developing country interests to a significant extent, highlighting the negative impact of EU agricultural policies on developing-country agricultural sectors.[32] As a result of this developing-country focus, the issue of global hunger and rising livestock demand from global population growth (predominantly in developing countries) are addressed and more closely discussed alongside sustainability issues. In other words, this production-side approach is often used to promote efficiency improvements in production to 'free up' agricultural capacity to tackle food security issues in developing countries, in addition to satisfying the increasing demand for animal products in these regions from their growing middle classes.

This can be seen clearly in the FAO's Strategic Framework from 2010 to 2019, which outlined 'sustainable intensification', and with regards to the livestock sector, 'increased sustainable livestock production' as strategic objectives.[33] Sustainable intensification is often ill-defined and considered contentious terminology – both for its environmental implications, but also its implication that more animals may be kept in poorer welfare conditions in its strive to intensify and streamline resource use.[34] However, definitions generally converge around the idea that sustainable intensification pursues improvements in production efficiency and reductions in the environmental externalities of agricultural production, though some suggest that it also pursues increased overall yields where necessary, which may bring increases in absolute emissions.[35]

The concept itself is uncertain and may vary in meaning depending on different local circumstances. In an environmental context, the FAO has stated that a 'sustainable food system' could ensure the positive or neutral effect of its activities on the natural environment with ecosystem and biodiversity being taken into consideration.[36] This may imply that sustainable livestock intensification in the FAO context would not pursue increases in output that would also increase absolute emissions. Resisting an increase in absolute emissions would avoid negative climate effects – though clarification on the FAO's standpoint on this issue would be beneficial.

Regardless, global hunger concerns are pressing, and it is therefore understandable why sustainable intensification has been offered as a viable solution to these issues as it increases access to food while using fewer natural resources. Sustainable intensification does also bring improvements in environmental efficiency, even if not necessarily in terms of absolute emissions. As the majority of livestock emissions come (and will continue to do so) from developing countries, efficiency improvements can produce significant emissions reductions for

[32] ibid 5–15.

[33] FAO, *Strategic Framework 2010–2019* (FAO 2009) C 2009/3,www.fao.org/3/k5864e01/k5864e01.pdf.

[34] See more in M Cardwell and F Smith, 'Renegotiation of the WTO Agreement on Agriculture: Accommodating the New Big Issues' (2013) 62 ICLQ 865, 872.

[35] ibid.

[36] A Mukhtar, *Policy Space for Sustainable Agriculture in the World Trade Organization Agreement on Agriculture* (FAO, 2020) 5.

the sector from business-as-usual pathways. However, as has been emphasised throughout this text so far, production inefficiency is only one layer of the problem underpinning the unsustainability of the agricultural sector. Whilst the FAO was historically formed to tackle hunger, policy interventions suggested by the FAO to address elevated consumption among higher-income countries or groups (both in developed *and* developing countries) are also relevant to consider when looking at the types of livestock emissions solutions promoted by the FAO.

Consumption-Side Livestock Emissions Mitigation under the FAO

The FAO has highlighted the role of consuming livestock goods in driving GHG emissions throughout its work on the livestock and the environment to some degree.[37] For example, the FAO highlights how the existence of market distortions in the agricultural sector may increase consumption. For example, when environmental externalities are not properly reflected in agricultural prices this can artificially increase demand for these goods by making prices cheaper than if externalities were properly accounted for. In one of their more recent livestock publications, *Five Practical Actions Towards Low-Carbon Livestock*, the FAO suggested that an 'undoing' of these market distortions is required in order to fully reflect environmental externalities.[38]

Generally, public policy interventions are highlighted as being particularly important in delivering the changes required to lower emissions in the livestock sector.[39] Giving an example of a possible public policy intervention that could address these market distortions, the FAO suggests that existing agricultural subsidies could be redirected towards incentivising farmers towards more efficient production (particularly referring to the role direct payments could play in achieving this if utilised under the right conditions).[40] Subsidisation of inefficient production (or production of less climate-friendly agricultural goods, such as beef) can lead to market conditions where the price of a good does not properly reflect its externalities as farmers actually operate at a loss.[41]

Proper emissions accounting in carbon pricing is also referred to as another way to address emissions externalities in the livestock sector, with a potential role for a well-designed meat tax discussed (comparing this with taxes that seek to reduce the health impact of sugary drinks and tobacco, though also noting its

[37] FAO (n 19) 13–15.
[38] ibid.
[39] ibid.
[40] ibid.
[41] For an EU example of this, see data on farm incomes for beef and dairy production in relation to cattle related Common Agricultural Policy (CAP) payments in Wageningen University et al, *Research for Agri Committee – The EU Cattle Sector: Challenges and Opportunities – Milk and Meat* (European Parliament, 2017) 281–84.

potential ineffectiveness).[42] 'Pull incentives' generally are referred to as a way to help 'generate market demand in support of shifts towards best practices' (namely, away from very inefficient livestock production).[43] For example, the potential effectiveness of stringent and reliable certification schemes for agri-food systems was also highlighted by the FAO as an option to raise consumer awareness and incorporate increasing consumer concerns about issues of animal welfare and sustainability into practical schemes.[44] In particular, when designed with 'rigorous traceability' and 'appropriate labelling systems' for livestock commodities at the point of sale, climate-smart certification schemes that involve 'benchmarking', 'monitoring' and 'evaluation' are seen as a way for governments, regulatory bodies, professional societies and cooperatives to respond to consumer pressure for markets to be more environmentally sustainable, including by ensuring higher levels of animal welfare.[45]

Through the identification and high-profile dissemination of potential consumer-side solutions such as these to policymakers,[46] the FAO has actively introduced the issue of consumption as a driver of livestock emissions within the international agricultural regime. This is because the issue of livestock emissions has been presented not only as an issue of production inefficiency (or of production-side factors) but also as one that can be tackled through addressing demand-side solutions, such as redirecting subsidies, or creating labelling schemes to address consumption-side issues related to livestock emissions. In particular, the FAO integrates its work on public health with the issue of sustainability to add additional weight to its promotion of policies that reorient food systems towards healthy and sustainable diets.

The FAO's Integration of Health Concerns into Consumption-Side Livestock Emissions Reduction

The way the FAO addresses the emissions associated with high consumption of resource-intensive dietary components in its work is often through its linking with human or public health concerns. Within FAO recommendations, dietary change is provided as a potential emissions solution for (1) excessive consumption of animal products that are linked with potentially increased risk of non-communicable diseases, such as colorectal cancer, and (2) overconsumption of foodstuffs generally (in parallel with eating too few fruits, vegetables and other healthy

[42] FAO (n 19) 13–15.
[43] ibid.
[44] ibid.
[45] ibid.
[46] And others not listed in the section, such as promoting a circular economy, cutting food waste and recycling waste output, in addition to the role of potential lab-derived meat replacement innovation that is being driven by consumer demand.

foods), which has led to the existence of what is labelled by the FAO as an 'obesity epidemic'.[47]

Reducing excessive consumption of resource-intensive livestock products should reduce the overall emissions produced by the average 'healthy diet' due to decreased consumption of these products and increased consumption of other more environmentally efficient sources of nutrition, such as fruits vegetables, legumes or wholegrains.[48] Moreover, it should also increase (or better balance) the consumption of these healthier foods, thereby contributing to improved individual and public health outcomes. However, as has been said previously, the FAO only recommends dietary change as a livestock solution where there are high or unhealthy levels of consumption of these goods, giving rise to negative health effects such as cancer risk, non-communicable disease or 'obesity'. This generally targets higher-income and developed countries, in contrast to the technical solutions promoted by the FAO that generally target developing or lower-income country producers (who generally have more inefficient livestock production, often in addition to food security issues). Even in the original *Livestock's Long Shadow* report in 2006, 'wealthy people' are explicitly referred to as the target of policies aimed at reducing excessive consumption of livestock products.[49] More recent FAO publications echo this sentiment, stating that 'overall protein consumption, and the contribution from livestock products, are closely linked to wealth with people in high-income countries generally consuming far more animal-source foods than in low to medium-income countries'.[50]

'Healthy, Sustainable Diets' under the FAO

Having established the FAO's boundaries and target groups for recommended dietary shifts, it is now possible to delineate the practical steps the FAO has taken to promote these solutions. A common theme raised so far across this text is the neglect of livestock emissions solutions for more developed global regions, with higher proportions of wealthy groups consuming high levels of resource-intensive dietary components, such as beef. The FAO begins to plug this gap through its integrative approach of bringing together sustainability (in this case, GHG emissions) and nutrition to strive for 'healthy, sustainable diets' in its work.[51]

[47] See more FAO (n 19) 11–12. The author does not endorse the use of terminology such as 'obesity' due to anti-fat bias in medicine, and the unreliability of the body mass index for all demographics. See further A Barnes, 'Overweight versus Obese: Different Risk and Different Management' (2015) 42 *Texas Heart Institute Journal* 237. However, due to the FAO's use of this word, it will be used to keep consistent terminology with the organisation.

[48] For more of the studies and data on the health impacts of meat and dairy consumption, see ch 1.

[49] Steinfeld et al (n 12) 269.

[50] FAO (n 19) 11.

[51] ibid.

One specific example of this approach being implemented in the FAO's work was its analysis of national food guidelines (where they exist) that were assessed to determine the extent to which they are consistent with health and sustainability goals.[52] The FAO found only 83 out of 215 countries had food-based dietary guidelines (FBDGs), and there was a particular absence of FBDGs in lower-income countries.[53]

However, the FAO highlighted that some countries were particularly forward-thinking in terms of health and sustainability in their FBDGs, including Germany, Brazil, Sweden and Qatar.[54] The FAO notes all of these countries emphasised the health and planetary advantages of a plant-based diet, despite some variation in emphasis and detail provided in this regard.[55] Sweden offers one of the strongest examples of integrated environmental and health guidelines of this kind. The Swedish guidelines provide specific advice on the types of plant-based foods to consume to promote sustainability, for example, encouraging long-life root vegetables over perishable salad greens (in terms of food waste).[56] The guidelines that include sustainability provisions all highlight the high environmental impact of meat, although Qatar only briefly refers to the impacts of meat consumption in health-related terms in its FBDGs.[57]

The FAO found that Brazilian FBDGs were unique in that they emphasized the 'social and economic' dimensions of what sustainable consumption entails for consumers. The guidelines advise Brazilians to be cautious in relation to food advertising and to avoid highly processed foods that are bad for health and undermine traditional Brazilian food cultures.[58] This is an interesting contrast to solely environmental definitions of sustainability, delving deeper into the socioeconomic drivers of consumption habits including the role of traditional diets, commercial food interests and advertising.[59]

The FAO's analysis of FBDGs from this integrated health and sustainability perspective demonstrates the gentle nudging[60] by the FAO to encourage Member States to change the eating habits of their populations away from high consumption

[52] See more FAO and WHO, *Sustainable Healthy Diets: Guiding Principles* (FAO and WHO, 2019).

[53] ibid 15.

[54] Others were found to have started to have conversations about sustainable diets in their FBDGs, but these were not yet official, eg Australia, the United States, the Netherlands, Estonia, the United Kingdom and France; see ibid 3.

[55] Gonzalez Fischer and Garnett (n 55) 17.

[56] ibid 28.

[57] ibid 33.

[58] ibid 23.

[59] The FAO itself has said that effective food and health education is often only afforded to the most elite in society, leaving many susceptible to the advertisements of 'unhealthy' foods. See ibid 56.

[60] Nudging in this sense refers to inducing behavioural change without coercion or strict obligation. FBDGs are a form of nudging that can utilised by Member States to improve consumption habits; see J Guthrie, L Mancino and C-T Jordan Lin, 'Nudging Consumers toward Better Food Choices: Policy Approaches to Changing Food Consumption Behaviors' (2015) 32 *Psychology & Marketing* 501; TM Marteau et al, 'Judging Nudging: Can Nudging Improve Population Health?' (2011) 342 *BMJ* d228; S Benartzi et al, 'Should Governments Invest More in Nudging?' (2017) 28 *Psychological Science* 1041.

of products such as red meat, and away from unhealthy or excessive consumption in general. There is a realisation that a nation's perspective on a 'healthy diet' is often learned through FBDGs, particularly when educating children in schools.[61] Thus, the FAO's analysis constitutes an attempt to highlight and showcase good national FBDG practices, in addition to providing information on how FBDGs can be improved from a health and sustainability perspective.[62] By engaging with these specific Member State examples, the FAO may be able to inspire a peer-learning process through its analysis.[63] Moreover, it demonstrates the FAO's broader recognition of the complexities of demand-side issues surrounding health and sustainability, and how to address them.

The Contentious Nature of Dietary Change as a Policy Solution under the FAO

Despite the FAO's work on the sustainability and healthiness of national diets, proposing dietary change as a livestock emissions solution is still a contentious issue for the FAO and its contributing stakeholders. Moreover, dietary change as a climate solution often does not receive the same traction as production-side technical solutions that seek to reduce the emissions produced by livestock, such as cattle. For example, while not discrediting dietary change as a mitigation solution, a few of the FAO's reports explicitly state that assessment on the implementation of this is outside their scope of research, despite supply-side mitigation strategies being presented.[64]

Other publications have appeared to distance themselves from dietary change as a possible livestock emissions solution. For example, one of the major FAO-facilitated stakeholder groups (the Global Agenda on Sustainable Livestock (GASL)[65]) posted a response to the publication of the aforementioned EAT-Lancet

[61] Children often learn their lifelong dietary habits at this age: see eg Elham Z Movassagh et al, 'Tracking Dietary Patterns over 20 Years from Childhood through Adolescence into Young Adulthood: The Saskatchewan Pediatric Bone Mineral Accrual Study' (2017) 9 *Nutrients* www.ncbi.nlm.nih.gov/pmc/articles/PMC5622750/, accessed 6 November 2019.

[62] This is often a soft law strategy to ensure compliance, see more on 'reputational costs' in KW Abbott and D Snidal, 'Hard and Soft Law in International Governance' (2000) 54 *International Organization* 421, 427–28.

[63] See discussion of the role of peer review in experimentalist governance, eg Gráinne De Búrca, Robert O Keohane and Charles Sabel, 'Global Experimentalist Governance' (2014) 44 *British Journal of Political Science* 477 and see DE Ho, 'Does Peer Review Work? An Experiment of Experimentalism' (2017) 69(1) *Stanford Law Review*.

[64] See Gerber and FAO (n 25) 45.

[65] GASL is a multi-stakeholder partnership with 111 institutional members, facilitated by the FAO. Stakeholders are grouped into seven clusters: the public sector, the private sector, non-governmental organizations (NGOs), donors, academia and research (A&R) centres, social movements and community-based organizations (pastoralist groups), and intergovernmental and multilateral organizations such as FAO, the World Bank, the International Livestock Research Institute, the International Organization for Animal Health, the UN International Fund for Agricultural Development and the

Commission report on healthy and sustainable diets.[66] The EAT-Lancet report offered similar mitigation options as the FAO itself – improving production efficiency, making dietary changes and other demand-side improvements, such as reducing food waste.[67] However, arguably the report had a dominant focus on dietary change as a climate solution[68] – particularly targeting high-income country diets.[69] Nonetheless, the EAT-Lancet report did make appropriate concessions to the dietary changes it proposed, including highlighting the need not to undermine agricultural livelihoods supported by livestock production, and recognising that dietary changes may not be appropriate for all stakeholders, such as those who need livestock products for nutritional reasons.[70]

The GASL statement in response to the report is somewhat defensive, making an effort to differentiate the GASL's actions from the EAT-Lancet proposals.[71] Instead, it highlights other possible mitigation options, even outlining the environmental benefits of some types of livestock production, in addition to discussing the nutritional benefits of livestock consumption.[72] Overall, the statement suggests that GASL was reluctant to endorse the EAT-Lancet report's dominant focus on dietary change as a solution for agricultural sector sustainability (even if only in high-income countries).

This report may not be representative of the FAO's livestock mitigation approach as a whole, as we saw some willingness to endorse dietary change among affluent actors as a mitigation solution earlier in this chapter. It is also interesting to note that dietary change as a livestock solution is largely only addressed by the FAO when it is providing synergies with public health outcomes. Even then the FAO remains tentative on this theme at times, instead often being more comfortable in making recommendations in relation to food security as discussed below.

African Union. Each cluster is represented by five members in a Guiding Group, led by the GASL Chair, who provides guidance in line with the GASL Action Plan.

[66] F Schneider, 'Statement by GASL on the EAT-Lancet Commission Report' (Global Agenda for Sustainable Livestock 2019).

[67] W Willett et al, 'Food in the Anthropocene: The EAT–Lancet Commission on Healthy Diets from Sustainable Food Systems' (2019) 393 *The Lancet* 447.

[68] The EAT forum itself is a non-profit funded by the Stordalen Foundation, the Stockholm Resilience Centre and the Welcome Trust. Their vision is for a 'fair and sustainable global food system for healthy people and planet – leaving no one behind' with a mission 'to transform our global food system through sound science, impatient disruption and novel partnerships'. They have a self-confessed 'conviction' to 'deliver disruptive solutions, where others can't' – perhaps underpinning why they were so bold and focused with their dietary-focused solutions in the EAT-Lancet Report whereas others, including the FAO, are more tentative in letting discussions of dietary change and livestock emissions dominate the discourse.

[69] Willett et al (n 67) eg 479 and 482.

[70] ibid 482.

[71] Schneider (n 66) 1, 'GASL's approach to the sustainability of food and agriculture in general and of livestock agri-food systems in particular differs from that of the EAT-Lancet Commission in a number of important ways: it is multidimensional, multistakeholder, multifaceted, and it embraces the enormous diversity of livestock agrifood systems globally.'

[72] ibid 2.

Livestock as a Food Security and Poverty Eradication Solution under the FAO

The FAO is constantly balancing its food security objectives against its more recently established agri-environmental objectives. As was discussed in the introduction to this section, the FAO was created as an institution to end global hunger during wartime food scarcity. Whether it be in the FAO's Constitution[73] or its commitment to achieving the UN SDGs,[74] it is clear that the FAO is committed to tackling food security issues, such as hunger or nutrition. Even on the most basic symbolic level, the FAO's emblem shows an ear of wheat alongside their motto, *fiat panis*, 'let there be bread'. The FAO has since further narrowed its hunger-ending mandate into a more specific low-income food security workstream in relation to livestock production.

The FAO attempts to target food security issues that more commonly affect lower-income groups and countries, such as hunger and malnutrition. More specifically, in this work, the FAO presents livestock production as an avenue for eradicating hunger and malnutrition, alleviating poverty and providing livelihood support, and not only as a source of environmental externalities, such as methane emissions. For example, consistent references are made to the dietary role of meat and animal products in preventing malnutrition in the most vulnerable populations globally (particularly women and children) due to their high levels of protein and key micronutrients, such as iron.[75]

The FAO also makes an effort to show the interlinkages between livestock production, food security and eradicating poverty. In particular, the FAO frequently references smallholder livestock farmers in developing countries, and how livestock consumption actually helps protect the livelihoods of these farmers and their families.[76] For instance, in 2001, the FAO launched the 'Pro-Poor Livestock Policy Initiative' (PPLPI) which aims to create policy and institutional changes in the livestock sector for the purpose of benefiting the poor.[77] This targeted developing-country agricultural sectors in particular to exemplify the development benefits that livestock can have, especially on the poorest producers in these countries.[78]

[73] For example, see 'raising the levels of nutrition and standards of living'; 'bettering the condition of rural population'; 'contributing toward an expanding world economy and ensuring humanity's freedom from hunger' in the FAO Constitution.

[74] The FAO is committed to achieving SDGs such as ending poverty and hunger: 'SDG Progress Report' (FAO, undated) www.fao.org/sdg-progress-report/en/, accessed 8 October 2020.

[75] See eg FAO, Animal Production and Health Division, *Shaping the Future of Livestock; Sustainably, Responsibly, Efficiently* (FAO, 2018) 3.

[76] See *FAO, Developing Sustainable Value Chains for Small-Scale Livestock Producers* (FAO 2019) 3 and 10 for more on who are classed as small-scale livestock producers.

[77] FAO, *Pro-Poor Livestock Policy Initiative: A Living from Livestock Sector Policies and Programmes in Developing Countries: A Menu for Practitioners* (FAO, 2010) www.fao.org/3/i1520e/i1520e00.pdf.

[78] eg ibid 1.1–1.2.

The framing of livestock production as a poverty and food insecurity eradication strategy can have co-benefits in improving the environmental efficiency of production in some cases. By improving the efficiency of production, more food can be produced with fewer resources to nourish vulnerable populations and address food shortages while also improving agri-environmental footprints. Additionally, supporting the livestock production of the most vulnerable smallholder farmers (particularly in developing countries) can have many socioeconomic benefits for their livelihoods, including providing subsistence and increasing their resilience to supply shocks (such as a reduction in harvest yield due to severe drought caused by climate change).[79]

While this food-security-focused workstream strives to increase and stabilise access to livestock goods for vulnerable populations, its objectives do not necessarily clash with other livestock emissions solutions promoted by the FAO such as dietary change. In fact, these solutions can work together simultaneously in a complementary fashion. This is because calls for dietary change for sustainability and health reasons target wealthier and higher-income consumers, more frequently in developed countries. Food security and poverty strategies that involve improving production efficiency, by contrast, target poorer and more vulnerable populations, commonly in developing countries.

Boundaries between wealthy and poorer groups may be blurred in developing countries where there is income inequality, and wealthier middle classes exist alongside groups that are more financially vulnerable or disadvantaged in terms of food security.[80] Tensions may also exist if dietary change is imposed on vulnerable groups (such as pregnant women), or excessively high consumption of these goods is pursued under the veil of food security. However, the tensions and boundaries of these approaches (such as the target demographic of their solutions) are clearly defined by the FAO. Though, of course, the extent to which these solutions are up taken appropriately by policymakers may be beyond the remit of the FAO's role in international agri-climate governance.

The FAO's Role in International Agri-climate Governance

Information Provision

The FAO's role as an international institution in international agri-climate governance may somewhat differ from other UN institutions discussed so far due to its

[79] FAO (n 76) s 2.

[80] For more on income equality globally, see United Nations, *Inequality – Bridging the Divide* (United Nations, undated) www.un.org/en/un75/inequality-bridging-divide, accessed 3 September 2021.

expansive research and outreach role. Under Article 1 of the FAO Constitution, the FAO is mandated to undertake several actions to support global agricultural needs, including: (1) collecting, analysing, interpreting and disseminating information relating to nutrition, food and agriculture; (2) promoting and recommending national and international action with respect to, inter alia, scientific, technological, social and economic research relating to nutrition, food and agriculture, the conservation of natural resources and the adoption of improved methods of agricultural production; and (3) providing technical assistance to governments if requested.[81] As a consequence, the FAO can be seen to play a significant information-providing and expert role for an international institution through its gathering and disseminating of agricultural data and best practice – completed by its large Secretariat, reported to consist of 1,738 professional staff and 1,510 support staff.[82]

Since the FAO's formation it has undertaken several significant activities to pursue this mandate. This includes completing World Food Surveys in addition to creating FAOSTAT to provide statistics and information on the global state of agriculture, including forests.[83] GLEAM also provides a good example of the FAO's role in providing information in relation to the livestock sector. The GLEAM framework is evidence of its work to help realise environmental improvements in key stakeholders in the agricultural sector through technical capacity building and information provision.[84] As mentioned previously, GLEAM is a 'modelling framework that simulates the interaction of activities and processes involved in livestock production and the environment'.[85] It operates on various levels of governance and enables estimations of lifecycle GHG emissions from different livestock products, different stages of livestock production, different livestock species and so forth to help facilitate improvements in agri-environmental practices – with its data being used by numerous research institutes and the IPCC in their reports.[86]

This technical support is particularly helpful in the livestock sector given that members have highlighted elsewhere (such as Nationally Determined

[81] Art 1 FAO Constitution 1945. Other objectives include: the promotion and recommendation of national and international action with respect to inter alia scientific, technological, social and economic research relating to nutrition, food and agriculture; the conservation of natural resources, the adoption of improved methods of agricultural production, and the development of policies for the provision of adequate agricultural credit and with respect to agricultural commodity arrangements; provision of technical assistance as governments may request; organisation, in cooperation with the governments concerned, of missions that may be needed to assist them in fulfilling the obligations arising from their acceptance of the recommendations of the United Nations Conference on Food and Agriculture and of the Constitution.

[82] FAO Legal and Ethics Office, *International Regulatory Co-Operation and International Organisations: The Case of the Food and Agriculture Organization of the United Nations* (FAO) (OECD/FAO, 2016) 29.

[83] FAOSTAT was known as AGROSTAT until the mid-1990s; it is viewed as the most comprehensive source of agricultural information and statistics, see O'Broin et al (n 3) 26.

[84] See more nn 21 and 22 above.

[85] See more in nn 17 above.

[86] See more in nn 21 and 22 above.

Contributions (NDCs) under the Paris Agreement) that a lack of technical capacity impedes their ability to address livestock emissions. For example, Argentina highlighted in its first NDC that it struggled to implement correct accounting methodologies to gain reliable information on the scale of its livestock emissions.[87] As a result, it can be said that GLEAM plays a key role in helping to improve the reporting and accounting of livestock emissions, including informing IPCC practices for data in a sector where data collection is more complex.[88]

Data and policy solutions disseminated in seminal documents published by the FAO, such as *Livestock's Long Shadow*, have also become key reference documents for other research and publications on livestock emissions mitigation. This take-up of the FAO's work provides evidence of the FAO's institutional 'credibility' as a policy influencer.[89] The fact, then, that the FAO does not entirely neglect consumption as a driver of livestock emissions unlike other regimes explored in this volume is significant. Through its work on healthy and sustainable diets, there is not a complete lacuna among international or UN bodies on the role of dietary change in reducing the impact of livestock, such as cattle, on the climate.

The FAO's Institutional Capabilities

Despite its dominant reputation as an international technical body, the Conference or the Council of the FAO[90] under Article XIV of the FAO Constitution does actually have the legal authority, by a two-thirds majority of the votes cast, to approve and submit to Member Nations international treaties concerning matters

[87] Argentina 'Nationally Determined Contribution – Argentina' (Government of Argentina, 2021) https://unfccc.int/sites/default/files/NDC/2022-05/Traduccio%CC%81n%20NDC_Argentina.pdf.

[88] See earlier in this chapter at nn 21 and 22.

[89] Benford and Snow state that a policy frame is credible, based on consistency, empirical credibility and the credibility of the frame articulator. RD Benford and DA Snow, 'Framing Processes and Social Movements: An Overview and Assessment' (2000) 26 *Annual Review of Sociology* 611.

[90] The FAO is comprised of 194 Member States, as well as the European Union, Faroe Islands and Tokelau. Three entities form the top level of FAO's governance structure: the Conference, Council, and Director-General. The FAO Conference is the plenary body of Member States. It meets every two years to review the FAO's work, approve a Work Programme and Budget for each biennium, elect the Council and Director-General when necessary, and take other decisions as appropriate. Each Member State receives one vote in the Conference, with most decisions being made by simple majority, and constitutional changes requiring a two-thirds majority. Normally, the Conference approves the proposals presented to it unanimously, though recently budgetary matters have been more contentious. The Council has the responsibility for operations and management policies. The Director General sits as the head of the FAO Secretariat and its senior management. The Office of the Director-General is responsible for budget preparations, strategic plans, and other proposals for approval by the governing bodies, as well as final responsibility for the day-to-day management of the FAO.

relating to food and agriculture.[91] Currently, 17 treaties have been approved under Article XIV of the Constitution and are in force, spanning animal production and health, fisheries, genetic resources for food and agriculture, and plant production and protection.[92] The OECD states these Article XIV treaties most commonly include obligations relating to sharing information, surveys and research; surveillance, early-warning systems and crisis management; and compliance assessment and settlement of disputes.[93] The FAO can also create voluntary instruments, such as the prevalent Codex Alimentarius for food safety, to help encourage best practices from stakeholders.[94] The OECD highlights the significant work done by the FAO to strengthen these voluntary initiatives, such as improving participation in voluntary instruments such as this through capacity-building or keeping instruments updated and revised in light of new technical information developed.[95]

Creating a treaty with mitigation targets or requirements for the livestock sector likely falls out of the typical scope of obligations in the Article XIV-permitted treaties noted above. More broadly, Guiding Principles for sustainable and healthy diets have been created by the WHO and FAO[96] but again do not amount to a voluntary instrument, but rather simply guidance that could be considered by states. As a result, the FAO's role in the international legal order for cattle and climate change has largely focused to date on its research and dissemination role, providing recommendations in publications and attempting to 'nudge' behavioural change (such as highlighting best practices or specific Members' actions as exemplars[97]), in addition to providing technical capacity building (such as training with GLEAM modelling). This does not mean this influence is not significant – as mentioned previously, the FAO is viewed as an expert authority on the environmental impact of agriculture. This influence alone has already led to the broad use of GLEAM and the frequent citing and reliance upon reports such as *Livestock's Long Shadow* when discussing the environmental impact of livestock.[98] Moreover,

[91] The OECD highlights the importance of these binding decisions in Regional Fisheries Management Organisation: 'These binding measures are particularly significant in the context of Regional Fisheries Management Organizations (RFMOs). 50 RFMOs adopt binding regulatory measures to, inter alia, govern fishing methods and gears, prescribe minimum sizes for specified species, define protected species, and establish fishing seasons and the amount of total catch for each Party. Their regulatory role is, in fact, essential for the purposes of conservation and resource management. For example, as of June 2016, the General Fisheries Commission for the Mediterranean (GFCM) had adopted 40 binding recommendations and resolutions for fisheries conservation.' See more in FAO Legal and Ethics Office (n 82) 63–67.

[92] FAO Legal and Ethics Office (n 82) 63–67.

[93] ibid.

[94] See Joint FAO/WHO Codex Alimentarius Commission, *Codex Alimentarius: Cereals, Pulses, Legumes and Vegetable Proteins* (WHO/FAO, 2007).

[95] FAO Legal and Ethics Office (n 82) 62.

[96] FAO and WHO (n 52).

[97] See the previous example of the FBDGs analysis by the FAO in Gonzalez Fischer and Garnett (n 55).

[98] See earlier in this chapter, eg at n 12.

this does not undercut the potential of the FAO's influence in other formal legal processes – such as the international climate regime – to encourage appropriate mitigation solutions.

The FAO's Role in Other Legal Processes in the International Legal Order

As part of its mandate, the FAO has been invited to partake in the legal processes of other UN bodies, such as international climate governance in the UNFCCC forum. A key example of this is the aforementioned KJWA established under the Paris Agreement.[99] Whilst the FAO regime does not have its own legal framework relating to agriculture and climate, its expertise was embedded in the international climate regime through this joint work.[100] As a result, the FAO played a direct role in delineating the scope of agri-climate measures within the UNFCCC process – bringing with it the potential to influence the Paris Agreement's implementation with respect to agriculture. There were, of course, no obligations created for parties under the KJWA decision. However, through the institutional linking of the two regimes, normative content and facilitation provided by the FAO may be able to help inform NDCs and national action on livestock emissions in the future.

Although the KJWA's mandate has now ended, the work path has been picked up by the Sharm El Sheikh joint work on the implementation of climate action on agriculture and food security.[101] The KJWA is referred to several times in the Sharm El Sheikh Joint Work decision, though the FAO's role in this new joint work is not entirely clear (and at the very least, is not yet as enshrined as its role under the previous KJWA decision).[102] Moreover, the extent to which the FAO's gap-filling dietary shift recommendations will be included in this new phase of international agri-climate governance is vague.

The FAO has instead found itself at the centre of other key informal agri-climate initiatives at more recent COPs, including those mentioned in the previous chapter. For example, the FAO was a critical partner in supporting the COP27 presidency in forming the aforementioned I-CAN.[103] As the FAO integrates the concept of healthy diets with livestock emissions mitigation through the concept of 'healthy and sustainable' diet, this could provide an avenue for the FAO to provide information that will influence the direction of the informal initiative. Beyond this, the FAO jointly launched the aforementioned FAST Initiative with the Egyptian presidency at COP28.[104] The initiative aimed to improve the quantity

[99] 'Decision 4/CP.23, 'Koronivia Joint Work on Agriculture', FCCC/CP/2017/11/Add.1.

[100] ibid.

[101] Decision 3.CP/27, 'Sharm El Sheikh Joint Work on Implementation of Climate Action on Agriculture and Food Security', FCCC/CP/2022/10/Add.1.

[102] eg at paras 1–6 of the Sharm El Sheikh Decision, ibid.

[103] See more in the previous chapter from n 110.

[104] See more in the previous chapter at n 108.

and quality of climate finance contributions towards food systems by 2030 – again, providing another forum in which the FAO's expertise on agri-climate matters could be utilised.[105]

However, these are all still informal initiatives surrounding the main formal texts from the UNFCCC process. Unless there are developments under the Sharm El Sheikh Joint Work, there is little formal requirement for states actually to introduce measures that target full food systems and require controversial dietary shifts in wealthier groups. Nonetheless, the overall value of the FAO in the international governance of livestock emissions and research cannot be dismissed, particularly in relation to its role as a technical expert and in disseminating information and recommendations.

Conclusion

Overall, the FAO is one of the few international legal institutions that does actively recognise the need for demand-side food systems strategies, such as dietary shifts, to tackle the climate impact of livestock goods, such as beef. Largely through the integration of public health concerns surrounding 'obesity' and non-communicable diseases, the FAO recognises the importance of pursuing sustainable healthy diets within developed countries' wealthier populations and non-vulnerable groups. There are instances of the FAO-facilitated stakeholder dialogues trying to distance itself from controversial reports mandating dietary change, such as the EAT-Lancet report. Nevertheless, the FAO does take a fuller food systems approach, recognising the importance of agri-climate measures to both support food security and poverty eradication, but also the need to respond to livestock consumption as a driver of livestock emissions among certain global demographics. Alongside the strong institutional influence of the FAO as an international expert in agri-environmental issues, the influence of the FAO in international agri-climate discourse is significant – as can be seen through formal UNFCCC decisions on agriculture, such as the KJWA, the long-standing impact of seminal reports such as *Livestock's Long Shadow* and the widespread utilisation of GLEAM.

The FAO does not currently have any relevant conventions or voluntary initiatives in place regarding livestock emissions. Therefore, the FAO's most significant influence stems from its role in more formal governance processes of other regimes, such as the UNFCCC in the climate regime, or as an information provider more generally in agri-climate discourse. While the influence of these roles is significant, more embedded legal requirements and norms – such as the economic growth-focused norms discussed in chapter six on the international agri-trade regime – can place limitations on the influence the FAO can have on state actors in these capacities while stronger

[105] 'FAST Initiative' <http://example.com/index.htm> accessed 14 July 2023.

legal rules exist in the broader international legal order for climate change and cattle. Nevertheless, its role in international agri-climate governance as an information provider has provided useful normative developments for agri-climate action to date, and undoubtedly will do so in the future. Before discussing the aforementioned international agri-trade regime, the following chapter will first turn attention to the international forest regime and its approach to livestock and climate governance.

4

Climate Change and Cattle in the International Forest Regime

Increasingly it is clear that forests and the agricultural sector are intrinsically intertwined.[1] The main global driver of deforestation and degradation is frequently reported as being agricultural expansion.[2] In particular, large-scale commercial agriculture (primarily cattle ranching and the cultivation of soy and palm oil) accounted for 40 percent of all tropical deforestation between 2000 and 2010.[3] South America in particular has been highlighted as a hotspot for deforestation relating to the livestock sector, whether that be for feed production or cattle ranching itself.[4]

Crucial forest ecosystems exist in South America, including the Amazon rainforest (which spans across eight countries) and other regions, such as the Cerrado in Brazil. The Amazon is reported to host at least '40,000 species of plants and trees, and 390 billion individual trees; 2.5 million species of insects, and 2,000 species of mammals and birds, at least half of which live in the forest canopy'.[5] Moreover, in recent years, Amazonia has now been considered a carbon source rather than a carbon sink due to deforestation and its impact on the forest to absorb carbon and act as the 'worlds' lungs'.[6]

Other smaller regions in South America, such as the Cerrado, have important carbon neutralising roles yet are often forgotten in the debate on reducing deforestation. The Cerrado region is 200 million hectares (ha) in size and covers nearly 25 percent of Brazil's landmass. It is the country's second largest biome and contains a wide range of varied landscapes, including grasslands, savannah and

[1] C Soto Golcher and IJ Visseren-Hamakers, 'Framing and Integration in the Global Forest, Agriculture and Climate Change Nexus' (2018) 36 *Environment and Planning C: Politics and Space* 1415.

[2] See more E Goldman et al, *Estimating the Role of Seven Commodities in Agriculture-Linked Deforestation: Oil Palm, Soy, Cattle, Wood Fiber, Cocoa, Coffee, and Rubber* (WRI, 2020).

[3] FAO and UNEP, *The State of the World's Forests 2020: Forests, Biodiversity and People* (FAO and UNEP, 2020) www.fao.org/documents/card/en/c/ca8642en, accessed 6 October 2020, xvi.

[4] See generally A Muller and L Bautze, *Agriculture and Deforestation: The EU Common Agricultural Policy, Soy, and Forest Destruction: Proposals for Reform* (Fern, 2017).

[5] C Müller, 'Brazil and the Amazon Rainforest' (European Parliament, 2020) www.europarl.europa.eu/RegData/etudes/IDAN/2020/648792/IPOL_IDA(2020)648792_EN.pdf, 9.

[6] LV Gatti et al, 'Amazonia as a Carbon Source Linked to Deforestation and Climate Change' (2021) 595 *Nature* 388.

dry forests.[7] Soy and cattle production is heavily concentrated in the Cerrado, and agricultural success in the region has resulted in substantial degradation, with reports that 'more than half of the Cerrado [being] cleared of its native vegetation, with most … taking place since the 1970s'.[8] Between only 2003 and 2008, one study suggests 'deforesting and burning of the Cerrado released 1,449 million metric tons of carbon-dioxide equivalent ($MtCO_2$-eq) into the air' – roughly equivalent to the pollution emitted by 422 coal-fired power plants in a year.[9] Moreover, it has been reported that the creation of pasture was reported to be responsible for more than half of this clearance.[10]

This chapter seeks to assess the extent to which agricultural-driven land use and land use change emissions (agricultural-LULUCF emissions), such as those generated by expanding cattle pasture or soy production, are addressed by climate measures within the international forest regime. Firstly, the nature of international forest governance is described on a general level to provide context for the subsequent analysis. Then, the fundamental clash between forest protection and the agricultural sector is outlined, before delineating the extent to which agricultural-LULUCF emissions are specifically addressed in the international forest regime, as compared with broader LULUCF emissions mitigation. This chapter builds on previous analysis of legal regimes within the international legal order for climate change and cattle, offering insight into the muddied landscape of agri-forest governance and utilising a case study of forest governance in Brazil to demonstrate the roadblocks that exist globally in forest governance for agri-climate matters.

Characterising International Forest Governance

The Multifunctional Nature of Forests

The nature of international forest governance has arguably been widely investigated. Typically, international forest governance is characterised as inadequate or insufficient.[11] Many of these reported issues are cited to stem from the fact that forests are multifunctional.[12] For example, Chazdon et al describes that forests can be viewed as a source of timber, an ecosystem for biological diversity, a home for indigenous forest communities, a carbon sink, a source of various ecosystem services,

[7] Union of Concerned Scientists, 'The Importance of Brazil's Cerrado' (2016) www.ucsusa.org/sites/default/files/attach/2016/11/cerrado-fact-sheet-ucs-october-2016.pdf, accessed 8 September 2021.

[8] DM Lapola et al, 'Pervasive Transition of the Brazilian Land-Use System' (2013) 4 *Nature Climate Change* 27, 35.

[9] Union of Concerned Scientists (n 7) 9.

[10] Bustamante et al in ibid.

[11] See generally L Giessen, 'Reviewing the Main Characteristics of the International Forest Regime Complex and Partial Explanations for its Fragmentation' (2013) 15 *International Forestry Review* 60.

[12] RL Chazdon et al, 'When Is a Forest a Forest? Forest Concepts and Definitions in the Era of Forest and Landscape Restoration' (2016) 45 *Ambio* 538, eg 542.

a social or ecological system –and can serve all of these functions, or a combination of them, depending on the interests promoted.[13] Consequently, what constitutes a 'forest' and forest protection varies from different perspectives, making it difficult for any individual instrument to govern all issues relating to forest protection. This is particularly the case when a number of forest functions can fundamentally clash with each other in terms of the objectives they pursue (eg using forests for timber products and preserving forests for biodiversity conservation).[14]

Chazdon et al go on to highlight the range of different management objectives and forest definitions that currently exist and the multitude of international instruments and institutions that are relevant in codifying and promoting these different objectives.[15] For example, viewing forests as a carbon sink can be delineated from the UNFCCC's provisions on forests.[16] Defining forests as a home and site of cultural importance can be delineated from provisions and targets outlined by the UN Permanent Forum on Indigenous Issues.[17] It is clear here that there is no single unique use or conceptualisation of forests on the international level, but rather a plethora of institutional interests and objectives for forests exist in its place.

This being said, Chazdon et al suggest that forest management has generally shifted from the 1960s onwards, from largely timber-industry-focused objectives towards broader environmental and social objectives, including conservation, climate change mitigation and earth stewardship.[18] Unsurprisingly perhaps, no singular overarching international treaty exists for forest protection as is the case for other environmental issues, such as climate change. It is difficult for an individual legal instrument to cover this wide range of interests whilst still ensuring forest protection. However, an additional layer of complexity is added to forest law-making when Global North and South forest-related interests are also considered.

Global North and South Dynamics in Forest Policy-Making

One commonly cited reason why the development of forest law on the international level has been limited is the 'prevailing paradigm' of state sovereignty over

[13] ibid eg 541.

[14] C Rodríguez Fernández-Blanco, SL Burns and L Giessen, 'Mapping the Fragmentation of the International Forest Regime Complex: Institutional Elements, Conflicts and Synergies' (2019) 19 *International Environmental Agreements: Politics, Law and Economics* 187, eg from 196.

[15] Chazdon et al (n 12) from 541.

[16] For more on the UNFCCC and forests, see later in this chapter and FAO, *From Reference Levels to Results Reporting: REDD+ under the United Nations Framework Convention on Climate Change* (FAO, 2020) www.fao.org/documents/card/en/c/cb1635en, accessed 8 September 2021.

[17] For more on indigenous rights and forestry in international law, see H Abidin, *The Protection of Indigenous Peoples and Reduction for Forest Carbon Emissions: The REDD+ Regime and International Law* (Brill Nijhoff, 2015); UN ECOSOC Permanent Forum on Indigenous Issues, 'Indigenous People's Rights and Safeguards in Projects Related to Reducing Emissions from Deforestation and Forest Degradation (REDD+)' (2013)E/C.19/2013/7.

[18] Chazdon et al (n 12) 941.

natural resources, including forests.[19] In other words, a state's policies on forest exploitation or conservation are often not deemed to be subject to international law. [20]

However, the global picture of forest governance is more complex than this. Although deforestation has global climate impacts, the majority of the world's forests are in the Global South and previous attempts at developing international forest law were often met with suspicion by Global South countries which feared continuing ecological imperialism by the Global North.[21] As a result, a Global North/South dynamic or divide exists within international forest governance.

Maintaining the Global South's control of their forests to balance their own development and environmental goals is important in light of 'colonial residue' in forest management from eras of colonial control where Global North countries systematically accumulated wealth from the Global South's natural resources.[22] Forest depletion or mismanagement in developing countries itself is often at least partly, if not entirely, a remnant of colonial control.[23] Beyond this, as highlighted by Natarajan and Dehm, Northern understandings of economic development were eventually 'universalised' by the decolonisation process by conditioning Southern independence upon a commitment to industrial development – often through the extraction of natural resources, such as forests.[24] They highlight that even across the political spectrum of communist to capitalist postcolonial states, any state that failed to reject the Northern ideal of industrial development was denied self-sovereignty, particularly in the case of indigenous and tribal peoples.[25]

Still to this day, consumption in Global North countries drives demand for the extraction and exploitation of natural resources from the Global South.[26] Examples

[19] See J Brunnée and A Nollkaemper, 'Between the Forests and the Trees – An Emerging International Forest Law' (1996) 23 *Environmental Conservation* 307, 108. Also, Principle 2 Rio Declaration 1992, 'States have, in accordance with the Charter of the UN and the principles of international law, the sovereign right to exploit their own resources pursuant to their own environmental and developmental policies, and the responsibility to ensure that activities with their own jurisdiction or control do not cause damage to the environment of other States or of areas beyond the national limits of national jurisdiction.' See also Principle 2(a) of the UN Forest Principles.

[20] Though attempts to regulate forests beyond a nation's domestic jurisdiction have been attempted where harm from forest degradation has been deemed to extend beyond the territory of the forest being degraded. See an example, also discussed in ch 6, of the EU's new proposed due-diligence regulation for forest and ecosystem risk commodities. G Marín Durán and J Scott, 'Regulating Trade in Forest-Risk Commodities: Two Cheers for the European Union' [2022] *Journal of Environmental Law* eqac002.

[21] HM Schally, 'Forests: Towards an International Legal Regime' (1993) 4 *Yearbook of International Environmental Law* 308.

[22] For more on 'colonial residue', see Y Ariadne Collins, 'Colonial Residue: REDD+, Territorialisation and the Racialized Subject in Guyana and Suriname' (2019) 106 *Geoforum* 38.

[23] See various discussions in N Myers and R Tucker, 'Deforestation in Central America: Spanish Legacy and North American Consumers' (1987) 11 *Environmental Review* 55; A Bandopadhyay, 'The Colonial Legacy of Forest Policies in India' (2010) 38(1/2) *Social Scientist* 53–76.

[24] U Natarajan and J Dehm, *Locating Nature: Making and Unmaking International Law* (Cambridge University Press, 2022) 6.

[25] ibid 7.

[26] ibid.

from the livestock sector include the European Union's high demand for soybean meal from South America for animal feed, often grown in high-risk deforestation areas.[27] Amidst a landscape of Global North countries historically failing to pull their 'weight' in terms of their own international environmental legal responsibilities, and their promotion of so-called green solutions that continue to fuel unsustainable capitalist models, it is perhaps unsurprising that Global South countries view attempts at governing forests internationally with scepticism.[28] This is particularly the case when past Southern responses to environmental challenges attempted to articulate alternative visions of a more just international economic order were met with 'sustained resistance' by Northern states.[29] Even the Global North's adoption and imposition of environmental standards has been deemed to have detrimental 'chilling' effects on the Global South due to the prejudiced nature of the international legal order and its broader conceptualisation of environmental protection.[30] Consequently, the global political landscape for forest management is one fraught with tensions between Global North and South histories and interests, making the negotiation of any international forest treaty particularly contentious, with a significant risk of negative impacts for Global South states.

A Fragmented International Forest Regime

In place of an international forest treaty commanding wide support amongst states in this contentious context, a vast number of piecemeal international policies and instruments (both public and private) have emerged to form a transnational forest regime.[31] This section does not intend to outline all of these policies and instruments, as this stretches beyond the scope of the chapter, which intends to instead provide general context to international forest governance and surrounding literature, before addressing agriculture-specific analysis that is often neglected in academic study. Nonetheless, some prominent examples of forest governance instruments at the international level will be outlined.

For instance, softer law principles, such as the UN Forest Principles 1992, or voluntary instruments, resolutions and decisions of international organisations (eg the FAO, the United Nations Environment Programme (UNEP), United Nations

[27] See more in the subsequent chapter on the EU's due diligence regulation, or ch 2 for statistics on the consumption of global agricultural goods.

[28] Natarajan and Dehm (n 24) provide the example of the reluctance by the United States to engage in UNFCCC processes.

[29] Natarajan and Dehm (n 24) 7.

[30] See eg C Gonzalez, 'Bridging the North–South Divide: International Environmental Law in the Anthropocene' (2015) Seattle University School of Law Research Paper No 16-02; R Eckersley, 'The Big Chill: The WTO and Multilateral Environmental Agreements' (2004) 4 *Global Environmental Politics* 24.

[31] C Overdevest and J Zeitlin, 'Assembling an Experimentalist Regime: Transnational Governance Interactions in the Forest Sector: Assembling an Experimentalist Regime' (2014) 8 *Regulation & Governance* 22.

Forum on Forests (UNFF), exist in place of harder forest law on the international level.[32] In some cases (particularly those concerning forest conservation for environmental and social as opposed to economic reasons), attempts to plug these international policy 'gaps' have been made made by private initiatives, such as the Forest Stewardship Council (FSC) certification and labelling scheme.[33]

The FSC Scheme – A Non-governmental Attempt at Global Forest Governance

The FSC was launched in 1993 in an attempt to address global deforestation following failed efforts to agree on a multilateral convention on forests at the Rio Summit in 1992. It was seen as a 'non-state regulatory experiment' – a transnational multi-stakeholder initiative administering a global ecolabelling scheme for timber and forest products.[34] This is an opt-in scheme under which businesses and retailers can have their wood products certified against FSC principles so they can use the FSC logo to market their products to consumers, often with a higher price tag due to the recognition of higher environmental and social standards of wood production.[35] The FSC principles themselves refer to issues such as environmental impact, indigenous peoples' rights and workers' rights.[36]

Academic reflection on the FSC scheme suggests that it has facilitated and brokered some new multisectoral forest standards and has likely achieved improvements against a 'business as usual' baseline.[37] However, many studies suggest that this initiative has failed to meaningfully transform commercial forestry practices or tropical deforestation,[38] with issues with the FSC process being highlighted in academic commentary over the years, including: a disparity in the representation of stakeholders from different geographical regions;[39] a disparity in the uptake of certification between developed and developing countries;[40] power imbalances between dominant economic actors and other

[32] United Nations Forest Principles 1992; Soto Golcher and Visseren-Hamakers (n 1) 1421.

[33] See more here, BEFSCI, *FSC Principles and Criteria for Forest Stewardship* (FAO, 2011).

[34] See generally S Moog, A Spicer and S Böhm, 'The Politics of Multi-stakeholder Initiatives: The Crisis of the Forest Stewardship Council' (2015) 128 *Journal of Business Ethics* 469, eg in the Introduction.

[35] Premiums for FSC-certified wood are reported to be as high as 20 percent. See FSC, 'FSC-Certified Wood and Products Fetch Higher Prices' (2020) https://fsc.org/en/newsfeed/fsc-certified-wood-and-products-fetch-higher-prices, accessed 25 June 2020.

[36] See more at BEFSCI (n 33).

[37] For more on the complexity of evaluating the impact of the FSCS Scheme, see C Romero et al, 'Evaluation of the Impacts of Forest Stewardship Council (FSC) Certification of Natural Forest Management in the Tropics: A Rigorous Approach to Assessment of a Complex Conservation Intervention' (2017) 19 *International Forestry Review* 36.

[38] See Moog et al (n 34).

[39] See more in K Dingwerth, 'North–South Parity in Global Governance: The Affirmative Procedures of the Forest Stewardship Council' (2008) 14 *Global Governance* 53, 59, 61.

[40] ibid.

actors (eg indigenous communities[41]); failure to account for resource imbalances in the scheme given the neoliberal global marketplace for forest goods;[42] failure to ensure adequate biodiversity protection;[43] limited effectiveness against illegal logging;[44] and general limitations of market-based governance[45] and ecolabelling, including the diminishing returns of the proliferation of forest certification schemes[46] and the high costs of certification or market access in the FSC context.[47]

The range and breadth of these issues raised are representative of the challenge being confronted by the FSC, reflecting the complex causality and array of interests at stake in forest management and protection. Using the FSC scheme and its shortcomings as an example, it is understandable why these attempts at global forest governance have been generally characterised as fragmented, weak, hollow and even failed.[48]

Overlapping Forest Regimes

Although not covered by a single treaty, forest protection is technically covered by other international treaties or laws, even if it is not the primary objective or subject of that instrument. This also contributes to the fragmentation of the global forest regime as this leads to piecemeal solutions to forest issues.[49] For example, the Convention on Biological Diversity (CBD) does not explicitly refer to forests in its text, but a number of its provisions are 'directly' or 'indirectly' relevant for the protection of forests.[50] The general mandate of the CBD is aimed at a 'wide range' of forest uses, including biological diversity protection, habitat protection, and protection of natural heritage and cultural and spiritual values.[51] In light of this, forests are deemed as an ecosystem that is included within that mandate.

[41] See more, M Colchester, 'Do Commodity Certification Systems Uphold Indigenous Peoples' Rights? Lessons from the Roundtable on Sustainable Palm Oil and Forest Stewardship Council' (2016) 21 *Policy Matters* 150–65, eg 153.

[42] Moog et al (n 34) 484.

[43] D Schepers 'Challenges to Legitimacy at the Forest Stewardship Council' (2010) 92 *Journal of Business Ethics* 288; see also H Garrelts and M Flitner, 'Governance Issues in the Ecosystem Approach: What Lessons from the Forest Stewardship Council?' (2011) 130 *European Journal of Forest Research* 395.

[44] Schepers (n 43) 288. See also more case studies in Richard Conniff, 'Greenwashed Timber: How Sustainable Forest Certification Has Failed' (Yale E360, 2018) https://e360.yale.edu/features/greenwashed-timber-how-sustainable-forest-certification-has-failed, accessed 21 August 2023.

[45] P Pattberg, 'The Forest Stewardship Council: Risk and Potential of Private Forest Governance' (2005) 14 *Journal of Environment & Development* 356, 369.

[46] Moog et al (n 34) 484.

[47] Schepers (n 43) 287.

[48] See more in L Giessen, 'Reviewing the Main Characteristics of the International Forest Regime Complex and Partial Explanations for its Fragmentation' (2013) 15 *International Forestry Review* 60.

[49] H van Asselt, 'Managing the Fragmentation of International Environmental Law: Forests at the Intersection of the Climate and Biodiversity Regimes' (2012) 44 *International Law and Politics* 1205–1278.

[50] ibid 1266.

[51] ibid 1225.

Van Asselt outlines the expanding and deepening of the inclusion of forests within the CBD's activities from 1996 onwards to demonstrate how the treaty's coverage of forests has translated into an ongoing work programme.[52] However, the extent to which overlapping components of the international forest regime can be beneficial for a particular forest problem is not a given and must be individually evaluated in different contexts. As will be highlighted subsequently in this chapter, the overlaps between forest–climate policies and agriculture do not necessarily receive the same policy-making traction as the forest–biodiversity overlaps mentioned above. As a result, active integration (eg by policymakers) is required to ensure the potential maximisation of mutual benefits that can flow from productive overlaps between different international policies.

The Effectiveness of Fragmented Regimes

As suggested above, sometimes synergies can occur within highly fragmented regimes to create positive effects. A legal regime that is largely fragmented does not necessarily correlate with a lack of substantive action in pursuit of its various objectives. Some academics suggest that progress has been made in this fragmented forest context despite inaction often being assumed at first glance. For example, Overdevest and Zeitlin suggest that the European Union's Forest Law Enforcement, Governance and Trade (FLEGT+) Scheme[53] has actually been positively influenced transnationally by multilateral institutions, NGO campaigns and interactions with third countries.[54] Moreover, they state that the architecture of the EU FLEGT+ initiative has 'fostered productive, mutually reinforcing interactions both with public timber legality regulation in other consumer countries and with private certification schemes'.[55] This echoes similar lines of argument that suggest hope is not lost due to the fragmentation of environmental regimes, with progress being made despite fragmentation or a softer legal regime.[56] Cottrell and Trubek in particular suggest that the assumption that greater degrees of obligation, precision and delegation in legal rules will lead to more compliance and greater cooperative gains is not always true.[57] Moreover, they state 'precision [in legal rules] may

[52] ibid 1266.

[53] Council Regulation (EC) No 2173/2005 of 20 December 2005 on the Establishment of a FLEGT Licensing Scheme for Imports of Timber into the European Community 2005. See also the EU Timber Regulation in conjunction with this, Regulation (EU) No 995/2010 of the European Parliament and of the Council of 20 October 2010 laying down the obligations of operators who place timber and timber products on the market Text with EEA relevance adopted on 20 October 2010.

[54] See generally Overdevest and Zeitlin (n 31).

[55] J Zeitlin and C Overdevest, 'Experimentalist Interactions: Joining up the Transnational Timber Legality Regime' [2020] *Regulation & Governance* 687.

[56] See, for just one example, KW Abbott, 'Orchestrating Experimentation in Non-state Environmental Commitments' (2017) 26 *Environmental Politics* 738.

[57] MP Cottrell and D Trubek, 'Law as Problem Solving: Standards, Networks, Experimentation and Deliberation in Global Space' (2012) 21 *Transnational Law and Contemporary Problems* 359, 364.

actually reduce compliance as precise rules may create resistance in situations where open-ended standards, allowing for diversity, would not'.[58]

However, it has been argued that the many policies and agreements in the current global forest regime do not necessarily achieve this. For example, a broader analysis of *all* potential forest-protecting synergies within the regime labels these synergies as superficial,[59] very general, content-poor, unspecific and non-concrete, despite being high-level, politically well-visible institutional elements of the regime.[60] Additionally, the aforementioned conflicts between forest functions are particularly prominent between different components of the global forest regime, particularly when the conflict involves free-trade interests (and consequently, forest-harvesting interests), such as WTO rules, which will be discussed in the next chapter.[61] Lastly, the progress outlined by Overdevest and Zeitlin was specified in a timber-producing context, targeting illegal timber production. As will be seen in subsequent analysis, agricultural drivers of deforestation and forest degradation have not necessarily gained the policy-making traction that illegal timber production has thus far. This overall policy weakness may be in part underscored by fundamental clashes between forest-protection and agricultural-sector interests outlined below.

The Fundamental Clashes between Forest Protection and the Agricultural Sector

It has previously been stated that there are often clashes in policy objectives within the international forest regime. This is no different in the case of forest protection and the agricultural sector. A clash in objectives exists between forest protection and the agricultural sector on a fundamental level.[62] Land is required for agricultural production. Therefore, in a landscape where global hunger exists and the global population is rising, achieving food security across the world can translate to a perceived requirement to increase the amount of land being used for agricultural production. As a result, it is common to see direct clashes in the current global landscape between forest protection and agricultural policies such as those relating to food security and agricultural trade.[63] Additionally, as noted, the majority

[58] ibid 365.

[59] Colchester (n 41).

[60] Rodríguez Fernández-Blanco et al (n 14), 199.

[61] ibid 200.

[62] C Soto Golcher, B Arts and I Visseren-Hamakers, 'Seeing the Forest, Missing the Field: Forests and Agriculture in Global Climate Change Policy' (2018) 77 *Land Use Policy* 627.

[63] Historically, even in pre-industrial times, agriculture has been found to have some degree of environmental manipulation – even if to a lower extent than modern industrial methods. Developments such as the use of fire, growth and relocation of human population (including colonialism), and trade in goods such as gunpowder had early effects on land and its transformation for agricultural or even hunter-gathering purposes – with varying levels of direct and indirect impacts on land depending on the location, extent and context of their use in pre-industrial societies globally. See discussion of

of the world's forests are located in the countries in the Global South. Many of these countries (1) may have comparatively higher national hunger indexes, and (2) have agricultural systems more vulnerable to the impacts of climate change that may affect their future food security.[64] Forest-protection policies being implemented against this backdrop can be harmful to food security and development objectives in these nations if not carefully implemented.

Additionally, agricultural trade is also frequently a large economic sector for forest-rich countries in the Global South.[65] It plays a crucial role in poverty eradication and economic development by providing food, fuel, fibre, timber and other forest products for subsistence and income generation.[66] The FAO reports that 252 million people living in forests and savannahs have incomes of less than US$1.25 per day and forests provide more than 86 million green jobs and support the livelihoods of many more people.[67] This adds another layer of complexity when trying to promote forest conservation, as forest protection can directly clash with these countries' broader economic (and often consequently socioeconomic) development goals if agricultural production is limited in some way. This complexity (along with the fragmented nature of the international forest regime) has meant attempts on the international level to target forest-related agricultural emissions have been relatively limited thus far, as reflected in the analysis in the rest of this chapter.

Agricultural Emissions Mitigation in the International Forest Regime

There have been some attempts to address agricultural-LULUCF emissions on the international level, but these have been relatively sparse and have failed to gain policy-making traction. That being said, a few attempts have been made to integrate agriculture into the forest regime.

Soto Golcher and Visseren-Hamakers highlight a number of key attempts at integrating agricultural considerations into forest governance from interviews with key stakeholders.[68] For example, the International Union of Forest Research Organizations (IUFRO) tried to raise awareness about the role of forests in

IG Simmons, 'Transformation of the Land in Pre-industrial Time' in *Land Transformation in Agriculture* (Scope, 1987). This source has global observations, though largely relying on sources from Western academic observations.

[64] See generally AA Golub et al, 'Global Climate Policy Impacts on Livestock, Land Use, Livelihoods, and Food Security' (2013) 110 *Proceedings of the National Academy of Sciences of the United States of America* 20894.

[65] A Kalfagianni and S Duyck, *The Evolving Role of Agriculture in Climate Change Negotiations: Progress and Players* (CCAFS, 2015) 22.

[66] FAO and UNEP (n 3) eg 58.

[67] ibid 60.

[68] Soto Golcher and Visseren-Hamakers (n 1).

achieving food security, highlighting the gap that exists on the international level for strategies to tackle this; Principles for Responsible Investment Agriculture and Food Systems exist as part of the Committee on World Food Security (CFS); the World Agroforestry Centre has been trying to actively promote the integration of trees into agriculture; the Intergovernmental Science-Policy Platform on Biodiversity and Ecosystem Services (IPBES) has also tried to integrate forests and agriculture through linking both with biodiversity; and the United Nations Convention to Combat Desertification (UNCCD) also refers to agricultural land degradation, including sustainable land-management and agroforestry practices.[69] However, Soto Golcher and Visseren-Hamakers suggest that efforts to integrate agriculture into current forest considerations have not led to 'significant results' due to the lack of an overarching framework for forests and the multitude of institutions functioning in the governance space.[70]

Agricultural-LULUCF Mitigation in the International Climate Regime

Perhaps more obvious traction between agriculture and forest governance has been seen within the international climate regime's agri-climate work. The aforementioned KJWA, the mandate of which ended at COP27, attempted to target agricultural-LULUCF emissions mitigation more explicitly within the existing Paris Agreement framework.[71] While the KJWA did not refer explicitly to LULUCF emissions in its 'work topics', in broader FAO projects and reports it is clear that agricultural-LULUCF emissions were highlighted as an agricultural driver of climate change by the FAO.[72] Deforestation itself was only referred to briefly as a driver of poor soil quality under the KJWA's Work Topic 2(c) on 'improved soil carbon, soil health and soil fertility under grassland and cropland as well as integrated systems, including water management'.[73] The FAO does highlight that the KJWA was not limited to the six topics outlined in its work path. However, given the significant contribution of the agricultural sector to deforestation it is surprising more direct attention was not given to forests under the KJWA, and more correlation between deforestation and climate change was not highlighted.

[69] ibid.

[70] ibid 1427.

[71] See more discussion of the KJWA in ch 3.

[72] For example, in the FAO's analysis of NDCs and agriculture, the LULUCF commitments of the Paris Agreement's parties were analysed, demonstrating the FAO's recognition of LULUCF's relevance when looking at agriculture's climate impact. R Strohmaier et al, 'The Agriculture Sectors in the Intended Nationally Determined Contributions – Analysis' (FAO, 2016) Environment and Natural Resources Working Paper No. 62.

[73] FAO, *Koronivia Joint Work on Agriculture – Summary of Workshop on Topic 2(c) : Improved Soil Carbon, Soil Health and Soil Fertility under Grassland and Cropland as Well as Integrated Systems, Including Water Management* (FAO, 2020) www.fao.org/publications/card/en/c/CA8943EN/, accessed 7 December 2021.

This (albeit soft) divide created between the agricultural sector and forest-related issues is not limited to the KJWA. This divergence in approach in the submission process may be because definitions of forest and agricultural-related emissions can be considered somewhat fragmented themselves, despite the two areas being treated together by the IPCC from 2006 as the 'agriculture, forestry and other land use' (AFOLU) sector.[74] For example, the FAO in one of its analysis reports in relation to the KJWA provided this summary of the varied definitions relating to agricultural emissions, depending on the institution involved:

> Agriculture or the agricultural sectors, when used by the FAO, comprises the sub-sectors of crops, livestock, fisheries and aquaculture and forestry. The terms agriculture or the agricultural sector in the UNFCCC domain are defined in accordance with Intergovernmental Panel on Climate Change (IPCC) terminology and cover emissions from enteric fermentation, manure management, rice cultivation, prescribed burning of savannas and grassland, and from soils (ie agricultural emissions). Emissions and removals from grassland and cropland are covered under LULUCF (Land Use, Land Use Change and Forestry). In the IPCC 2006, the two sectors (ie agriculture and LULUCF) are treated together in the Agriculture, Forestry and Land Use sector.[75]

These different ways of determining the scope of agricultural-LULUCF emissions may contribute to the overall lack of clear or consistent agricultural emissions coverage in the international climate regime to date. There are overlaps between what are considered emissions from the agricultural sector and what are LULUCF emissions, leading to somewhat muddied categorisation of emissions in reality – as was the case in some previous NDCs. Alongside the lack of more direct coverage of forest issues in the initial KJWA workplan, international climate law references to address agricultural-LULUCF mitigation were incoherent.

In terms of COP27 developments in agricultural-LULUCF mitigation in the international climate regime, land-related goals are more specifically referenced throughout the Sharm El Sheikh Joint Work Decision on the Implementation of Climate Action on Agriculture and Food Security.[76] Increased references are made to 'enhancing sinks on pasture and grazing land' as a contribution to achieving long-term climate objectives.[77] In particular, the importance of farmers' and pastoralists' knowledge of 'sustainable land management' is referred to, in addition to highlighting that approaches adaptation, adaptation co-benefits and mitigation can have positive direct links with broader goals, such as biodiversity and food security.[78]

As a result, it is promising to see the inclusion of forests in the main decision on agriculture in the international climate regime, and that work on agriculture

[74] Koronivia Joint Work on Agriculture, Analysis of Submissions on Topic 2(d) (FAO, 2020) www.fao.org/documents/card/en/c/ca9169en, accessed 29 June 2020.

[75] ibid 4.

[76] Decision 3.CP/27, Sharm El-Sheikh Joint Work on Implementation of Climate Action on Agriculture and Food Security Decision 3.CP/27, FCCC/CP/2022/10/Add.1.

[77] ibid Art 2(j).

[78] ibid Art. 2 (t).

and climate has continued into the future international climate regime after the KJWA. Arguably, forests have a greater mention in the Sharm El Sheikh Joint Work when compared with its predecessor – even if the Sharm El Sheikh Joint Work was criticised in previous chapters.[79] In combination with the historical muddying of forests and agricultural emissions in NDCs, it will be interesting to note if and how the new decision translates into agri-forest action relating to livestock in NDCs.

General LULUCF Emissions Mitigation in the International Forest Regime

Beyond the analysis above, it is important to also address other attempts to address LULUCF emissions more broadly under the international forest regime – not only agricultural – LULUCF specifically. Through the creation and implementation of the Reducing Emissions from Deforestation and Forest Degradation (REDD+) programme, forests are embedded into international climate law by framing forests as carbon sinks and as a tool for mitigation.[80] The REDD+ programme was not solely designed to address LULUCF emissions from agriculture. Nonetheless, it is worth analysing the applicability of its provisions and uptake within the agricultural sector, after initially setting out the historical development of the programme.

The Development of REDD+

Regarding forests as carbon sinks and as a source of emissions (when cut down) can be linked to the development of the global climate regime and the role of forests within this. Under the UNFCCC, parties[81] are required to report their annual emissions by source and also any removals by sinks.[82] Parties are also supposed to promote the 'sustainable management of all carbon sinks and reservoirs that includes forests'.[83] The Kyoto Protocol continued to develop the concept of LULUCF emissions and treated forests as carbon sinks. For example, Article 3.3 of the Protocol permitted using forests as a sink to meet the emissions reduction targets of Annex 1 parties, stating that 'net changes in greenhouse gas

[79] See more on weaknesses in this Decision for fair and effective agri-climate solutions in ch 2.

[80] FAO (n 16).

[81] The UNFCCC reporting guidelines on annual inventories for parties included in Annex I to the Convention (Decision 24/CP.19) provide guidance reporting emissions by sources and removals by sinks of greenhouse gases not controlled by the Montreal Protocol caused by LULUCF activities. The guidance introduces a land-based approach, in that reporting under the UNFCC covers all emissions and removals from the lands included in the LULUCF sector.

[82] Art 4(a) United Nations Framework Convention on Climate Change 1992.

[83] ibid.

emissions by sources and removals by sinks resulting from direct human-induced land-use change and forestry activities, limited to afforestation, reforestation and deforestation since 1990, measured as verifiable changes in carbon stocks in each commitment period, shall be used to meet the commitments'.[84] In 2001, the Marrakesh Accords settled any unresolved issues related to forest sinks, and agreed on a number of principles for implementing LULUCF activities, as well as defining terms such as 'afforestation', 'reforestation' and 'deforestation'.[85] Some problems around the inclusion of LULUCF issues in the Kyoto Protocol's Clean Development Mechanism (CDM) existed, but in 2003 it was finally agreed that the CDM would include afforestation and reforestation.[86]

In 2005, following a proposal from Papua New Guinea and Costa Rica to discuss reducing emissions from deforestation in tropical countries, the concept of REDD was created.[87] Emissions from deforestation in developing countries became a formal negotiation point for the new international climate treaty (what would be the Paris Agreement) in the Bali Action Plan 2007.[88] REDD+[89] provisions were fleshed out further at COP15 in 2009 and COP16 in 2010, but the greatest clarity on the practical implementation of the initiative was achieved at COP19 in 2013 under the Warsaw Framework for REDD+.[90] This included decisions on results-based finance, coordination of support for implementation, and modalities for national forest monitoring systems.[91] REDD+ was then included in the Paris Agreement which was agreed at COP21 in 2015, solidifying its role in the global climate regime.[92]

REDD+ itself is a voluntary programme that seeks to 'reduc[e] emissions from deforestation and forest degradation in developing countries, and [highlights and encourages] the role of conservation, sustainable management of forests, and enhancement of forest carbon stocks in developing countries'.[93] After setting up the necessary national technical and monitoring capacity, institutional frameworks and scaling up their forest programmes, the involved developing countries receive results-based finance as an incentive for their efforts.[94] As a result, developing

[84] Art 3.3 Kyoto Protocol 1997.

[85] Asselt (n 52) 1219.

[86] ibid.

[87] ibid 1221.

[88] ibid 1222.

[89] Ahead of the agreement of the Bali Action Plan, REDD was expanded to REDD+, broadening the initiative's scope to include increasing forest cover through both reforestation and the planting of new forest cover, and promoting sustainable forest resource management.

[90] Decision 1/CP.19, 'Work programme on results-based finance to progress the full implementation of the activities referred to in decision 1/CP.16, paragraph 70', FCCC/CP/2013/10/L.5REDD+ goes beyond REDD as it not only includes reducing emissions from deforestation in developing countries, but also forest degradation and the role of conservation sustainable management of forests and enhancement of forest carbon stocks in these countries.

[91] ibid.

[92] See Art 5(2) Paris Agreement.

[93] Decision 1/CP.19 (n 90)..

[94] See more on results-based finance in s III in C Voigt and F Ferreira, 'The Warsaw Framework for REDD+: Implications for National Implementation and Access to Results-Based Finance' (2015) 9 *Carbon & Climate Law* Review 113.

countries in theory maintain some sovereignty[95] over their forests through the opt-in component of their implementation and domestic 'crystallisation' of their own forest plans.[96] Moreover, any economic opportunity costs of their forest programmes are intended to be offset by results-based payments from developed countries.[97] There are still discussions raised and arguments made about the extent to which REDD+ does actually permit developing countries to have sovereignty over their own forest resources, in addition to whether REDD+ has properly respected indigenous community rights.[98]

Nonetheless, the creation of the REDD+ programme in the international climate and forest regime (even imperfectly[99]) demonstrates a collective willingness to address forest issues in the international climate regime. Through years of negotiations and COP decisions, the REDD+ programme includes 'hard law' references in the Paris Agreement[100] that add additional weight to its provisions, even if the initiative itself is opt-in.[101] Although being 'opt-in', through the fleshing out of the programme over the years, considerable prescriptive detail exists within REDD+ to direct and guide parties' behaviour – including requirements for the involved developing-country parties and provisions for financing the programme.[102]

Moreover, as the initiative is based on results-based payments, measures to ensure enforcement[103] in developing countries' actions are provided, in addition to technical capacity-building requirements for developing countries to ensure adequate accountability under the scheme.[104] The institutional backing of the UNFCCC and of the parties to the Paris Agreement provides additional institutional legitimacy to REDD+.[105] When compared with alternatives in the global

[95] See n 111 for critical sources that talk about the implementation of REDD+ in practice.

[96] Voigt and Ferreria (n 9=4) eg 117.

[97] ibid.

[98] See for just one example, L Wallbott and E Recio, 'Practicing Human Rights across Scale: Indigenous Peoples' Affectedness and Recognition in REDD+ Governance' (2018) 3 *Third World Thematics* 785.

[99] See ibid for an example of this.

[100] Including potential linking with carbon markets following COP27. See Carbon Brief Staff, 'COP27: Key Outcomes for Food, Forests, Land and Nature at the UN Climate Talks in Egypt', *Carbon Brief*, 24 November 2022, www.carbonbrief.org/cop27-key-outcomes-for-food-forests-land-and-nature-at-the-un-climate-talks-in-egypt/, accessed 10 January 2023.

[101] eg Art 5(2) Paris Agreement 2015.

[102] 'Report of the Conference of the Parties on its Nineteenth Session, Held in Warsaw from 11 to 23 November 2013' FCCC/CP/2013/10/Add.1.

[103] By enforcement and accountability, the author refers to these terms in relation to Abbott and Snidal's conceptualisation of the possibilities of 'legalisation' – where commitments can be 'hardened' through delegation to third-party decision-makers. See KW Abbott and D Snidal, 'Hard and Soft Law in International Governance' (2000) 54 *International Organization* 421, 430.

[104] Art 5(2) Paris Agreement.

[105] See Benford and Snow's discussion of institutional legitimacy as a factor that determines the perceived credibility of a policy by stakeholders. This credibility can be identified through things such as the institution's historical experience in the policy matter, financial or technical expertise in the policy matter, and so forth; see RD Benford and DA Snow, 'Framing Processes and Social Movements: An Overview and Assessment' (2000) 26 Annual Review of Sociology 611.

forest regime, such as the FSC initiative, REDD+ has been created and negotiated by state parties during its development and has a public Secretariat and further COP negotiations to follow up on its progress.[106] As a result, REDD+ can be seen to have more legitimacy than private initiatives that are not necessarily accountable to any nation or body of citizens.

This being said, political will is still required on the national level to effectively implement REDD+ which can be complicated when considering the aforementioned trade-offs between forests and agriculture. Compared with other initiatives in the international forest regime, REDD+ and its coverage of forest emissions are comparatively strong, though as will be shown subsequently, a lack of political will exists to tackle drivers of forest degradation from the livestock sector.

Livestock Emissions under REDD+

As noted previously, livestock farming can impact land in two ways: requiring pastureland for grazing; and requiring agricultural land for feed production (most often soybean due to its protein-rich nature). Although the scope of REDD+ can in theory include agricultural-LULUCF emissions from these activities, in practice mitigation of these emissions has not been uniformly included in REDD+ national strategies to date.[107] Kissinger has noted that the agricultural sector is generally absent from the national strategies of all REDD+, particularly in terms of smallholder agricultural coverage.[108] This being said, in Brazil – a 'hotspot' of forest degradation from the agricultural sector – the reported REDD+ strategy coverage is better.[109] In fact, Brazil was often called the 'poster child' of REDD+, being classed as one of the most successful REDD+ parties in the world, having received US$1 billion from Norway through the Amazon Fund.[110]

The subsequent analysis utilises Brazil's REDD+ strategy as a case study to assess the extent to which livestock emissions are addressed under REDD+, and where weaknesses lie in this coverage.

[106] See discussions of 'delegation to third party for decision makers' in Abbott and Snidal (n 102) eg 449. Also, for more on the FSC's governance process, see Pattberg (n 45) from 179.

[107] See generally, G Kissinger, 'Linking Forests and Food Production in the REDD+ Context' in M Behnassi, O Pollmann and G Kissinger (eds), *Sustainable Food Security in the Era of Local and Global Environmental Change* (Springer, 2013) http://link.springer.com/10.1007/978-94-007-6719-5_4, accessed 20 January 2020.

[108] ibid 13.

[109] See ibid from 24. See also General Coordination for Developing Brazil's National REDD+ Strategy, Secretariat of Climate Change and Environmental Quality, and Ministry of the Environment, 'Brazil's National REDD+ Strategy' (2016) http://redd.mma.gov.br/images/publicacoes/enredd_english_web.pdf.

[110] This was part of the Forest Investment Programme, not the World Bank Forest Carbon Partnership Facility (FCPF) process, see Kissinger (n 107) 11.

Agricultural-LULUCF Emissions in Brazil's REDD+ Strategy

As has been said, agriculture is included in Brazil's REDD+ strategy. The political motivation to include agricultural emissions in Brazil's forest strategies probably stems from two factors: (1) agriculture being a major sector and driver of emissions in Brazil; and (2) international pressure to protect the Amazon, the 'world's lungs', from deforestation.[111] Cattle ranching has been reported to generate 44 percent of Brazil's GHGs, and Brazil is the second biggest exporter of beef and soybeans globally.[112] Moreover, Brazilian soybean production was reported to have increased 196 percent between 1990 and 2008,[113] with land conversion to soy crops said to account for up to 18 percent of deforestation in Brazil.[114] As a result, when drawing up national forest plans, it was apparent both domestically and internationally that the forest impacts of Brazil's agricultural sector should not go unnoticed.

In Brazil's REDD+ plan and Biennial Climate Update Reports, there is a recognition of the impact of livestock (particularly cattle) and soy on forests shown through the accounting of these different subsectors.[115] Specific plans are created to tackle agricultural forest emissions, including the National Plan for Low Carbon Emission in Agriculture or the 'ABC Plan' – a programme that encourages the uptake of more environmentally friendly technologies and practices by farmers through offering loans[116] to implement these actions.[117]

Other deforestation-tackling programmes have also been created, not specifically targeting the agricultural sector alone (like the ABC Plan) but targeting deforestation issues more generally in Brazil, not excluding livestock-driven forest impacts.

[111] P Moutinho, R Guerra and C Azevedo-Ramos, 'Achieving Zero Deforestation in the Brazilian Amazon: What Is Missing?' (2016) 4 *Elementa* 000125.

[112] E Batista et al, 'Large-Scale Pasture Restoration May Not Be the Best Option to Reduce Greenhouse Gas Emissions in Brazil' (2019) 14 *Environmental Research Letters* 125009.

[113] Kissinger (n 107) 26. Though this rate stagnated due to the Soy Moratorium, see more on the Soy Moratorium later in this chapter when discussing the Bolsonaro administration.

[114] BS Filho et al, *Challenges for Low-Carbon Agriculture and Forest Conservation in Brazil* (Inter-American Development Bank, 2012) 5.

[115] Much of Brazil's REDD+ strategy has been linked to its climate commitments under the Paris Agreement, hence the use of the Biennial Update Reports here. Brazil Ministry of Environment, 'National Strategy for Reducing Emissions from Deforestation and Forest Degradation, and the Role of Conservation of Forest Carbon Stocks, Sustainable Management of Forests and Enhancement of Forest Carbon Stocks' (Brazilian Government, 2016) https://redd.unfccc.int/files/brazil_national_redd__strategy.pdf; Brazil Ministry of Foreign Affairs and Ministry of Science, Technology, Innovations and Communications, 'Brazil's Third Biennial Report to the UNFCCC' (Brazilian Government, 2019).

[116] There has only been a small budget for ABC loans thus far, as farmer demand for ABC credit is reported to have been limited. The loans provided to farmers by the ABC programme are less appealing than other existing agricultural loans for farmers, as there are stricter environmental standards attached, such as proving compliance with Brazil's Forest Code. See more in G Medina, 'Where Are Governments Leading Their Agricultural Sectors? Comparative Lessons from Agri-environmental Measures Promoted in the US, Europe and Brazil' (2019) 27 *Estudos Sociedade e Agricultura* 5.

[117] Ministry of Foreign Affairs and Ministry of Science, Technology, Innovations and Communications, 'Brazil's Third Biennial Report to the UNFCCC' (2019) 21.

These include: the Action Plan for the Prevention and Control of Deforestation in the Legal Amazon (PPCDAm) which aims to decrease deforestation and forest degradation in the Brazilian Amazon by promoting more sustainable use of forests and agricultural practices;[118] and the Action Plan for the Prevention and Control of Deforestation and Forest Fires in the Cerrado biome[119] (PPCerrado) which has a similar general objective to the PPCDAm but is more specifically targeted at the biome.

Consequently, the existence of Plans such as these demonstrates the consideration of agriculture and livestock in Brazil's forestry and REDD+ strategies. Despite these references, Brazil's inclusion of the agricultural and livestock sectors in its REDD+ strategies relies heavily on the national political context. In the case of Brazil, this context is outlined below as deficient particularly due to its lacking permanence, leaving it susceptible to political changes in the Brazilian government in recent years.

Brazil's Forest Protection Administrative and Legal Permanence

Elements of Brazil's agroforestry administration have lacked permanence: they can be altered and changed depending on the government in power.[120] So, whilst Brazil is one of the few countries to cover agriculture in its REDD+ strategies (albeit imperfectly), this inclusion is dependent on the state of political leadership in Brazil. Even though Brazil's forest strategies were not always exclusively created for the REDD+ programme, changes in leadership can alter the approach taken to forests in this and other global 'hotspots'.[121] For Brazil, the presidential leadership of Jair Bolsonaro had a significant impact on environmental policymaking in Brazil, particularly in relation to forests.[122]

Bolsonaro's administration was detrimental to the protection of Brazilian forests in a number of ways. Bolsonaro generally had little to no climate change mitigation mandate, even making a pre-election promise to take Brazil out of the Paris Agreement (which luckily was not followed through – although he did

[118] Brazil, 'National Strategy for Reducing Emissions from Deforestation and Forest Degradation, and the Role of Conservation of Forest Carbon Stocks, Sustainable Management of Forests and Enhancement of Forest Carbon Stocks' (Brazilian Government, 2016) 23.

[119] For more on the climate, deforestation, biodiversity and socioeconomic importance of protecting the Brazilian Cerrado see more in Union of Concerned Scientists (n 7). See the Third Biennal Report (n 117) for more on the PPCerrado Plan.

[120] Also see more on the deterioration of administration and funding under Bolsonaro in the Climate Action Tracker: https://climateactiontracker.org/countries/brazil/policies-action/.

[121] See more earlier in this chapter or in Kissinger (n 107).

[122] See T Phillips, 'Amazon Deforestation Surges to 12-Year High under Bolsonaro', *The Guardian*, 30 November 2020, www.theguardian.com/environment/2020/dec/01/amazon-deforestation-surges-to-12-year-high-under-bolsonaro, accessed 11 December 2020.

withdraw Brazil's bid to host COP25[123]).[124] His cabinet equally lacked a climate-change agenda, with his foreign minister, Ernesto Araujo, denying a 'climate catastrophe' during the high-profile fires in the Amazon in 2019.[125]

Bolsonaro's administration also greatly altered the Brazilian government departments that dealt with climate change and environmental issues, weakening their powers and abilities. For example, as Araújo helpfully outlines, the Brazilian Forest Service (a department with 'managerial autonomy' that handles forest concessions) and the Rural Environmental Registry (CAR) were transferred to the Ministry of Agriculture, Livestock and Supply (Mapa) whilst Bolsonaro was president.[126] Later in his term, a presidential decree completed the transfer of public forest management to the Mapa, including the overall management of forest concessions.[127] Mapa arguably prioritises agricultural interests (eg producing more agricultural goods and boosting the agricultural sector) rather than any sustainability prioritisations.[128] In terms of other changes to departmental organisation, the Ministry of Environment (MMA) secretariat focused on climate change[129] and the environmental education department were also abolished during the Bolsonaro administration.[130]

Reductions in budgets for environmental issues were also made, including a reported 95 percent cut to the climate budget; with only 0.03 percent of Brazil's $6.8 trillion budget in 2020 said to be dedicated to environmental protection; 25.3 percent less was reported to be set aside in 2020 than in 2019 for inspections by the Brazilian Institute for the Environment and Renewable Resources (IBAMA); and the budget for the implementation of Federal Conservation Units (covering 9.32 percent of the Brazilian land area) was said to be cut by 32.7 percent from 2019 to 2020.[131]

[123] 'Bolsonaro Requested Not to Hold Climate Summit in Brazil', *Folha*, 29 November 2018, www1.folha.uol.com.br/internacional/en/brazil/2018/11/bolsonaro-requested-not-to-hold-climate-summit-in-brazil.shtml, accessed 14 December 2020.

[124] 'Will President Bolsonaro Withdraw Brazil from the Paris Agreement? (Commentary)' https://news.mongabay.com/2019/01/commentary-will-president-bolsonaro-withdraw-brazil-from-the-paris-agreement/, accessed 14 December 2020.

[125] 'Brazil Foreign Minister Says "There Is No Climate Change Catastrophe"', *Reuters* {2019}, https://uk.reuters.com/article/us-brazil-environment-araujo/brazil-foreign-minister-says-there-is-no-climate-change-catastrophe-idUKKCN1VW2S2, accessed 14 December 2020; H Escobar, 'Amazon Fires Clearly Linked to Deforestation, Scientists Say' (2019) 365 *Science* 853; 'Emmanuel Macron Says He Will Block EU Trade Deal with Brazil over Amazon Forest Fires', *The Independent* {2019}, www.independent.co.uk/news/world/europe/macron-amazon-forest-fires-veto-mercosur-eu-trade-deal-brazil-a9076181.html, accessed 6 January 2020; 'EU Piles Pressure on Brazil over Amazon Fires', *Reuters*, 23 August 2019, https://uk.reuters.com/article/uk-eu-mercosur-ireland-idUKKCN1VD0PV, accessed 6 January 2020.

[126] S Mara Vaz Guimarães de Araújo, 'Environmental Policy in the Bolsonaro Government: The Response of Environmentalists in the Legislative Arena' (2020) 14 *Brazilian Political Science Review* 2.

[127] ibid 3.

[128] ibid.

[129] There were also threats from Bolsonaro initially to completely abolish the MMA itself, though following a backlash this did not happen.

[130] ibid 3.

[131] ibid 3.

Bolsonaro also backed the abolition of certain agroforestry measures during his term.[132] Although not explicitly part of its REDD+ strategy, during his presidency Bolsonaro supported the end of the Soy Moratorium in Brazil, a voluntary agreement between the soy industry, civil society and government to remove deforestation from the supply chain of soy produced in the Brazilian Amazon region.[133] Between 2004 and 2012, multiple policies contributed to a reported 84 percent decrease in the rate of Brazilian Amazon deforestation.[134] Among the most prominent of these policies was the Amazon Soy Moratorium. The Soy Moratorium has been heralded as particularly successful, contributing to deforestation reductions while also increasing soy production by 400 percent through the utilisation of existing agricultural lands.[135]

Nonetheless, some Brazilian farmers pushed to end the moratorium and this was backed by Bolsonaro during his presidency.[136] He sided with an already prominent farming lobby in the Brazilian political arena, and given that similar initiatives for different crops, such as sugarcane, were also already scrapped, it was worrying to see the potential impact of Bolsonaro's administration on the Moratorium.[137] Although NGOs and the Brazilian Congressional Environmental Coalition were able to restrict the use of Bolsonaro's executive powers to weaken environmental protection,[138] Bolsonaro's intention to 'productivise' Brazil's forests[139] was prominent during his term in office.

The election of Luiz Inácio Lula da Silva at the beginning of 2023 may reverse the anti-climate sentiment of the previous administration, with much of his campaign pledge focusing on addressing the country's emissions, which largely stem from its forests and forest management.[140] Lula announced his government would readjust its international climate commitments back to that pledged in 2015, where Brazil committed to reduce emissions by 37 percent by

[132] HK Gibbs et al, 'Brazil's Soy Moratorium' (2015) 347 *Science* 377; 'Brazil Farmers Push Traders to End Amazon Soy Moratorium', *Reuters*, 5 November 2019, https://uk.reuters.com/article/us-brazil-soybeans-moratorium-idUKKBN1XF2J6, accessed 14 July 2020; 'Brazil Agriculture Minister Calls Amazon Soy Moratorium "Absurd"', *Reuters*, 13 November 2019, www.reuters.com/article/us-brazil-soy-moratorium-idUSKBN1XN2LM, accessed 14 July 2020; R de Aragão Ribeiro Rodrigues et al, 'The Actions of the Brazilian Agricultural Sector in the Context of Climate Change Negotiations' (2019) 10 *Sustentabilidade em Debate* 28.

[133] 'Brazil Agriculture Minister Calls Amazon Soy Moratorium "Absurd"' (n 132).

[134] See R Heilmayr et al, 'Brazil's Amazon Soy Moratorium Reduced Deforestation' (2020) 1 *Nature Food* 801.

[135] See Abiove and Agrosatelite, 'Soy Moratorium: Monitoring Soy Crops in the Amazon Biome using Satellite Images' (Abiove and Agrosatelite, 2018).

[136] 'Brazil Farmers Push Traders to End Amazon Soy Moratorium' (n 132).

[137] 'Brazil Agriculture Minister Calls Amazon Soy Moratorium "Absurd"' (n 132).

[138] See more on the role of the Congressional Environmental Coalition's role in Araújo (n 126).

[139] 'Bolsonaro Government Reveals Plan to Develop the "Unproductive Amazon"', *Mongabay Environmental News*, 28 January 2019, https://news.mongabay.com/2019/01/bolsonaro-government-reveals-plan-to-develop-the-unproductive-amazon/, accessed 11 December 2020.

[140] Meghie Rodrigues, 'Will Brazil's President Lula Keep His Climate Promises?' (2023) 613 *Nature* 420.

2027 and 43 percent by 2030 – commitments that Bolsonaro had scaled back.[141] In June 2023, Lula's administration also unveiled a plan to end illegal deforestation by 2030, pledging to achieve net zero deforestation through restoring native vegetation stocks as compensation for legal vegetation removal.[142] These new measures mark the fifth phase of the aforementioned PPCDAm, originally created by Lula's previous administration and largely abandoned during Bolsonaro's time as leader.[143] The plan's new measures to increase monitoring and law enforcement of new conservation units are largely a response to recent congressional limitations on Brazil's environment minister driven by agribusiness interests.[144]

Although there are indications of promising developments for the future of the Brazilian Amazon's climate governance during Lula's term, the sharp changes of direction seen with changes of administration in Brazil highlight the fragility of forest governance in the region and the lack of influence of international governance in the face of national priorities and policy-making. Whilst references to livestock-driven deforestation climate impacts do exist, (albeit weakly) on the international level through initiatives such as REDD+, their durability is further weakened by the susceptibility of the commitments in light of national political will.[145] Further weaknesses of the REDD+ programme are highlighted below.

REDD+'s Developing Country Focus

A general point can also be made about the weakness of the REDD+ programme, namely that it only focuses on producers in developing countries (in line with the UNFCCC regime's overall use of production-based accounting[146]). In the case of many agricultural commodities, such as soy, beef and palm oil, demand for these goods is driven from outside these deforestation 'hotspots', such as South

[141] 'Brazil's Lula Unveils Plan to Stop Deforestation in Amazon by 2030', *Reuters*, {2023} www.reuters.com/world/americas/brazils-lula-launches-plan-stop-deforestation-amazon-by-2030-2023-06-05/, accessed 6 June 2023.

[142] Associated Press, 'Brazil's Lula Lays out Plan to Halt Amazon Deforestation', *POLITICO*, 6 June 2023, www.politico.com/news/2023/06/06/brazils-lula-lays-out-plan-to-halt-amazon-deforestation-00100342, accessed 13 September 2023.

[143] M Rodrigues, 'How Is Brazil's President Lula Doing on Climate? Experts Rate His Performance' (2023) 620 *Nature* 474.

[144] ibid.

[145] See more on climate policy durability generally in AJ Jordan and B Moore, *Durable by Design? Policy Feedback in a Changing Climate* (Cambridge University Press, 2020) www.cambridge.org/core/books/durable-by-design/635638C9209435D8C8491EB3EC288081, accessed 6 November 2021.

[146] For more on the relevance of production vs consumption-based accounting processes for the agricultural sector and responsibility attribution see Mengyao Han et al, 'Agricultural CH_4 and N_2O Emissions of Major Economies: Consumption- vs Production-Based Perspectives' (2019) 210 *Journal of Cleaner Production* 276.

America.[147] Although the REDD+ programme is supposed to tackle all drivers of deforestation, the fact that these goods are driven by demand in regions (such as soy imports to the European Union for livestock feed) is often bypassed, even though they are often the nations funding the results-based payments in the programme. Some positive domestic environmental benefits can be achieved through targeting demand for exports – for example, in the past Argentina placed a 35 percent export tax on soybean exportation, with its National Forest Law (2007) deforestation programme being funded via a 2 percent tax imposed on exported agricultural commodities, resulting in curbing of deforestation by 60 percent in one hotspot.[148]

However, a clash still exists between (1) the high demand for agricultural goods in regions such as the European Union and the profitability of this demand for agricultural global 'hotspots', such as Brazil or Argentina (ironically, Argentina has since slashed soy export taxes in an attempt to stimulate income from soy exports[149]), and (2) protecting forests in these 'hotspot' regions. As a result, at least on the fundamental design level of REDD+, the consumption side of the issue is not properly addressed. Some 'gap-plugging' attempts do exist separately to the REDD+ programme, such as the aforementioned Soy Moratorium.[150] Much of the public interest in securing soy-free deforestation chains ahead of the Moratorium came from an exposé on large corporations using soy from deforested areas in mainstream consumer brands or products (the most referenced perhaps being the Chicken McNugget).[151]

However, as stated previously, national initiatives such as this Moratorium are fragile as it is a voluntary initiative and has already been threatened in the past by farming lobbyists and the previous Bolsonaro administration.[152] As things stand, high importation and/or consumption of these agricultural goods in Global North regions remain largely unaddressed by REDD+, and their effects may even be worsened through the conclusion of bilateral trade agreements, like the EU-Mercosur Agreement.[153] Whilst consumption remains unaddressed in REDD+, its approach to livestock emissions cannot be classed as comprehensive, thereby compromising the breadth and depth of agri-climate governance with the international forest regime.

[147] For an example in the EU, see more in Muller and Bautze (n 4).

[148] Kissinger (n 107) 18.

[149] H Bronstein and M Heath, 'Argentina Cuts Soy Export Tax Rate in Bid to Boost FX Reserves', *Reuters*, 3 October 2020, https://uk.reuters.com/article/us-argentina-grains-taxes-idUKKBN26N03R, accessed 15 December 2020.

[150] Or the European Union's new due diligence regulation discussed further in the next chapter.

[151] Greenpeace, 'Eating Up the Amazon' (Greenpeace, 2006) 44.

[152] See earlier analysis, eg n 132.

[153] See the weakness in the enforcement mechanisms of the Sustainable Development provisions in the Agreement in principle in F Colli, 'The EU–Mercosur Agreement: Towards Integrated Climate Policy?' (2019) 57 *European Policy Brief* 5.

Conclusion

Generally, the international forest regime is characterised by fragmentation and multiple soft legal instruments. Due to the multifunctionality of forests, the principle of national sovereignty and colonial residue in forest governance, no single forest treaty exists on the international level. Sometimes forests are covered by other overlapping areas of international law, such as biodiversity protection and the CBD 1992. However, generally, focalised forest protection is not present on this international level.

This being said, through the creation and implementation of REDD+ under the UN climate regime, attempts to address LULUCF emissions are being made within the international forest regime. However, the coverage of agricultural-LULUCF emissions within the REDD+ programme is limited, or in many cases non-existent. Whilst agricultural-LULUCF emissions are covered in the REDD+ strategies of many 'hotspot' countries, such as Brazil, in non-hotspot regions they are less prominent.

Moreover, even the 'hotspot' or 'poster child' country commitments often fall short in terms of ambition and design to meaningfully mitigate agricultural-LULUCF emissions. Through a case study on Brazil's forest governance, Brazil's national strategies were found to be very susceptible to political change where economic interests were at stake, despite these international commitments. This was most strongly seen in Jair Bolsonaro's disruptive changes to national forest programmes and governance during his term, though may have similarities to other right-wing political turns in other developing countries' environmental protections.

Lastly, it was highlighted how the REDD+ programme focuses on agricultural producers rather than consumers – sidelining the impact of high consumption of agricultural goods, such as soy, from regions like the European Union that drive production (and consequently, often deforestation or land-use change) in these countries. Whilst some developed regions fund the results-based payments under the programme, attempts to address agricultural emissions through REDD+ fail to include the full range of driving forces behind deforestation in these 'hotspot' areas – once again leaving complex structural changes to food systems to the responsibility of developing countries, despite the contribution of developed countries in driving and establishing these forest extraction processes – as has been highlighted throughout the book so far.

The following chapter focuses on a less-fragmented regime that is relevant to the global livestock sector – the international agricultural-trade regime. It focuses primarily on relevant WTO law and how (or if) it addresses livestock emissions mitigation.

5

Climate Change and Cattle in the International Agricultural Trade Regime

Most beef and dairy products are not internationally traded but rather domestically consumed in the country in which they are produced. Nonetheless, the world's biggest dairy and beef exporting countries are reported to export between 10 and 20 percent of their domestically produced beef and dairy.[1] This percentage is often far more in terms of trade in soy, which is commonly used for livestock feed. Whilst it is reported that the United States only exports 10 percent of its soy production, Argentina and Brazil are reported to export 95 and 45 percent of their soy production, respectively.[2] More generally, increased free trade in agricultural goods has the potential to cause agri-environmental impacts. A global trade dynamic is therefore present in the production of agricultural goods production, making international trade laws relevant when looking to mitigate the climate impacts of the international cattle sector.

This chapter identifies how the issue of livestock emissions is addressed within the international agricultural trade regime (and more specifically in the WTO context) and determines whether and how livestock emissions reductions may be achieved in a manner that is compatible with WTO law. It does this by analysing the provisions of WTO Agreements and relevant 'case law' relating to agricultural production and environmental protection (or a lack thereof). Through this analysis, it is possible to determine the extent to which the WTO regime permits or encourages emissions mitigation for livestock goods that are traded internationally. Additionally, it builds on previous chapters by analysing a rules-based and more economic-focused legal regime within the international legal order for climate change and cattle, and delineating how this aligns with agri-climate goals.

Firstly, the historical development of WTO law and agricultural commodities is summarised. Then, an overview of the Agreement on Agriculture 1994 (AoA) is provided for ease of understanding the subsequent analysis. The dominant agricultural trade liberalisation mandate of the Agreement on Agriculture is delineated

[1] See more USDA Foreign Agricultural Service, 'Livestock and Poultry: World Markets and Trade' (USDA, 2018); and USDA Foreign Agricultural Service, 'Dairy: World Markets and Trade' (USDA, 2018).'

[2] ibid.

before outlining the agri-economic literature that exists on the environmental impact of agricultural trade liberalisation. The 'legalised'[3] nature of the international agri-trade regime, compared with other international legal regimes, is highlighted before outlining provisions under the Agreement on Agriculture and General Agreement on Tariffs and Trade 1947 (GATT) that are relevant for Member States to consider when undertaking WTO-compliant livestock emissions mitigation measures. This includes the outlining and analysis of various provisions that either permit or limit agri-environmental protection and food security under WTO Agreements. Lastly, the chapter concludes with overall takeaways on the extent to which the international agri-trade regime works at odds with livestock emissions goals.

The History of WTO Law and Agriculture

Aside from preferential trade agreements, international trade rules are largely dominated by the WTO. The WTO is a rules-based system with 164 members currently and is designed to encourage international trade in goods and services.[4] The issue of agricultural trade was 'effectively excluded' from the GATT at an early stage due to a consensus that agriculture was a unique sector of the economy and could not be treated like other sectors for national food security reasons.[5] Some authors suggest this 'exclusion' was largely to avoid two large, protectionist agricultural sectors being included in the GATT's general free-trade agenda, namely those of the United States and the countries that would later form the European Union.[6] The act of sidelining the protectionist agricultural policies[7] of these developed countries later led to significant trade-distorting effects as overproduction occurred in these regions due to the existence of production-based subsidies.[8] For example, at the time of the Uruguay Round, the European Union's surplus cereal stock was 33.4 million tonnes,

[3] See more on the concept of 'legalisation' in KW Abbott and D Snidal, 'Hard and Soft Law in International Governance' (2000) 54 *International Organization* 421, eg 427.

[4] This is a simplified conception of what much of the literature on the GATT and WTO describes. For a summary of the numerous narratives and conceptions of the purpose and objectives of international trade law, such as 'trade and' debates in international trade law, see ATF Lang, 'Reflecting on "Linkage": Cognitive and Institutional Change in the International Trading System' (2007) 70 *Modern Law Review* 523.

[5] S Healy et al, 'An Overview of the Negotiations on Agriculture', in *The implications of the Uruguay Round Agreement on Agriculture for Developing Countries: A Training Manual* (FAO, 1998) www.fao.org/3/w7814e/W7814E04.htm, accessed 30 August 2020, 1.1.3. See n 56 for a definition of protectionism.

[6] F Smith, 'Regulating Agriculture in the WTO' (2011) 7 *International Journal of Law in Context* 233, eg 234.

[7] For example, Smith (ibid) 234 states that 'Although the GATT rules on quantitative restrictions and subsidies theoretically applied to the CAP, uncertainty surrounding the scope of the Article XXIV GATT regional trading arrangements exemption meant the CAP was not really successfully challenged in the GATT era.'

[8] Further analysis of this will be found later in this chapter.

not including the 36 million tonnes that had already been exported outside of the Union.[9]

The Uruguay Round is probably best known as the multilateral trade negotiation that led to the creation of the WTO. However, it was also during this negotiation that GATT signatories also decided they needed a separate international trade agreement on agriculture, and agricultural trade 'was placed firmly on the GATT negotiating table' – though certain agricultural products did previously appear in the negotiations as individual commodities.[10] The European Union and the United States had many differences in their desired approach to agriculture in the Uruguay Round which often led to a stagnation in negotiations. However, by November 1992 they settled many of these differences, including agreeing upon an agricultural deal often referred to as the 'Blair House Agreement'.[11]

After this breakthrough, it was possible for an international trade agreement to be made on agriculture, namely the AoA.[12] The AoA's aim was 'to establish a fair and market-oriented agricultural trade system'.[13] The AoA was a framework agreement, designed to be fleshed out by WTO members to realise its trade liberalisation goal following further negotiations. Beef, dairy and soy are all classed as agricultural products as per the Article 2 and Annex 1 of the AoA.[14] Over the years, WTO members have met to complete these negotiations, but progress has often been slow and specific negotiations have sometimes failed.[15] More recently, some concerns have been raised as to whether the AoA is still fit for purpose because the global agricultural trade landscape is now very different to that at the time of the conclusion of the initial agreement.[16] As will be seen in subsequent analysis, the AoA was largely created as a response to protectionist agricultural regimes in

[9] See European Commission, *The Agricultural Situation in the Community: 1993 Report* (European Commission, 1994) 52–3 in M Cardwell and F Smith, 'Renegotiation of the WTO Agreement on Agriculture: Accommodating the New Big Issues' (2013) 62 *ICLQ* 865.

[10] For example, The Dillon Round succeeded in cutting tariffs on soya beans, cotton, vegetables and canned fruit to very low levels, and the International Wheat Agreement and the International Dairy and Meat Agreement were negotiated under the auspices of the Kennedy Round. In general, though, agricultural commodities remained outside the negotiating agenda, see Healy et al (n 5) 1.1.3.

[11] US–EC Blair House Agreement (September 1993).

[12] Agreement on Agriculture (15 April 1994) LT/UR/A-1A/2.

[13] ibid Preamble and Art 20(c).

[14] ibid Art 2 and Annex 1. For the WTO's harmonised customs classification code, see WTO, 'Current Situation of Schedules of WTO Members' (2013) G/MA/W/23/Rev.9.

[15] The Doha Agenda began with a ministerial-level meeting in 2001, in Doha, Qatar. The Doha Round's broad objective was to reduce distortions in agricultural trade caused by high tariffs and other barriers, export subsidies, and certain aspects of domestic support, taking particular concern for the needs of developing countries. Ministers met again multiple times between 2003 and 2008, though ultimately these negotiations broke down in 2008 due to political differences between developed agricultural economies (such as the United States and the European Union) and developing agricultural commodities (such as Brazil, China and India) – particularly in relation to the United States' and the European Union's maintenance of agricultural subsidies. Attempts were made in 2008 by the United States, China, and India to overcome these differences through further negotiation; however, ultimately these negotiations failed. See more details in A Charlton, 'The Collapse of the Doha Trade Round' (CentrePiece, LSE, 2006) https://cep.lse.ac.uk/pubs/download/CP210.pdf.

[16] See generally, Cardwell and Smith (n 9).

developed countries and their trade-distorting impacts.[17] However, there is now an increased focus on what are called 'non-trade issues' beyond the goal of liberalising the global agricultural market, such as food security and environmental protection.[18]

This section of the chapter will initially set out the basic provisions of the AoA – the main instrument currently regulating international trade in agricultural goods – and the key decisions that have been made on agricultural trade since its conclusion. Additionally, as the AoA is an often-unfamiliar component of WTO law, outlining its core provisions provides useful context for the rest of the analysis. Lastly, avenues and roadblocks to securing livestock emissions reduction under the WTO law are outlined, demonstrating to what extent agri-climate measures for the livestock are feasible under the international agri-trade regime given its various trade and non-trade mandates.

An Overview of the Agreement on Agriculture

As mentioned above, some essential information needs to be provided to make sense of the discussion later in this chapter on livestock-specific issues. In particular, an explanation of the AoA is needed to for ease of understanding the subsequent analysis of its provisions.

As previously noted, the objective of the AoA was 'to establish a fair and market-oriented agricultural trading system', particularly against the backdrop of overproduction and market distortion from protectionist domestic agricultural policies in developed countries at the time.[19] To achieve greater liberalisation of global agricultural trade, three so-called pillars were established under the AoA: (1) the Market Access Pillar; (2) the Domestic Support Pillar; and (3) the Export Competition Pillar. All of these pillars contain policies which were designed to decrease the existence of trade-distorting agricultural policies in Member States.

Market Access

The Market Access Pillar was designed to provide greater access to the global agricultural market by making trade restrictions and barriers more transparent.[20] The main process that is provided for under the Market Access Pillar is known

[17] ibid eg 878.

[18] For a more critical discussion on the conceptualisation of so-called 'non-trade' interests in international trade literature and how these relate to so-called 'trade interests' again, see Lang (n 4).

[19] Agreement on Agriculture (15 April 1994) LT/UR/A-1A/2, Preamble.

[20] For more context on the negotiation and intentions of the AoA, see W Hett, 'US Corn and Soybean Subsidies: WTO Litigation and Sustainable Protections' (2008) 17 *Transnational Law & Contemporary Problems* 775, 779.

as 'tariffication', or the conversion of non-tariff barriers into a tariff equivalent.[21] A prescribed uniform method of 'tariffication' was created to make trade barriers more clear, transparent and easy to compare. As a result of the increased transparency through tariffication, it became possible for WTO members to make comprehensive tariff-reduction commitments, the implementation of which could be monitored and evaluated for compliance.[22] As with many provisions under the AoA, concessions were made for developing countries[23] which are more likely to have larger economic reliance on their domestic agricultural sectors (in addition to more food security issues due to wealth disparity or geographical susceptibility). This is normally referred to as 'special and differential treatment for developing countries' (SDT).[24] An example of SDT for developing countries under the Market Access Pillar is the Special Agricultural Safeguard (SSG).[25] This mechanism allows developing countries to temporarily increase tariffs to suppress import surges or price falls.[26] It was particularly created for agricultural imports that can cause damage to farmers' livelihoods in developing countries.[27]

Domestic Support

Measures under the Domestic Support Pillar limit the use of domestic subsidies on agricultural goods that can distort world trade.[28] Domestic support refers to any subsidy or benefit that is provided to producers but has no effect on exports, such as minimum price support for a specific commodity.[29] Domestic support measures like these often artificially increase the production of an agricultural commodity, thereby driving down global prices.[30] This in turn can often 'insulate' producers

[21] Agreement on Agriculture (15 April 1994) LT/UR/A-1A/2, Art 4(2). See also Cardwell and Smith (n 9) 877.

[22] Hett (n 20) 799.

[23] There are no WTO definitions of 'developed' and 'developing' countries. Members announce for themselves whether they are 'developed' or 'developing' countries. However, other members can challenge the decision of a member to make use of provisions available to developing countries. The WTO recognises as least-developed countries (LDCs) those countries which have been designated as such by the United Nations.

[24] For more on Special and Differential Treatment, see S Switzer, 'A Contract Theory Approach to Special and Differential Treatment and the WTO' (2017) 16 *Journal of International Trade Law and Policy* 126.

[25] Agreement on Agriculture (15 April 1994) LT/UR/A-1A/2, Art 5.

[26] Nairobi Ministerial Declaration 2015 (WT/MIN(15)/DEC).

[27] See more, J-J Hallaert, 'Special Agricultural Safeguards: Virtual Benefits and Real Costs – Lessons for the Doha Round' (IMF, 2016) www.imf.org/en/Publications/WP/Issues/2016/12/31/Special-Agricultural-Safeguards-Virtual-Benefits-and-Real-Costs-Lessons-for-the-Doha-Round-18328, accessed 11 July 2023.

[28] Agreement on Agriculture (15 April 1994) LT/UR/A-1A/2, Art 6.

[29] Hett (n 20) 780.

[30] See S Mitra and T Josling, 'Agricultural Export Restrictions: Welfare Implications and Trade Disciplines, IPC Position Paper (International Food and Agricultural Trade Policy Council 2009) 1, eg 3.

from global prices. This incentivises the maintenance of high levels of production, or increased production, even when the real market value of goods would correlate with lower levels of production.

Domestic support is subject to reduction commitments under the AoA.[31] A calculation of members' Aggregate Measure of Support (AMS) is used to quantify levels of domestic support in order to facilitate these reductions. Article 1 of the AoA defines AMS as 'the annual level of support, expressed in monetary terms, provided for an agricultural product in favour of the producers of the basic agricultural product[,] or non-product specific support provided in favour of agricultural producers in general'.[32] An initial base level of AMS was calculated at the time of the Uruguay Round,[33] and members agreed to reduce this level over subsequent years (for example, the initial commitment was a 20 percent reduction in AMS by 2000 for developed countries).[34]

Not all domestic support measures are required to be reduced. Whether or not reduction commitments are required is determined by provisions under three 'boxes' in the Agreement, (1) the Amber Box, (2) the Blue Box and (3) the Green Box. Some so-called developmental measures are also exempt under the Agreement. Each of these categories is discussed below.

Amber Box

The Amber Box covers domestic support that is considered highly trade-distorting and is therefore subject to reduction commitments. The Amber Box measures include price supports and other measures directly related to production.[35] A de minimis exemption to this reduction commitment exists if the specific support is not greater than 5 percent of the total value of production of an agricultural good.[36] This is also applicable to non-product-specific support, where the total value of production is less than 5 percent.[37] This threshold is raised to 10 percent for developing countries, but the de minimis exception essentially exists to avoid trivial or minor support being subject to reduction commitments.[38]

[31] Agreement on Agriculture (15 April 1994) LT/UR/A-1A/2, Art 6.

[32] ibid Art 1.

[33] It is worth noting that base years used saw very high levels of subsidisation which reduces the utility of reduction commitments. OECD, *The Uruguay Round Agreement on Agriculture: An Evaluation of Its Implementation in OECD Countries* (OECD, 2001) www.oecd-ilibrary.org/agriculture-and-food/the-uruguay-round-agreement-on-agriculture_9789264192188-en, accessed 11 July 2023.

[34] See GATT, Modalities for the Establishment of Specific Binding Commitments under the Reform Programme, MTN.GNG/MA/W/24, 20 December, paras VIII, XV and XVI as referenced in Cardwell and Smith (n 9) 880.

[35] Hett (n 20) 780.

[36] Agreement on Agriculture (15 April 1994) LT/UR/A-1A/2, Art 6(4).

[37] ibid.

[38] Cardwell and Smith (n 9) 880.

Blue Box

Blue Box measures are similar to Amber Box measures in that they are considered market distorting. However, because Blue Box measures require farmers to limit production (as opposed to incentivising production) they are considered less market-distorting and, thus, are not subject to reduction commitments.[39]

For example, the European Union's past production-limiting programmes (such as land set-aside policies) were Blue Box exempt as they involved limiting agricultural production on farming land (largely due to agricultural surpluses at the time, but also to prevent environmental degradation).[40] This policy technically did distort trade as it had the effect of lowering production levels. However, it did not distort trade to the same extent as the European Union's other more trade-distorting subsidies which encouraged production at levels higher than those determined by market forces due to subsidised production. This subsidised production arguably had more negative effects on other members' agricultural sectors due to its depressing effect on global agricultural prices.[41] The Blue Box was initially negotiated as a compromise to blanket reduction commitments on all forms of domestic support. In particular, it was seen as a way for the US and EU Member States to maintain these 'traditionally valued' (or sometimes labelled 'protectionist') subsidies without being faced with reduction commitments.[42]

Green Box

Green Box measures are exempted from reduction commitments and are found under Annex 2 of the AoA.[43] Green box measures must have no, or at most minimal, trade-distorting effects or effects on production.[44] They must be funded publicly through government programmes, not involve transfers from consumers, or have the effect of providing price support to producers.[45] Any level of expenditure is permitted for the Green Box measures as long as these conditions are satisfied, and they apply equally to developed- and developing-country members. Green measures listed under Annex 2 include:

[39] For more on Blue Box support, see S Kumar Sharma et al, 'Demystifying Blue Box Support to Agriculture Under the WTO: Implications for Developing Countries' (2021) 22 *South Asia Economic Journal* 161.

[40] Cardwell and Smith (n 9) 881.

[41] See more in S Leetmaa, 'Effects of Eliminating EU Export Subsidies' in M Burfisher (ed), 'Agricultural Policy Reform in the WTO – The Road Ahead' (Market and Trade Economics Division, Economic Research Service, USDA, 2001) Agricultural Economic Report No 802.

[42] Hett (n 20) 781.

[43] Agreement on Agriculture (15 April 1994) LT/UR/A-1A/2, Annex 2.

[44] ibid Annex 2, para 1.

[45] ibid.

- general services, including research, pest and disease control, training, extension, inspection, marketing and promotion services, and infrastructural services;
- public stockholding for food security purposes;
- domestic food aid; and
- direct payments to producers, including decoupled income support, income insurance and safety-net programmes, disaster relief, producer or resource retirement schemes, investment aids, environmental programmes, and regional assistance programmes.[46]

Developmental Measures

Although not categorised under the 'Box' system, developmental measures are also excluded from reduction commitments under Article 6 AoA.[47] Developmental measures, whether direct or indirect, are designed to 'encourage agricultural and rural development' and are an 'integral part of the development programmes of developing countries'.[48] This includes:

- investment subsidies which are generally available to agriculture in developing countries;
- agricultural input subsidies generally available to low-income or resource-poor producers in developing countries; and
- domestic support to producers in developing countries to encourage diversification from growing illicit narcotic crops.[49]

Figure 4 Domestic support pillar measures and their exemption status

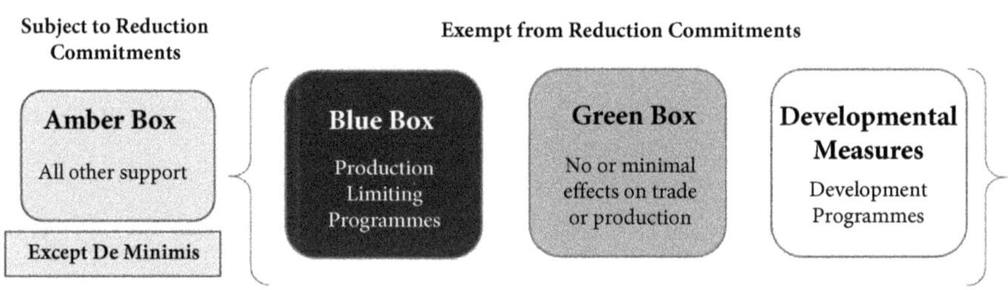

[46] ibid Annex 2.
[47] ibid Art 6.
[48] See more 'WTO Agriculture – Explanation of the Agreement – Domestic Support' (WTO, undated) www.wto.org/english/tratop_e/agric_e/ag_intro03_domestic_e.htm.
[49] Agreement on Agriculture (15 April 1994) LT/UR/A-1A/2, Art 6(2).

Export Competition

The final pillar under the AoA is the Export Competition Pillar which sought to restrict the use of export subsidies for agricultural goods. Export subsidies are defined as support measures conditioned upon 'export performance' or 'upon the use of domestic over imported goods'.[50] They are normally designed with the purpose of aiding a country's trade by bolstering exports. These subsidies were also subject to reduction commitments under the AoA, with differentiated rates for developed and developing countries and special provisions in place under Article 10 of the AoA to avoid circumvention of these reductions.[51] However, as of 2015 and the Nairobi Package, all export subsidies should have been eliminated in developed WTO member countries.[52] Moreover, developing-country members should have eliminated all export subsidies by 2018.[53] Although export subsidies were consistently being reduced before the Nairobi Package, this decision ensures that export subsidies will not be used in the future in response to agricultural commodity price drops.[54]

Agricultural Trade Liberalisation under the AoA

As mentioned previously, the WTO regime has over time increasingly sought to include both trade and so-called 'non-trade' concerns, such as environmental protection. Nevertheless, trade liberalisation provisions are prominent in the AoA, as with the general provisions under the GATT. A number of components of the AoA promote agricultural trade liberalisation within the agricultural trade regime. Trade liberalisation involves opening up domestic economies to global trade and investment, particularly by reducing 'protectionist' domestic measures.[55] Protectionism can be defined as when an economy seeks to protect its domestic firms from foreign competition using policy measures.[56] Traditional protectionist policy measures include tariffs and quotas that are generally prohibited under trade agreements unless they follow the specific rules[57] of different trade agreements such as the GATT.[58]

[50] Agreement on Subsidies and Countervailing Measures 1869 UNTS 14, Art 3(1).
[51] Agreement on Agriculture (15 April 1994) LT/UR/A-1A/2, Art 10.
[52] Notwithstanding a few exceptions. Developing-country members shall continue to benefit from the provisions of Art 9.4 AoA until the end of 2023, ie five years after the end date for elimination of all forms of export subsidies. Least-developed countries and net food-importing developing countries listed in G/AG/5/Rev.10 shall continue to benefit from the provisions of Art 9.4 AoA until the end of 2030. See Ministerial Decision of 19 December 2015: WT/MIN(15)/45 – WT/L/980, para 8.
[53] Ministerial Decision of 19 December 2015: WT/MIN(15)/45 – WT/L/980, para 8.
[54] WTO, 'Tenth WTO Ministerial Conference – Nairobi' (Briefing Note, 2015) www.wto.org/english/thewto_e/minist_e/mc10_e/briefing_notes_e/brief_agriculture_e.htm, accessed 25 August 2023.
[55] IMF Staff, 'Global Trade Liberalization and Developing Countries' (IMF Issues Brief, 2001).
[56] For more on protectionism generally, see AO Sykes, 'Regulatory Protectionism and the Law of International Trade' (1999) 66 *University of Chicago Law Review* 1.
[57] For example, see the process of 'tariffication' referred to in the summary of the AoA at the start of this chapter.
[58] Again, see more in Sykes (n 56).

Agricultural trade liberalisation follows a similar definition to trade liberalisation, but instead focuses solely on the opening up of global trade in agricultural goods. Agricultural trade liberalisation may be (and has been) pursued for a number of reasons, including (1) supporting the economic development of developing countries which often rely heavily on the economic growth generated by their agricultural sectors,[59] and (2) minimising the impacts of 'protectionist' domestic agricultural measures in developed countries on developing countries.[60]

The AoA itself is formulated around an overarching goal of establishing a 'fair and market oriented agricultural trade system'.[61] Cardwell and Smith have delineated the meaning of fair in the AoA's context to mean one where 'market conditions prevail'.[62] In essence, the supply of agricultural goods will only fluctuate in response to demand for them and vice versa, and this balance should not be distorted by the domestic agricultural policies of members. As was seen in the summary of the provisions above, a considerable number of measures were created under the AoA to reduce agricultural protectionism and distortion of trade, particularly from developed-country members that historically had a strong track record of protectionist domestic agricultural regimes, such as the European Union.

Improving market access (under the Market Access Pillar), eliminating export subsidies and support (under the Export Competition Pillar) and decreasing market-distorting domestic support (under the Domestic Support Pillar) all contribute towards the AoA's goal of agricultural trade liberalisation while avoiding protectionist agricultural policies. The agricultural trade liberalisation is balanced against other environmentally focused provisions and exceptions under the Agreement that will be discussed in subsequent sections. However, before this, the environmental impacts of agricultural trade liberalisation (as per agricultural economics literature) will be outlined to determine the extent to which the AoA's agricultural trade liberalisation goal can hinder emissions mitigation in the agricultural sector and for climate change mitigation more generally.

The Environmental Effects of Agricultural Trade Liberalisation

There are surprisingly few empirical studies on the impact of agricultural trade liberalisation on the environment. It is a relatively new field of study, with economic

[59] Healy et al (n 5) 1.1.6.

[60] Though even with the AoA, there are issues with this, see later in this chapter but also generally in L Stuart and T Riechert, *Green but Not Clean: Why a Comprehensive Review of Green Box Subsidies Is Necessary* (Action Aid, Caritas, CIDSE, Oxfam, 2005); C Galperín and I Miguez, 'Green Box Subsidies and Trade-Distorting Support: Is There a Cumulative Impact?' in R Melendez-Ortiz et al (eds) *Agricultural Subsidies in the WTO Green Box* (Cambridge University Press, 2009).

[61] Agreement on Agriculture (15 April 1994) LT/UR/A-1A/2, Preamble.

[62] Cardwell and Smith (n 9) 874.

research on the topic only really beginning in the mid-1990s.[63] A number of the earlier seminal economic works on agricultural trade and environment did not address more contemporary environmental issues relating to agriculture, particularly climate change and enteric fermentation stemming from agricultural (and especially livestock) production.[64] As a result, earlier economic research on the impact of liberalising global agriculture on the environment is 'decidely upbeat'.[65] Since then, Balogh and Jámbor have published a systematic literature review of all the studies on the impact of agricultural trade on the environment.[66] They found there were only 65 articles written on agricultural trade and the environment between 1990 and 2019, with only 38 of these on climate change and four on land-use change.[67] Moreover, only 21 of these 65 articles approached their study from a global environmental perspective (as opposed to a regional case study, which may not fully address the transboundary impact of emissions production from agriculture).[68] In more recent years, there has been increased recognition that agricultural trade can be more detrimental to the environment than initially suggested in these earlier works, and an even clearer causal relationship found between general trade liberalisation (as opposed to solely agricultural trade) and increases in GHG emissions.[69] The details of these studies and their underlying logic are outlined below.

Agricultural Trade Liberalisation and Climate Change

On a broad, synthesising level, Schmitz et al report that most of the 'saved economic costs' of trade liberalisation are achieved 'at the expense of the environment and climate'.[70] A study on the impact of agricultural trade liberalisation on GHG emissions by Verburg et al conclude that emissions increased by 6 percent under a full agricultural trade liberalisation scenario compared with a 'no new policy scenario'.[71] Schmitz et al's study found a similar increase, though using a longer time scale for full agricultural liberalisation to occur.[72]

[63] C Schmitz et al, 'Trading More Food: Implications for Land Use, Greenhouse Gas Emissions, and the Food System' (2012) 22 *Global Environmental Change* 189.

[64] See eg K Anderson, 'Agricultural Trade Liberalisation and the Environment: A Global Perspective' (1992) 15 *World Economy* 153.

[65] C Tisdell and A Dragun, 'Agriculture and Sustainability: The Impact of Trade Liberalisation' in *Sustainable Agriculture and Environment: Globalisation and the Impact of Trade Liberalisation* (Edward Elgar, 1999) 1–6.

[66] J Máté Balogh and A Jámbor, 'The Environmental Impacts of Agricultural Trade: A Systematic Literature Review' (2020) 12 *Sustainability* 1152.

[67] ibid 2–4.

[68] ibid.

[69] Schmitz et al (n 63) eg 189.

[70] ibid 199.

[71] R Verburg et al, 'The Effect of Agricultural Trade Liberalisation on Land-Use Related Greenhouse Gas Emissions' (2009) 19(4) *Global Environmental Change* 434, from 438.

[72] Schmitz et al (n 63) from 193.

When the geographical shifts in production experienced under an agricultural trade liberalisation scenario are also considered alongside this emissions increase, agricultural trade liberalisation can be seen as particularly damaging (both ecologically and from a more ethical standpoint, as will be explained). For example, it is reported that this liberalisation causes a shift in export shares in favour of regions that have a comparative advantage in agriculture.[73] Comparative advantage in the case of livestock production can be considered as having more land on which animals such as cattle can be reared and grazed. As a result, global agricultural trade liberalisation has been reported to lead to expansion of deforestation in ecologically sensitive areas in the Amazon, and to generate more environmental pressures across regions of Latin America.[74] Conversely, certain studies suggest environmental conditions actually improve in more developed regions following this liberalisation, including the European Union.[75] Balogh and Jámbor have verified this trend, identifying from the literature that the countries that are most negatively influenced by agricultural trade liberalisation are *developing* regions (China, Indonesia, India, Mexico, Brazil, Thailand, Malaysia, Vietnam) or *least-developed poor* regions[76] (the Maghreb, the Middle East, sub-Saharan Africa, Latin America, the Caribbean).[77] By contrast, they found that studies suggested *developed* countries, such as those in the European Union and the United States, benefited the most from the potential positive environmental effects of this liberalisation (particularly due to trading shifts in biofuel, soybean and palm oil).[78]

As was mentioned above, agricultural comparative advantage usually arises where there is more land available for agricultural production. More developed regions, such as the European Union and the United States, often have more densely populated land. Consequently, when agricultural trade liberalisation occurs, agricultural production is reported to shift from these areas to less densely populated countries with more 'available' land, such as ecologically sensitive regions in the Brazilian Amazon.[79] Overall, 'dramatic shifts' in land use are reported to

[73] ibid.

[74] See a range of studies, such as C Schmitz et al, 'Agricultural Trade and Tropical Deforestation: Interactions and Related Policy Options' (2015) 15 *Regional Environmental Change* 1757–1772; DJ Lee and J Zhang, 'Efficiency, Equity, and Environmental Implications of Trade Liberalization: A Computable General Equilibrium Analysis' (2009) 18 *Journal of International Trade & Economic Development* 347; I Flachsbarth et al, 'The Role of Latin America's Land and Water Resources for Global Food Security: Environmental Trade-offs of Future Food Production Pathways' (2015) 10 *PLoS ONE* e0116733; R Defries et al, 'Deforestation Driven by Urban Population Growth and Agricultural Trade in the Twenty-First Century' (2010) 3 *Nature Geoscience* 178.

[75] See H van Meijl et al, 'The Impact of Different Policy Environments on Agricultural Land Use in Europe' (2006) 114 *Agriculture, Ecosystems & Environment* 21; B Eickhout et al, 'The Impact of Environmental and Climate Constraints on Global Food Supply' in TW Hertel, SK Rose and RSJ Tol (eds), *Economic Analysis of Land Use in Global Climate Change Policy* (Routledge, 2009); Balogh and Jámbor (n 66).

[76] Defined by the authors as the Maghreb, the Middle East, sub-Saharan Africa, Latin America and the Caribbean.

[77] Balogh and Jámbor (n 66) 10.

[78] ibid.

[79] See more Anderson (n 64).

occur in developing regions and only small land-use shifts occur in regions such as Europe.[80] Earlier studies suggest the gains in environmental improvements in these more densely populated countries outweighs (if cumulative benefits rather than site-specific losses can even be deemed a fair measure[81] of the impacts of environmental degradation) the losses in these less densely populated countries.[82] However, the majority of studies have now disproven this hypothesis, showing that overall environmental losses appear to outweigh environmental gains.

Overall, agricultural trade liberalisation can be found to lead to ecologically detrimental shifts in trading patterns and overall increases in emissions production. Moreover, concerns can be raised about the fairness and socioeconomic impact of this liberalisation worsening environmental degradation in developing countries more than developed countries. Developing countries (and particularly least-developed poor countries) historically have contributed less to climate change (and often continue to do so), and this therefore raises ethical questions about the fairness of these countries being subject to environmental degradation in the name of global trade liberalisation.[83] In a climate change context, this does raise issues surrounding the concept of 'common but differentiated responsibilities and respective capabilities in light of different national circumstances', as embodied in the Paris Agreement.[84] This notion of 'fairness' will not be expanded upon here but will be considered further in the Conclusion alongside other issues surrounding the fairness of agricultural emissions mitigation identified across this book.

Nonetheless, the literature does draw attention to further factors to take into account when considering these shifts caused by agricultural trade liberalisation. For example, increased consumption from economic and population growth, rather than solely liberalisation of the agricultural sector, does have a role to play in the potential environmental impact of the global agricultural sector. By way of illustration, when considering nitrates pollution (such as that from livestock manure), some authors have reported that large increases in nitrogen waste in China in their liberalisation scenarios were linked to their domestic economic growth rather than trade liberalisation per se.[85] In terms of non-CO_2 agricultural emissions, Schmitz et al attribute some of the shifts in production within China to

[80] Schmitz et al (n 74) 1758.

[81] There is further discussion in the Conclusion of this book of what 'fair' means in relation to agricultural emissions mitigation.

[82] Anderson (n 64).

[83] For more discussion on this developed/developing country dynamics in environmental or climate change mitigation, see more on the concept of common but differentiated responsibilities and climate justice, eg S Caney, 'Two Kinds of Climate Justice: Avoiding Harm and Sharing Burdens: Two Kinds of Climate Justice' (2014) 22 *Journal of Political Philosophy* 125; S Klinsky and H Dowlatabadi, 'Conceptualizations of Justice in Climate Policy' (2009) 9(1) 88–198 *Climate Policy*; L Rajamani, *Differential Treatment in International Environmental Law* (Oxford University Press, 2006). Alternatively, see the Conclusion of this book for a discussion of the principle in the context of its analysis.

[84] Paris Agreement on Climate Change 2015.

[85] See Anderson (n 64); AN Rae and A Strutt, 'Livestock Production and the Environment: Some Impacts of Growth and Trade Liberalisation' (2001) 35 *New Zealand Economic Papers* 176.

increasing domestic demand for livestock products in the region, probably stemming from increasing wealth levels.[86] Thus, increasing consumption can be seen to have a role to play in increased production levels and shifts in production patterns (and its consequential environmental impacts).

Nonetheless, in some circumstances, the full environmental impacts of goods consumed in a country may be externalised beyond its borders. Studies have reported that including 'imported emissions' in some regions' GHG emissions accounts results in higher emissions levels than solely production-based accounting,[87] including the European Union, Western Europe, the United States and Japan.[88] Consequently, there is a 'producing country' and 'consuming country' dynamic that is relevant to consider when addressing emissions from agricultural trade. In fact, Drabo reports that the higher the proportion of primary commodity exports a country has for agricultural production, the higher its GHG emissions.[89] This supports the idea that trade policy is not the only driving factor behind environmental degradation from agricultural production, but consumption patterns (particularly those driven by population and economic growth) do have a role to play in understanding how agricultural trade liberalisation may increase agricultural emissions.

Another factor that affects the impact of agricultural trade liberalisation on the environment is the extent to which sufficient and well-enforced environmental protections are put in place domestically in regions where comparative advantage for resource-intensive agricultural production exists, such as Latin America. Lopez has reported that trade increases resource degradation in producing countries if negative environmental externalities are not properly accounted for in product prices.[90] The FAO has also highlighted the importance of embodying environmental 'bads' in the costs and prices of traded products.[91]

Nevertheless, the aforementioned empirical studies have demonstrated that agricultural trade liberalisation can induce negative environmental consequences. As a consequence, the agricultural trade liberalisation goal of the AoA in theory will be detrimental to the goals of climate change mitigation. Of course, empirical studies and projections can only provide so many predictions of what will happen in reality. Brazil may not necessarily produce fewer agricultural goods under

[86] Schmitz et al (n 63) 199.

[87] Production-based accounting methods add all the emissions that are produced within that country. If emissions associated with the goods and services consumed within that country are added instead, this is considered consumption-based accounting. See the following footnote for the implications of different accounting methods for agricultural emissions responsibility attribution.

[88] M Han et al, 'Agricultural CH_4 and N_2O Emissions of Major Economies: Consumption- vs Production-Based Perspectives' (2019) 210 *Journal of Cleaner Production* 276; B Zhang et al, 'Consumption-Based Accounting of Global Anthropogenic CH_4 Emissions' (2018) 6 *Earth's Future* 1349.

[89] See A Drabo, 'Climate Change Mitigation and Agricultural Development Models: Primary Commodity Exports or Local Consumption Production?' (2017) 137 *Ecological Economics* 110.

[90] See R Lopez, 'The Environment as a Factor of Production: The Effects of Economic Growth and Trade Liberalization' (1994) 27 *Journal of Environmental Economics and Management* 163.

[91] J Bruinsma and Food and Agriculture Organization of the United Nations, *World Agriculture: Towards 2015/2030: An FAO Study* (|FAO, 2017) eg 39.

a non-trade liberalisation scenario and the European Union may not necessarily increase its consumption of these goods under a non-trade liberalisation scenario (for example, trends away from meat eating may alter consumption habits).[92]

However, the general consensus of agri-environmental economists highlighted thus far is that there will be an increase in negative environmental impacts as agricultural trade liberalisation increases. As a result, tensions can be identified between climate change mitigation goals and the agri-trade liberalising components of the AoA. More literature on this will hopefully be undertaken in the coming years, but broader literature on climate change and *general* trade liberalisation (across all sectors) will be outlined below to provide greater context to this conclusion.

General Trade Liberalisation and its Climate Change Impacts

As was mentioned previously, only a small amount of literature exists on the environmental impacts of agricultural trade liberalisation specifically. However, slightly more research on general trade liberalisation and its climate change impacts has been undertaken. This section will summarise this literature because although it is not specific to the agricultural trade context,[93] it does provide some additional material from which to understand the climate impacts of trade liberalisation more generally.

The literature outlines three main ways that trade liberalisation can affect GHG emissions: the scale effect, the composition effect and the technique effect.[94] These effects can be positive or negative in nature. The scale effect refers to the expansion of economic activity that comes from trade opening up and the effect of this on GHG emissions.[95] As trade opens up, levels of economic activity and consequent energy and resource use increase, thereby increasing levels of GHG emissions.[96] The composition effect can also have similar negative effects of increasing GHG emissions. The composition effect describes the way that opening trade can change the structure of a country's production as a response to changes in relative prices, and how this impacts emissions levels. Whether this change in the structure (or location) of production causes an increase in emissions will depend on whether any country has a comparative advantage in emissions-intensive sectors and

[92] See the rising statistics of decreased meat eating in Europe, 'Europe: Vegetarianism & Veganism among Young Adults 2021' (Statista, 2021) www.statista.com/statistics/768475/vegetarianism-and-veganism-among-young-adults-in-selected-european-countries/, accessed 4 September 2021.

[93] For example, food is not just a tradable commodity, but perhaps can even be considered a public good and its supply a socioeconomic necessity. See C Runge and et al, 'Liberal Agricultural Trade as a Public Good: Free Trade vs Free Riding under GATT' (Staff Paper Series P87-11, University of Minnesota 1987) as a historic example of the perceived importance of agricultural trade as public good.

[94] For a comprehensive overview of the literature on this, see H Abaza et al, *Trade and Climate Change: A Report by the United Nations Environment Programme and the World Trade Organization* (WTO, UNEP 2009).

[95] ibid 49–53.

[96] ibid.

whether these industries are growing or contracting.[97] It also depends on how well environmental degradation is regulated in these economies.[98]

Copeland and Taylor developed the 'pollution haven hypothesis' (PHH) which predicts that countries with weaker environmental regulations will specialise in polluting industries, and high-emissions industries may relocate to countries with less-stringent environmental protection policies.[99] A number of empirical studies[100] have reported the existence of the PHH, particularly in China but also in other regions.[101] Lastly, the technique effect refers to the potential improvement in methods of production that will reduce the emissions intensity of goods and services.[102] This is the main way trade liberalisation could help mitigate climate change. Firstly, it can help to lower the costs and increase the availability of climate-friendly goods and services (such as feed additives in the case of livestock emissions).[103] Secondly, some studies suggest when income levels rise from trade opening, this may result in public demand to reduce GHG emissions.[104] Other authors suggest that increased

[97] ibid 52.

[98] See discussions of pollution haven hypothesis following, or ibid 51.

[99] See BR Copeland and MS Taylor, 'Trade, Growth and the Environment' (2004) 46 *Journal of Economic Literature* 7.

[100] Some governance theories (rather than being necessarily empirical) have suggested that 'governance spillovers' may exist. When one country 'exports' its regulations to the producing country this might lead to a 'trading up' effect in environmental regulation as is postulated by the California or Brussels Effect. This may be an external factor to consider when considering the dynamics between nations in relation to environmental standards and environmental degradation. As mentioned previously, this has not been empirically studied to the same extent as the pollution haven hypothesis. Nonetheless, many governance scholars have written on this concept. For example, on the Brussels Effect, see generally A Bradford, *The Brussels Effect: How the European Union Rules the World* (Oxford University Press, 2020). For more on the positive effect of EU trade rules on third-party countries see G Marín-Durán, *The Role of the EU in Shaping the Trade and Environment Regulatory Nexus: Multilateral and Regional Approaches' in The EU's Role in Global Governance* (Oxford University Press, 2013). For a study demonstrating no evidence of the causal effect of including non-trade provisions (such as environmental provisions) in EU preferential trade agreements on indicators of non-trade outcomes (eg environmental degradation), see A Ferrari et al, 'EU Trade Agreements and Non-Trade Policy Objectives' (EUI Working Papers No 48, 2021).

[101] S Solarin et al, 'Investigating the Pollution Haven Hypothesis in Ghana: An Empirical Investigation' (2017) 124 *Energy* 706; D Zheng and M Shi, 'Multiple Environmental Policies and Pollution Haven Hypothesis: Evidence from China's Polluting Industries' (2017) 141 *Journal of Cleaner Production* 295; J Shen et al, 'Does Migration of Pollution-Intensive Industries Impact Environmental Efficiency? Evidence Supporting "Pollution Haven Hypothesis"' (2019) 242 *Journal of Environmental Management* 142; U Bulut, G Ucler and R Inglesi-Lotz, 'Does the Pollution Haven Hypothesis Prevail in Turkey? Empirical Evidence from Nonlinear Smooth Transition Models' (2021) 28 *Environmental Science and Pollution Research* 38563; M Akif Destek and I Okumus, 'Does Pollution Haven Hypothesis Hold in Newly Industrialized Countries? Evidence from Ecological Footprint' (2019) 26 *Environmental Science and Pollution Research* 23689; M Bu et al, 'Corporate Social Responsibility and the Pollution Haven Hypothesis: Evidence from Multinationals' Investment Decision in China' (2013) 20 *Asia-Pacific Journal of Accounting & Economics* 85; A Eser Guzel and İ Okumus, 'Revisiting the Pollution Haven Hypothesis in ASEAN-5 Countries: New Insights from Panel Data Analysis' (2020) 27 *Environmental Science and Pollution Research* 18157.

[102] Abaza et al (n 94) 49–53.

[103] ibid 51.

[104] See the following analysis of the existence of the environmental Kuznets curve.

income or wealth can sometimes provide a freedom to care about environmental quality rather than other aspects of their well-being.[105]

However, the positive link between per-capita income and environmental quality is not necessarily found in the case of climate change.[106] As GHG emissions are transboundary, the impacts of emissions production are often felt in a different location from where they were emitted, thereby reducing any strong incentive for a nation to reduce its emissions despite rising incomes of its citizens. Moreover, Grossman and Kreuger report that the relationship between per-capita income and environmental quality is not necessarily linear.[107]

The so-called 'Kuznets curve' has also gained significant research interest.[108] The environmental Kuznets curve represents the inverted U-shaped relationship between environmental quality and income – in other words, as income increases in a country, so does environmental degradation until a certain income threshold is met, then environmental quality should actually improve. This concept can also play into the aforementioned disproven hypothesis that higher per-capita incomes are associated with greater public demand for positive environmental outcomes. As it stands, empirical research on the environmental Kuznets curve for climate change has produced inconsistent results.[109] The World Bank has reported that per-capita CO_2 emissions always increase with income.[110] Another study has found that whereas some environmental indicators (such as water or sanitation) initially worsen with increases in income, they do improve eventually.[111] However, it was reported for CO_2 emissions that this was not the case, and as incomes increase these emissions get steadily worse over time.[112] Newer studies generally report no link between high income and lower CO_2 levels.[113] When studies differentiate between OECD and non-OECD countries, there only tends to be evidence of the environmental Kuznets curve for the former and not the latter (corroborating with developed/developing country dynamics in the aforementioned agricultural trade liberalisation literature).[114] Torras and Boyce actually found that countries with more equitable distribution of income and which achieved greater equality in literacy, political

[105] See an example of Mexico and trade opening in GM Grossman and AB Krueger, 'Environmental Impacts of a North American Free Trade Agreement' in PM Garber (ed), *The US–Mexico Free Trade Agreement* (MIT Press, 1993).

[106] Abaza et al (n 94) 49–53.

[107] Grossman and Krueger (n 105).

[108] For more on the general Kuznets curve, see S Kuznets, 'Economic Growth and Income Inequality' (1955) 45 *American Economic Review* 1.

[109] See WM Huang, GWM Lee and CC Wu, 'GHG Emissions, GDP Growth and the Kyoto Protocol: A Revisit of Environmental Kuznets Curve Hypothesis' (2008) 36 *Energy Policy* 239.

[110] See World Bank, *World Development Report 1992: Development and the Environment* (World Bank, 1992).

[111] See eg N Shafik, 'Economic Development and Environmental Quality: An Econometric Analysis' (1994) 46 *Oxford Economic Papers* 757.

[112] ibid.

[113] See WR Moomaw and GC Unruh, 'Are Environmental Kuznets Curves Misleading Us? The Case of CO_2 Emissions' (1997) 2 *Environment and Development Economics* 451.

[114] Huang et al (n 109) 245–46.

rights and civil liberties tended to have better environmental quality – rather than solely countries with higher income levels alone.[115] In the end, these authors report there is little evidence that supports the environmental Kuznets curve hypothesis. (Figure 5 illustrates the Kuznets curve.)

Figure 5 Environmental Kuznets curve example

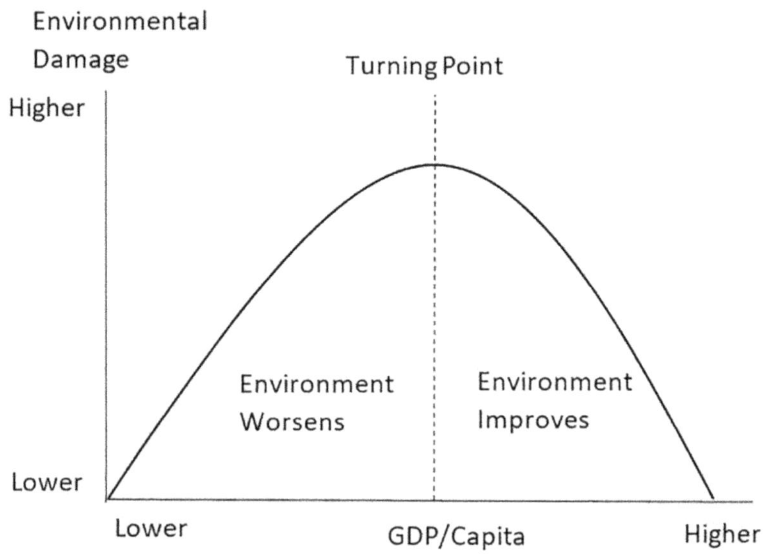

Overall, most studies report that trade liberalisation will most likely lead to increased CO_2 emissions, as the scale effect tends to 'dominate' or override the technique or composition effects.[116] However, there are reported differences between OECD and non-OECD countries (with environmental improvement noted in OECD countries, but deterioration observed in non-OECD countries with income increases).[117] Moreover, it is suggested that while the impact of trade on CO_2 emissions in the short term is small, over a longer time scale the reported impact is far larger.[118] Although not directly related to *agricultural* trade liberalisation, this review of the

[115] M Torras and J Boyce, 'Income, Inequality and Pollution' (1998) 25 *Ecological Economics* 147, 157–58.

[116] See generally, M Cole and R Elliott, 'Determining the Trade-Environment Composition Effect: The Role of Capital, Labor and Environmental Regulations' (2003) 46 *Journal of Environmental Economics and Management* 363; J Frankel and A Rose, 'Is Trade Good or Bad for the Environment? Sorting Out the Causality' (2005) 87 *Review of Economics and Statistics* 85; GR McCarney and WL Adamowicz, *The Effects of Trade Liberalization on the Environment: An Empirical Study* (Canadian Agricultural Economics Society, 2005) 34157, https://ideas.repec.org/p/ags/caes05/34157.html, accessed 17 February 2021; S Managi, 'Trade Liberalization and the Environment: Carbon Dioxide for 1960–1999' (2004) 17 *Economics Bulletin* 1.

[117] Managi (n 116) eg 4–6.

[118] ibid.

empirical literature can aid in understanding typical patterns relating to trade opening and levels of GHG emissions.

In combination with the aforementioned agricultural trade liberalisation study findings, it is understandable why agricultural free trade raises some concerns regarding increased levels of GHG emissions. This concern extends to the AoA's overarching goal of establishing a 'fair and market oriented agricultural trade system' in addition to its market access provisions, elimination of export subsidies and reduction in market-distorting domestic support that may have negative environmental impacts. An increase in GHG emissions and an ecologically detrimental shift in production on a broad level are reported to stem from agricultural trade liberalisation. As a result, tension exists between any attempts at agricultural emissions mitigation and the provisions facilitating agricultural trade liberalisation identified under the AoA – unless other avenues for agri-environmental protection are very well utilised.

Enforcement of the AoA

One thing to note in relation to the international agri-trade regime is that it practises comparatively strong enforcement of its legal rules for an international legal regime. This strong, legalised enforcement is not present with other international regimes discussed in this book so far which instead predominantly rely upon softer forms of governance, such as reporting requirements or information provision. The AoA itself is actionable under the WTO dispute-settlement procedure,[119] as per Articles XXII and XXIII of the GATT.[120] This section outlines why and how this dispute settlement procedure of the WTO adds additional weight to the potentially environmentally degrading norms stemming from the AoA's provisions, such as agricultural trade liberalisation.

Two aspects of the dispute-settlement procedure add particular strength to the enforcement of its provisions, namely (1) the existence of a judicialised Appellate Body offering opportunity for delegation to a third-party decision-maker for interpretation on the AoA's provisions; and (2) the existence of remedies and penalties (and monitoring thereof) to encourage compliance and enforcement of the AoA. More details on each of the components of this dispute-settlement

[119] Agreement on Agriculture (15 April 1994) LT/UR/A-1A/2, Art 19. Although the Agreement also provides for certain mechanisms that can be used by members to address their concerns without recourse to these procedures. For example, the review process of the Committee on Agriculture provides a forum for discussion and consultation. This process is mainly based on notifications and on a provision under Art 18.6 that permits any member to raise at any time any matter relevant to the implementation of the commitments under the reform programme as set out in the Agreement. A counter-notification provision also exists. Furthermore, the Working Procedures of the Committee allow members to request the Chairperson to mediate in concerns that may arise between them.

[120] ibid Art 19 and see more GATT 1947, Arts XXII and XXIII.

system are outlined below to illustrate how they confer strength on the aforementioned norms relating to the impacts of agricultural trade liberalisation on GHG emissions.

Appellate Body

Under the WTO's dispute-settlement procedure, an independent Appellate Body exists to help interpret, apply and elaborate on WTO rules. Abbott and Snidal refer to the existence of a dispute-settlement body such as this as 'delegation', where decision-making (eg on compliance) is delegated to a third-party decision-maker for interpretation.[121] The 'legalisation' of WTO law in this way[122] facilitates 'interpretation, application, and elaboration by setting relatively clear bounds on dispute resolution and negotiation'.[123] For example, if the initial Panel Report issued in any given dispute is appealed,[124] the dispute is transferred to the Appellate Body. The appeal itself is limited to addressing issues of law covered in the panel report and legal interpretation and application developed by the panel (as opposed to the establishment of facts or new factual evidence).[125] Three of the seven Appellate Body members serve on each appeal, and the seven members serve in rotation.[126] Appellate Body members are required to be individuals with recognised standing in the field of law and international trade and are not affiliated with any particular government (rendering them 'independent') and individual members serve four-year terms before being replaced.[127]

After an oral hearing, an Appellate Body report is written where the Appellate Body may uphold, modify or reverse the legal findings and conclusions of the panel.[128] The Dispute Settlement Body (DSB) must adopt, and the parties must unconditionally accept, the Appellate Body report unless the DSB decides by consensus not to adopt the Appellate Body report within 30 days following its circulation to members (although members still have a right to express their views on an Appellate Body report[129]). From this report, the DSB addresses a 'recommendation and ruling' to the losing party (in case of a successful violation complaint) to bring itself in compliance with WTO law or (in the case of a successful non-violation complaint) to find a mutually satisfactory adjustment.[130]

[121] Abbott and Snidal (n 3) eg 433.
[122] Abbott and Snidal also refer to other factors when determining whether international law is 'harder' or 'softer' including a 'precision of rules' and 'creation of obligations'.
[123] Abbott and Snidal (n 3) 430.
[124] See Dispute Settlement Understanding, Annex 2 to WTO Agreement 1994, Art 17.
[125] Dispute Settlement Understanding, Annex 2 to the WTO Agreement 1994 Art 17(6).
[126] ibid Art 17(1).
[127] ibid Art 17(3).
[128] ibid Art. 17(13).
[129] Ibid, Art. 17(14).
[130] eg ibid Art 3(4).

Article 21.1 of the Dispute Settlement Understanding (DSU) emphasises that prompt compliance with these recommendations or rulings is essential to effectively resolving disputes.[131] The DSB then supervises the implementation of the panel and Appellate Body reports.[132]

The role of the Appellate Body in the WTO's dispute-settlement procedure helps to strengthen norms and provisions that are imbued by the AoA's rules, such as agricultural trade liberalisation.[133] For example, the Appellate Body's role as an independent third party to WTO rule interpretation and application enables the obligations and behaviour expected of WTO members to be more precisely defined, thereby facilitating future compliance and assessment of compliance.[134] The independent and expert nature of the Appellate Body members may also contribute to the credibility[135] of trade norms as imbued through the WTO's dispute-settlement procedure. This is not only due to the Appellate Body members' recognised standing in the field, but also due to their independence from any national affiliation that enables less-biased interpretations of WTO rules to be made.[136] Moreover, through the existence of 'legalised'[137] Appellate Body members, these more precise commitments can be applied. This provides actors with a greater awareness of how to initiate legal proceedings over a dispute, in addition to creating incentives to invoke the rules under the WTO system.[138] Lastly, through the interpretation of WTO rules by an independent and legalised dispute-settlement body, such as the Appellate Body, legal coherence can be maintained, thereby ensuring that rules are consistently applied.[139] This could contribute to the ongoing permanence of rules and norms formed under the AoA, such as agricultural trade liberalisation, if legal rules are determined in relation to this as part of the WTO's dispute-settlement procedure.

Remedies, Penalties and their Monitoring

Beyond the role of the Appellate Body in interpreting WTO rules, the dispute-settlement procedure also contributes to the strength of the norms established by

[131] ibid Art 21(1).

[132] ibid Art 2(1).

[133] Although currently the Appellate Body is arguably in a period of crisis and is not functioning; see more B Hoekman and PC Mavroidis, 'Burning Down the House? The Appellate Body in the Centre of the WTO Crisis' (Global Governance Programme Working Paper No. RSCAS 2019/56, 2019) https://scholarship.law.columbia.edu/faculty_scholarship/2347.

[134] See more on these factors generally in Abbott and Snidal (n 3).

[135] See n 92 in ch 4 on the Agricultural Regime for more on 'credibility'.

[136] See more in S Charnovitz, 'Judicial Independence in the World Trade Organization' in *The Path of World Trade Law in the 21st Century* (World Scientific, 2014) ch 3.

[137] Abbott and Snidal (n 3) eg 427.

[138] For example, Abbott and Snidal state that: 'Legal rules and institutions operate both by changing material incentives and by modifying understandings, standards of behavior, and identities. In particular, they invoke doctrines and institutions that facilitate enforcement as well as social norms of obedience to law. Concerned actors strive to bring all these effects to bear, through techniques ranging from litigation and sanctions to persuasion, normative appeals, and shaming' (ibid 425).

[139] For more discussion on the impact of uncertainty on governance systems, see ibid from 441.

the AoA's provisions through the existence of enforcement mechanisms, such as remedies or penalties.

Firstly, linking to the aforementioned section on the interpretation of WTO rules, it is worth noting that with clear, binding decisions passed on WTO members' behaviour (or fewer 'grey areas' if you will), members are more publicly and definitively defined as 'in the right' or 'in the wrong' on the international political stage. As a result, this can have the effect of dissuading members from engaging in non-WTO-compliant behaviour as a result of concerns about damaging their international reputation following a non-WTO-compliant Appellate Body judgment.[140] Of course, reputational costs may form part of a cost–benefit analysis[141] undertaken by a non-compliant party.[142] If the financial gains of non-compliance are greater than its perceived reputational damage, this dissuasive effect may not be so strong. However, comparing the WTO regime to other international regimes without strongly legalised accountability systems (such as many of those discussed in this book[143]), there at least exists the possibility that a non-compliant party will incur reputational costs, as well as improved specificity in the interpretation of WTO rules.[144] The role of the Appellate Body in itself strengthens the norms stemming from the AoA due to the potential effect of this legalisation of the WTO's dispute-settlement procedure on enforcement of WTO rules.

However, in addition to Appellate Body decisions being made, penalties (or remedies) can be imposed under the WTO's dispute-settlement mechanism. For example, if a losing member fails to bring its measures into conformity with its WTO obligations within a 'reasonable period of time', the complainant is also entitled to resort to temporary measures including mutually acceptable compensation[145] or the suspension of WTO obligations (although full implementation of DSB recommendations and rulings are preferred[146]). Mutually acceptable compensation does not mean monetary payment, but the respondent is supposed

[140] Reputational costs can sometimes be explained in terms of 'naming and shaming' in that a particular party is 'shamed' or highlighted as being particularly non-compliant with certain legal rules or norms. See ibid 425.

[141] For more discussion of actual empirical scholarship in international law, see G Shaffer and T Ginsburg, 'The Empirical Turn in International Legal Scholarship' (2012) 106 *American Journal of International Law* 1.

[142] For a critical assessment of cost–benefit analysis in environmental regulation decision-making, see F Ackerman and L Heinzerling, 'Pricing the Priceless: Cost–Benefit Analysis of Environmental Protection' (2002) 150 *University of Pennsylvania Law Review* 1553.

[143] For example, the Paris Agreement, much FAO guidance on livestock emissions and many aspects of international forest governance do not have this more legalised or judicialised accountability system.

[144] For more on reputational costs in international legal governance, see JP Shimshack and MB Ward, 'Regulator Reputation, Enforcement, and Environmental Compliance' (2005) 50 *Journal of Environmental Economics and Management* 519; JM Karpoff, JR Lott, Jr and EW Wehrly, 'The Reputational Penalties for Environmental Violations: Empirical Evidence' (2005) 48(2) *Journal of Law and Economics* 653; MA Pollack and JL Dunoff, *Interdisciplinary Perspectives on International Law and International Relations* (Cambridge University Press, 2013); GW Downs and MA Jones, 'Reputation, Compliance, and International Law' (2002) 31 *Journal of Legal Studies* S95.

[145] Dispute Settlement Understanding, Annex 2 to the WTO Agreement, Art 22.

[146] ibid, see generally under Art 3.

to offer a benefit, such as a tariff reduction, which is equivalent to the benefit the respondent has impaired by applying its measures. This benefit must be consistent with WTO agreements and principles, such as the most-favoured-nation principle, perhaps suggesting why members have rarely managed to establish this compensation.[147] Moreover, if after 20 days after the expiry of the reasonable period of time compensation has not been agreed upon by the parties, the complainant can ask the DSB for permission to 'suspend … concessions or other obligations under the covered agreements'.[148] In other words, the winning party can ask for permission to impose trade sanctions against the respondent that has failed to implement the recommendations and rulings of the DSB. If permitted, the complainant is allowed to impose countermeasures that would otherwise be inconsistent with the WTO Agreement,[149] informally known as 'retaliation' or 'sanctions' (although only on a selective basis towards the member that has failed to bring its measures into conformity with WTO law).

This is the final and most serious consequence a non-implementing member can face under the dispute-settlement system. This punitive action is arguably particularly strong, with real financial consequences due to the ability of members to suspend trade concessions granted to trading partners found not to be in compliance with their obligations under WTO law.[150] All these sanctions can have a serious financial impact on a member, raising costs and affecting their ability to trade and import goods. As a result, the agricultural-trade-promoting provisions of the AoA are further backed up with the shadow[151] of these punitive measures to ensure compliance.

The recommendations and rulings of the Appellate Body are also monitored by the DSB from the time of judgment, further strengthening the enforcement of these penalties and remedies. The DSB keeps the implementation of the recommendations and rulings under surveillance, including a meeting six months after establishing the

[147] ibid Art 22(1).

[148] ibid Art 22(2).

[149] It is worth noting that the level of suspension of obligations authorised by the DSB must be 'equivalent' to the level of nullification or impairment (Art 22(4) DSU). In practice, the standard of 'appropriateness' has been found to permit countermeasures that may be higher than strictly 'equivalent' to the level of nullification or impairment caused by the prohibited subsidy. The sanctions should also be imposed in the same sector as that in which the violation or other nullification or impairment was found in accordance with the three parts of Annex 1 to the WTO Agreement (Art 22(3)(a) DSU). If the parties disagree on the complainant's proposed form of retaliation, arbitration can be requested (Art 22(6) and (7) DSU). See more generally: WTO,The Process – Stages in a Typical WTO Dispute Settlement Case in WTO, 'Dispute Settlement System Training Module' (WTO, undated) https://www.wto.org/english/tratop_e/dispu_e/disp_settlement_cbt_e/c6s1p1_e.htm accessed 5 December 2023.

[150] See, for further detail on the concept of responsive regulation and the enforcement pyramid, I Ayres and J Braithwaite, *Responsive Regulation: Transcending the Deregulation Debate* (Oxford University Press 1992), who show the 'hierarchy' of what actions or measures can be considered punitive – with 'incapacitation' (such as suspension of rights) being categorised as the most punitive.

[151] This terminology is also used in experimentalist governance literature, referring to the existence of the 'shadow of a penalty default' to encourage compliance with norms and rules in an governance system; see G De Búrca, RO Keohane and Charles S, 'Global Experimentalist Governance' (2014) 44 *British Journal of Political Science* 477, eg 478.

'reasonable' time (not exceeding 18 months).[152] A compliance review is also available under Article 21(5) of the DSU when the parties disagree on whether the losing member has correctly implemented the recommendations and rulings.[153] If sanctions or retaliation occur, the issue remains on the DSB's agenda until the request of the complaining parties is resolved,[154] and the suspension must be revoked once the member concerned has fully implemented the DSB's recommendations and rulings. Hence, in addition to the existence of punitive measures in the case of non-compliance, there is also a monitoring body to ensure that the DSU is followed accordingly.

When compared to other regimes covered in this book, the WTO regime is the main legal regime with possible recourse to stringent punitive measures in the case on persistent non-compliance. Other regimes covered in this book do have some sort of process for monitoring parties' behaviour, such as the Global Stocktake or Talanoa Dialogue (Peer Review) under the Paris Agreement.[155] However, unlike the dispute-settlement system of the WTO, financial or trade sanctions for non-compliance are not available. As a result, the existence of the dispute-settlement procedure under WTO law, and particularly the Appellate Body and penalties and remedies (and their enforcement), adds significant pervasiveness to the enforcement of AoA rules from which agricultural trade liberalisation goals are imbued.

This chapter thus far has largely focused on the role of the AoA and the surrounding enforcement mechanisms of the WTO regime in promoting the pervasiveness of agricultural trade liberalisation in the agri-trade regime. Nonetheless, there are some avenues under the AoA by which agri-environmental or agri-climate domestic measures can be considered WTO compliant. The extent to which these avenues are utilised and balanced alongside agricultural trade liberalisation provisions under the AoA is expanded upon further in the remaining sections of this chapter.

Agri-environmental Protection under the Agreement on Agriculture

In the Doha Declaration, non-trade concerns were specifically highlighted as an area to be taken into account by ministers when negotiating further modalities of the AoA.[156] Environmental protection was one of the examples of a non-trade concern provided in that Declaration.[157] Legal avenues for WTO-compliant

[152] This requires producing a status report of implementation under Art 21(6) Dispute Settlement Understanding, Annex 2 to the WTO Agreement.

[153] ibid Art 21(5).

[154] ibid Art 21(6).

[155] See the Climate Regime chapter of this book for more, eg page XX.

[156] WTO, Ministerial Declaration of 14 November 2001, WTO Doc WT/MIN(01)/DEC/1, 41 ILM 746 (2002) para 13.

[157] WTO, Doha Ministerial Declaration, WT/MIN(01)/DEC/I, 20 November 2001, from para 31.

agri-environmental protection measures can also be identified within the WTO regime, predominantly as a result of two features: (1) agri-environmental exceptions to baseline free-trade rules and principles; and (2) the adoption of 'Box-exempt' agri-environmental measures by states. Through these avenues, opportunities or instances of agri-environmental protection may be able to exist within the WTO regime alongside the aforementioned trade liberalisation agenda for the agricultural sector under WTO law. The discussion below will expand on the specific provisions that are relevant to provide avenues for agri-environmental protection under the international agri-trade regime.

Article XX Exceptions

Despite the prominence of trade-liberalisation principles in WTO law, some general exceptions do exist under Article XX that permit departure from the general obligations established under the GATT 1947 and incorporated in the GATT 1994.[158] Depending on the nature of these exceptions, these may weaken the dominance of agricultural trade liberalisation under the AoA because they result in environment-related trade-restricting measures being classed as WTO law compliant.

For exceptions to be granted on environmental grounds, Article XX(b) and (g) GATT are the most relevant.[159] Under these two paragraphs, WTO members are able to adopt measures that would otherwise be inconsistent with the GATT. They may do so where this is necessary to protect human, animal or plant life or health (paragraph (b)), or because the measures relate to the conservation of exhaustible natural resources (paragraph (g)). Cases about beef have been heard under these exceptions before but not in relation to the environmental impacts of their production.[160] To hypothetically contextualise using these exceptions in the context of livestock emissions, it could be possible for a member to argue, for example, that measures restricting imports of beef due to the high emissions intensity of the underlying production process can be justified as necessary to conserve exhaustible natural resources in the form of the global atmosphere. Likewise, measures requiring the labelling of beef produced with high emissions intensity or soy imports from deforested areas may be justified in a similar way.

For measures to pass muster under these GATT exceptions, they are required to meet the conditions of the exceptions which are laid down in the individual

[158] General Agreement on Tariffs and Trade 1994, Art XX. Annex 1A of the WTO Agreement contains the GATT 1994, which incorporates by reference the provisions of the GATT 1947, except for a few small adjustments to ensure the Agreement's practical functioning.

[159] General Agreement on Tariffs and Trade 1994, Art XX(b) and (g).

[160] See eg Korea – Measures Affecting Imports of Fresh, Chilled and Frozen Beef, United States and Canada (intervening) v Korea, Republic of, Appellate Body Report, WT/DS161/AB/R, Doc No 00-5347.

subparagraphs to Article XX as well as in the *chapeau*.[161] The latter is intended to ensure that measures are not applied in a manner which would constitute a 'means of arbitrary or unjustifiable discrimination between countries where the same conditions prevail' and are not a 'disguised restriction on international trade'.[162] Whether and how these exceptions might be relevant for members' measures seeking to reduce agricultural emissions is outlined below. It should be noted, however, this subsection focuses on GATT exceptions in the DSU context, rather than any standalone domestic environmental protection measures or provisions that exist under the AoA that will be addressed later on in this chapter. It has not always been entirely clear if the Article XX exceptions apply to the AoA, so this analysis is focused on environmental exceptions being made more generally under the GATT.[163]

Using the General Exceptions for Climate Change Mitigation Measures

No climate specific cases have been brought before the Appellate Body, let alone any focusing on the issue of agricultural emissions.[164] Nonetheless, previous cases considered by the Appellate Body have provided forms of analysis that may shed some light on how a member might be able to create GATT-compliant measures to promote climate change mitigation. The clearest provisions a member could utilise to achieve this would be Article XX(b) and (g).[165] In the *US – Gasoline* case,

[161] Otherwise known as the introductory clause of Art XX, General Agreement on Tariffs and Trade 1994.

[162] ibid.

[163] See discussion of the AoA 1994 in BJ Condon, 'Climate Change and Unresolved Issues in WTO Law' (2009) 12 *Journal of International Economic* Law 895; see also Y Ngangjoh-Hodu, 'Relationship of GATT Article XX Exceptions to Other WTO Agreements' (2011) 80 *Nordic Journal of International Law* 219, where Ngangjoh-Hodu highlights the relationship between the AoA and GATT 1994, noting that the AB in *EC – Export Subsidies on Sugar* observed that: 'Article 21 of the Agreement on Agriculture provides that: "[t]he provisions of [the] GATT 1994 and of other Multilateral Trade Agreements in Annex 1A to the WTO Agreement shall apply subject to the provisions of this Agreement. In other words, members explicitly recognised that there may be conflicts between the Agreement on Agriculture and the GATT 1994, and explicitly provided, through Article 21 that the Agreement on Agriculture would prevail to the extent of such conflicts"'. Moreover, Ngangjoh-Hodu highlights in a 'rather straightforward scenario' that a provision of an Annex 1A agreement 'may still prevail over a provision of GATT 1994 when there is an express derogation in such agreement. For instance, Article 5 of the Agreement on Agriculture permits WTO members to impose special safeguard measures which will be otherwise inconsistent with Article XIX of GATT 1994' (232).

[164] Although a number of policies have been found to fall within the realm of paragraphs (b) and (g) of Art XX: (i) policies aimed at reducing the consumption of cigarettes, protecting dolphins, reducing risks to human health posed by asbestos, reducing risks to human, animal and plant life and health arising from the accumulation of waste tyres (under Art XX(b)); and (ii) policies aimed at the conservation of tuna, salmon and herring, dolphins, turtles, petroleum, and clean air (under Art XX(g)).

[165] Although not mentioned in the main text here, Art XX (d) was used in India's defence in *India – Solar Cells*. Art XX(d) allows WTO members to maintain measures 'necessary to secure compliance' with GATT-consistent 'laws or regulations'. India made reference to its international legal obligations, including the UNFCCC. India also argued that it had 'an obligation to take steps to achieve energy security, mitigate climate change, and achieve sustainable development, and that this includes steps to

the panel agreed that a policy to reduce air pollution from the consumption of gasoline was a policy that concerned the protection of human, animal and plant life or health under Article XX(b).[166] Additionally, a policy seeking to reduce the depletion of clean air could be classed as a policy to conserve a natural resource under the meaning of Article XX(g).[167] As a result, measures seeking to achieve climate change mitigation could fall under paragraph (b) as they intended to protect humans from the impacts of climate change; or under paragraph (g) as they are intended to conserve exhaustible natural resources, such as the climate or plant and animals species whose survival is threatened by climate change, as per the Appellate Body's interpretation of exhaustible natural resources under the *US – Shrimp* case.[168]

Moreover, given that GHG emissions generated in one country will impact also on other countries, as well as globally, there would seem to be a 'sufficient nexus' between a member relying on an exception and emissions generated from within the territory of a different state. In *US – Shrimp*, the existence of a 'sufficient nexus' was found between the US and 'foreign' turtles, on the basis that the turtles sometimes entered US waters.[169] A similar nexus may be found to exist in relation to climate-change mitigation, as emissions are transboundary – meaning one state's emissions enter the territory of another state simply due to the nature of atmospheric pollution. As a result, measures adopted by one state aimed at reducing emissions generated within the territory of another state may similarly be found to constitute a 'sufficient nexus' in the same vein as in the *US – Shrimp* case, due to the fact one state's emissions territory can enter another's.[170] Consequently, there is generally wide scope for climate-change-related environmental measures to satisfy the conditions laid down in the exceptions if these exceptions are interpreted in a similar vein as in the

ensure the adequate supply of clean electricity, generated from solar power, at reasonable prices. See more in White & Case – Brendan McGivern, 'WTO Panel Report: India – Solar Cells and Modules', *Lexology*, 26 February 2016, www.lexology.com/library/detail.aspx?g=6ca4bac9-762f-4d47-be7e-a9dd6ff7ba49, accessed 11 July 2023. This may become increasingly relevant, for example, in relation to the Paris Agreement 2015 – as it in increasingly recognised as an instrument binding on national authorities, eg see *Urgenda Foundation v State of the Netherlands* [2015] HAZA C/09/00456689.

Similarly Art XX(a), which allows WTO members to maintain normally GATT-inconsistent measures necessary to protect public morals. An example may be where animal welfare (as seen in *EC – Seal Products*) aligns with agri-environmental improvements, perhaps in relation to the well-being of animals in intensive feed lots, or the impact of climate change (eg heatwaves or drought) on the well-being of livestock herds.

[166] United States – Standards for Reformulated and Conventional Gasoline – Status Report by the United States – Addendum WT/DS2/10/Add7, para 6(21). 1997.

[167] ibid para 6(37).

[168] *United States – Import Prohibition of Certain Shrimp and Shrimp Products*, Appellate Body Report, WT/DS58/AB/R, adopted 6 November 1998, DSR 1998:VII, 2755, para 142.

[169] ibid para 133.

[170] J Pauwelyn, 'US Federal Climate Policy and Competitiveness Concerns: The Limits and Options of International Trade Law' (Nicholas Institute, 4 February 2013) https://nicholasinstitute.duke.edu/climate/policydesign/u.s.-federal-climate-policy-and-competitiveness-concerns-the-limits-and-options-of-international-trade-law, accessed 24 February 2021, 35.

examples above. This opens up the potential for agri-climate measures to be pursued by members within the WTO regime in a way that is GATT compliant. This argument will be further substantiated below.

'Necessary for' and 'Relating to'

For a climate change mitigation measure to fall within the exceptions included in Article XX(b) and (g), a measure must also be either: *necessary* for the protection of human, animal or plant life or health (paragraph (b)) or *relating to* the conservation of exhaustible natural resources (paragraph (g)). When applying Article XX(b), a number of factors have been used and balanced (though no strong proportionality test is applied[171]) by the Appellate Body. These include 'the contribution made by the environmental measure to the policy objective pursued, the importance of the common interests or values protected by the measure, and the impact of the measure on international trade'.[172] Once this initial conclusion is drawn, the result must be compared with other alternative measures which may be less trade restrictive but capable of making the same contribution to achieving the objective pursued.[173] For example, in the *Brazil – Retreaded Tyres* case, the Appellate Body found that an import ban on retreaded tyres was 'apt to produce a material contribution to the achievement of its objective' of reducing the volume of tyre waste.[174] The Appellate Body found that proposed alternatives, such as waste management, were not real alternatives to the import ban which could avoid the accumulation of tyres.[175] In *EC – Asbestos* (a case that also refers to provisions under the Technical Barriers to Trade and Sanitary and Phytosanitary Agreements[176]), the Appellate Body also found that there was no reasonably available alternative to prohibiting trade in asbestos products, and the measure was designed for the level of value placed on health protection by France and which was found to be 'both vital and important in the highest degree'.[177] The Appellate Body emphasized that the more important the common interests

[171] D Regan, 'The Meaning of "Necessary" in GATT Article XX and GATS Article XIV: The Myth' (2007) 6 *World Trade Review* 347, 38.
[172] *Brazil – Measures Affecting Imports of Retreaded Tyres, European Communities v Brazil*, Appellate Body Report, WT/DS332/AB/R, Report No AB-2007-4, Doc No 07-2682, DSR 2007:IV, 1527, ITL 112 (WTO 2007), 3 December 2007, Appellate Body, para 178.
[173] ibid.
[174] ibid para 155.
[175] ibid paras 156–75.
[176] Agreement on Technical Barriers to Trade 1994; WTO Agreement on the Application of Sanitary and Phytosanitary Measures 1994.
[177] *European Communities – Measures Affecting Asbestos and Asbestos-Containing Products*, Appellate Body Report, WT/DS135/AB/R, adopted 5 April 2001, para 172.

or values pursued by a measure, the easier it was to accept it as a necessary measure designed to achieve those ends.[178]

With regards to what constitutes 'relating to' the conservation of natural resources under Article XX(g), a substantial relationship between the measure and the conservation of exhaustible natural resources must be established. The Appellate Body has stated that a member must demonstrate that the means (the chosen measure) must be 'reasonably related' to the ends (the objective of the policy seeking to conserve natural resources).[179] Additionally, any measures affecting imports must meet the even-handed requirement that any restrictions on imported goods must also exist for goods domestically produced. For example, in the *US – Gasoline* case, the United States had adopted a measure to regulate the composition and emissions effect of gasoline, with the objective of reducing air pollution in the country.[180] As the measure was 'primarily aimed' at the objective of conserving clean air in the United States, it fell within the scope of Article XX (g).[181] However, in the end, the Appellate Body ruled that the measure was an 'unjustifiable discrimination' and a 'disguised restriction' on international trade as the United States did not utilise established techniques for checking, verification, assessment and enforcement of data relating to imported goods from foreign gasoline refiners.[182]

Lastly, any exception (whether Article XX(b), (g) or otherwise) must be applied in line with the introductory clause of Article XX (the *chapeau*). More specifically, the measure must not be applied in a way that constitutes a 'means of arbitrary or unjustifiable discrimination' or a 'disguised restriction on international trade'.[183] As a result, any such measures must be applied in good faith – in *Brazil – Retreaded Tyres* the Appellate Body recalled that WTO members' right to avail themselves of exceptions is undertaken in good faith in order to protect legitimate interests, not as a means to sidestep one member's obligations towards other WTO members.[184] This ensures the balance between one member's right to invoke an exception and the rights of other members under the GATT. WTO cases have helped to understand under which circumstances a measure may be considered to be in compliance with the *chapeau*, as will be shown in the example below.

Overall, however, this analysis demonstrates that there is scope for domestic agri-environmental exceptions to be pursued and permitted within the WTO regime

[178] ibid.
[179] *United States – Import Prohibition of Certain Shrimp and Shrimp Products* (n 168) para 141.
[180] *United States – Standards for Reformulated and Conventional Gasoline*, Appellate Body Report, WT/DS2/AB/R, adopted 20 May 1996, DSR 1996:I, 3, 18.
[181] ibid.
[182] ibid 27.
[183] General Agreement on Tariffs and Trade 1994, Art XX.
[184] *Brazil – Measures Affecting Imports of Retreaded Tyres* (n 172) para 215.

through the existence of these exceptions. So long as the requirements of Article XX are met, there is potential for agri-environmental measures such as these to be WTO compliant and pursued domestically. To exemplify a possible national GATT-compliant measure that seeks to reduce emissions from agricultural imports, a brief example of a proposed EU trade regulation that could be permitted for climate mitigation purposes under Article XX exceptions of the GATT is provided, as outlined by Durán and Scott.[185] The proposed EU regulation places due-diligence requirements on all traders placing forest and ecosystem risk commodities (FERCs) on the EU market for the first time (such as soy for livestock feed), as well as financial institutions involved in the supply chain.[186]

Box 1 The possibility of national measures to reduce emissions from agricultural imports and the EU Commission's proposal for a regulation on deforestation-free products (author's own table)[187]

Summary of the Proposal	The Proposal seeks to introduce 'an EU legal framework based on mandatory due diligence, reporting, disclosure and third party participation requirements, as well as liability and penalties in case of breaches of obligations for all companies placing for the first time on the Union market commodities entailing forest and ecosystem risks and products derived from these commodities [such as soy used for livestock feed], and access to justice and remedy for victims of breaches of these obligations; that traceability obligations should be placed on traders on the Union market, in particular regarding the identification of the origin of the commodities and products derived thereof at the moment they are placed on the Union internal market, to ensure sustainable and deforestation-free value chains, as laid down in the Annex to this resolution; emphasises that the same legal framework should also apply to all financial institutions authorised to operate in the Union that are providing money to companies that harvest, extract, produce, process or trade forest and ecosystem-risk commodities and derived products.'

[185] G Marín Durán and J Scott, 'Regulating Trade in Forest-Risk Commodities: Two Cheers for the European Union' [2022] *Journal of Environmental Law* eqac002.

[186] See European Commission, 'Proposal for a Regulation of the European Parliament and of the Council on the Making Available on the Union Market as Well as Export from the Union of Certain Commodities and Products Associated with Deforestation and Forest Degradation and Repealing Regulation (EU) No 995/2010' (2021) COM(2021) 706.

[187] ibid.

Requirement	Application to due-diligence proposal
Article XX(g) measures relate to the conservation of exhaustible natural resources	Durán and Scott suggest that Article XX(g) is the most promising course of action for the exception.[188] This is because there is 'little doubt' that EU measures (as per *US – Shrimp*) are 'closely and genuinely related to' the conservation of natural forests, as they 'prohibit the placing on the EU market of illegally sourced timber and other FERCs' and thereby 'seek to reduce international demand for such commodities as a chief driver of global deforestation and forest degradation'.[189] They also suggest forests could constitute 'exhaustible natural resources' under Article XX(g) GATT considering the broad interpretation of this term in WTO law.[190] They emphasise that in *US – Shrimp* that the concept was interpreted 'dynamically' and 'in light of the contemporary concerns of the community of nations about the protection and conservation of the environment'.[191] Referencing several multilateral instruments, and the latest UNEP/Forest reports, they suggest deforestation and forest degradation would fall within the scope of these 'contemporary concerns'.[192]
'Sufficient nexus' between a member relying on an exception and the issue at hand	In *US – Shrimp*, the existence of a 'sufficient nexus' was found between the United States and 'foreign' turtles, on the basis that the turtles sometimes entered US waters. Durán and Scott suggest a similar nexus may be found to exist in relation to the European Union wanting to mitigate the climate impacts of their forest-risk imports, as climate change impacts are also transboundary.[193] For example, the degradation of the Amazon rainforest in South America will have climate impacts that are experienced globally due to the transboundary nature of GHG emissions.

[188] Marín Durán and Scott (n 187) 262.
[189] G Marin Duran and J Scott, 'Reducing the European Union's Global Deforestation Footprint through Trade Regulation' (European University Institute Working Paper, 2021) https://cadmus.eui.eu/handle/1814/73189, accessed 28 August 2023, 19.
[190] Marín Durán and Scott (n 187) 263.
[191] Marin Duran and Scott (n 191) 19.
[192] Marín Durán and Scott (n 187) 263.
[193] ibid.

The measure must not be applied in a way that constitutes a 'means of arbitrary or unjustifiable discrimination' or a 'disguised restriction on international trade', including the Even-Handedness Requirement	WTO cases have helped to understand under which circumstances a measure may be considered to be in compliance with these requirements, including: 'relevant coordination and cooperation activities' undertaken by the defendant at the international level in the trade and environment area[194] and the design of the measure including its flexibility to take into account different situations prevailing in different countries.[195] As Durán and Scott highlight, the due-diligence rules will apply to all FERCs on the EU Internal Market, so the even-handed requirement is satisfied in this respect.[196] However, it would need to be further assessed how this may affect foreign agricultural commodity producers compared with domestic producers, eg in terms of financial burden or ability to provide corporations on the EU internal market with sufficient data about the deforestation status of their products compared with domestic producers in the EU territory for different commodities, such as soy. When referring to international cooperation, and whether the European Union tried to engage in good-faith negotiations with affected third countries before undertaking a unilateral measure, Durán and Scott suggest the prospective Forest Due Diligence Regulation should 'provide the basis for negotiating similar partnership agreements with all countries having an export interest in the covered FERCs, as proposed by the European Parliament'.[197] Durán and Scott also highlight the flexibility requirement required under WTO law 'may be harder to meet since the underlying forest sustainability standards would be defined by the EU and apply to all exporting countries alike'.[198]

[194] For example, in *US – Shrimp* (Art 21(5)) the Appellate Body found that, in view of the serious, good-faith efforts made by the United States to negotiate an international agreement on the protection of sea turtles, including with the complainant, the measure was now applied in a manner that no longer constituted a means of unjustifiable or arbitrary discrimination. The Appellate Body also acknowledged that 'as far as possible' a multilateral approach is strongly preferred over a unilateral approach.

[195] For example, in the US – Shrimp case, the Appellate Body was of the view that rigidity and inflexibility in the application of the measure (eg by overlooking the conditions in other countries) constituted unjustifiable discrimination. It was deemed not acceptable that a WTO member would require another member to adopt essentially the same regulatory programme, without taking into consideration that conditions in other members' territories might be different, and that the policy solutions might be ill-adapted to their particular conditions.

[196] Marín Durán and Scott (n 187) 263.

[197] Marin Duran and Scott (n 191) 21.

[198] ibid 20.

As seen from the example above, it is possible for policies that seek to improve the climate or deforestation impact of trade to be GATT compliant, but they must be well designed in light of criteria and interpretations under WTO case law.[199] The subsequent section will, thus, balance the strong agricultural trade liberalisation mandate of the AoA against the utilisation of these Article XX exceptions for the purpose of Member States creating GATT-compliant derogations from general GATT principles for the purposes of agri-environmental protection, such as reducing emissions from traded livestock-related goods.

Agricultural Trade Liberalisation vs Article XX(b) and (g)

As was mentioned previously, this analysis is focused on the GATT because it is still unclear whether the Article XX exceptions apply to the AoA. This analysis nonetheless has provided a broader overview of the balance between environment and trade under the WTO case law to date, and how this can bolster or mitigate the ability of states to derogate from the agricultural trade liberalisation mandate of the AoA which can be environmentally degrading.

Overall, it is worth highlighting that the aforementioned provisions of the AoA that provide for agricultural trade liberalisation are not universal due to the existence of these general exceptions. As a result, while trade liberalisation is strongly embedded in the AoA's core provisions, the existence of these exceptions does reduce the universality of this mandate. Although there are no cases that have been heard regarding measures that aim to mitigate agricultural emissions (or even GHG emissions from any source), the above examples indicate the potential for members to implement measures that would reduce agricultural emissions in a manner that is GATT compliant.

However, these measure must be carefully designed and in line with the requirements outlined above. So far, this has proven to be quite a high threshold to satisfy, although, through trial and error, states have succeeded in having measures of this kind accepted, as in the case of the United States following the *US – Shrimp* case.[200] Moreover, the dispute-settlement process has motivated members to work multilaterally on environmental policy solutions,[201] perhaps suggesting all is not lost with regard to creating GATT-compliant environmental exceptions.

At the same time, Article XX is quite literally an 'exception' to the default trade-liberalisation principles that underpin the GATT (and the AoA) and the states relying on it bear the initial burden of justifying their measure as falling under

[199] And, in the case of the proposed EU Due Diligence Regulation, they address other concerns about the proposal, including human rights and land tenure rights coverage. See Duran and Scott (n 187) 257.

[200] Marín Durán and Scott (n 187) 265.

[201] WTO, *United States – Import Prohibition of Certain Shrimp and Shrimp Products* (Recourse to Article 21.5 by Malaysia), Report of the Appellate Body (21 November 2001) WT/DS58/AB/RW *US – Shrimp* (2001), paras 119 and 128.

the exception. There is no positive obligation for members to make use of these exceptions. While they have specific obligations to liberalise trade by eliminating quotas and discriminatory measures,[202] they do not have specific obligations to deploy trade instruments to protect the environment. This reflects the fact that the overall role of the WTO is merely to facilitate the wishes of its members electing to promote economic growth rather than, say, environmental protection. In addition, the WTO regime is particularly 'legalised' through the existence of its dispute-settlement procedure,[203] meaning the 'default' free-trade-oriented principles under the GATT (and perhaps also under the AoA) are particularly well embedded and more punitively enforced than other norms in different regimes on the international level. There are strong penalties for those not abiding by the recommendations and rulings (such as trade sanctions), thereby further entrenching core WTO principles that promote trade liberalisation (and potential consequent environmental degradation).

Consequently, it can be said that is not impossible to secure environmental exceptions to agricultural trade liberalisation provisions. However, there is a strong reliance on governments' political will to be proactive in creating well-designed environmental measures to tackle any trade-related degradation caused. Taking these observations together, the baseline position of the AoA as an instrument promoting agricultural trade liberalisation often outweighs the ability of members to create GATT-compliant exceptions for agri-environmental purposes. Debate exists regarding whether WTO law is the most appropriate forum to deal with environmental regulation, given that the WTO Agreement is primarily an agreement concerned with trade regulation[204] (although, of course, the two are not mutually exclusive).[205]

Nonetheless, free trade has been shown to cause increased emissions and environmental harm – meaning the trade liberalisation agenda pursued by the AoA and the GATT cannot be overlooked when considering the negative environmental impact of trade in beef and dairy production. The alternative avenues for members to secure agri-environmental provisions that could be classed at WTO compliant will be outlined further below.

Adoption of Box-Exempt Agri-environmental Measures by States

The AoA also contains a number of exemptions to provide opportunities for states to pursue agri-environmental programmes domestically that are exempt from the

[202] See earlier discussion in this chapter, eg the different Domestic Support Pillar Measures under the AoA and their Exemption Status.

[203] See earlier discussion by Abbott and Snidal (n 3) in relation to the dispute settlement mechanism and remedies under the WTO regime.

[204] See more in Lang (n 4) 534–35.

[205] *CF Runge, Environmental Effects of Trade in the Agricultural Sector; A Case Study* (Center for International Food and Agricultural Policy, 1992) eg from 35.

general trade-barrier-limiting liberalisation provisions of the AoA. The Green Box exemption for domestic support reduction commitments provides the main example of where adopting exempt programmes that could help to reduce livestock emissions may be pursued. In particular, the exemption of domestic environmental programmes, decoupled payments and resource retirement programmes are particularly relevant when locating avenues for members to pursue agri-environmental measures.[206]

Domestic Environmental Programmes

Under paragraph 12 of Annex 2, payments for domestic environmental programmes are exempt from restrictions under the AoA.[207] This is the clearest example of where agri-environmental measures are directly addressed under the AoA. For these payments to qualify for the exemption, they must be part of a 'clearly-defined' government environmental or conservation programme, and they must be dependent upon fulfilling specific requirements under the government programme, such as conditions relating to production methods.[208] Moreover, the 'amount of payment shall be limited to the extra costs or loss of income involved in complying with the government programme'.[209]

Cardwell and Smith provide the example of the US Conservation Reserve Programme (CRP) as an exempted domestic environmental programme.[210] The CRP is a 'voluntary program aimed at conserving soil, water and wildlife resources by removing highly erodible and environmentally sensitive lands from agricultural production and installing resource-conserving practices'.[211] The US Department for Agriculture (USDA) provides yearly rental payments for enrolling land in the CRP, and since 1987, it has made nearly US$50 billion in CRP payments to landowners.[212] Agri-environmental protection has clearly been on the global agricultural trade regime's agenda through the inclusion of the exemption that permits domestic payouts on programmes such as this. In the case of livestock or cattle emissions, a domestic pay-out programme for cattle farmers that prescribes more climate-friendly livestock production could hypothetically be exempted from AoA restrictions if a state 'clearly defines' this programme.

This being said, no baseline environmental standards are actually set out in Annex 2 to qualify for the exemption. In 2009, Steenblik and Tsai attempted to

[206] Cardwell and Smith (n 9) from 881.
[207] Agreement on Agriculture 1994, Annex 2 para 12.
[208] ibid para 12(a).
[209] ibid para 12(b).
[210] Cardwell and Smith (n 90) 885.
[211] See more J Newton, 'Change on the Horizon for the Conservation Reserve Program?' (2017) www.fb.org/market-intel/usda-resumes-conservation-reserve-program-enrollment, accessed 20 August 2020.
[212] ibid.

collate the (limited) studies that assessed the actual environmental benefits that have resulted from past domestic environmental programmes (while recognising the limitations of their approach given the few studies in this area).[213] Overall, some positives were found for implementing the programmes because improvements were seen in relation to the relevant environmental indicators.[214] However, both Ireland's Rural Environment Protection Scheme (REPS) and the European Union's agri-environmental policies were found to have shortcomings, such as lacking or inconsistent empirical baselines as a starting point for evaluating compliance with the programme, and lacking ecological expertise within the programme thereby limiting its overall efficacy.[215] In the evaluation of EU agri-environmental policies, it was found that the environmental benefits of these policies might be outweighed by other driving factors of production, such as the current prices of meat and livestock.[216]

As a result, it can be said that there is scope for a more detailed prescription of the environmental standards required to make exemptions for domestic environmental programmes under the AoA more environmentally effective or rigorous (and consequently more justified in being exempt from the AoA's broader liberalisation mandate). However, for now, it is unknown whether this could be a likely negotiation point for WTO members in the future or if the Appellate Body will ever be called on to interpret the scope, meaning and requirements of domestic environmental programmes more precisely and the impacts this could have on the efficacy of domestic environmental programmes.

It is also worth emphasising that domestic environmental programmes are reliant upon there being motivation in member nations to create an environmental programme in the first place. The domestic environmental programme is an 'opt-in' component of the AoA when compared with the reduction commitments under the Amber Box (in a similar vein to the 'exceptional' nature of Article XX(b) and (g)). As a consequence, the potential for this exemption is determined by individual members' political will to utilise it, including specifically in the livestock sector. Nonetheless, greater specificity or clarity in WTO rules on what would be classed as a 'clearly-defined government programme' could still contribute to ensuring more meaningful environmental protection in these programmes and enable their effective usage in reducing livestock emissions.

[213] See generally in R Steenblik and C Tsai, 'The Environmental Impact of Green Box Subsidies: Exploring the Linkages' in R Melendez-Ortiz, C Bellmann and J Hepburn (eds), *Agricultural Subsidies in the WTO Green Box* (Cambridge University Press 2009) www.cambridge.org/core/product/identifier/CBO9780511674587A029/type/book_part, accessed 20 August 2020, 457.

[214] ibid 450.

[215] ibid.

[216] ibid 451.

Decoupled Support and Direct Payments

Decoupled and direct payments are also free from restrictions under the Green Box exemption of the AoA. Shifting from production-based subsidies (seen under the Amber Box) towards these decoupled and direct payments (payments that are not attached to production levels) allows members to take environmental concerns into account. Decoupled or direct payments need not include environmental considerations, though Cardwell and Smith actually highlight the 'long association' of decoupled income support as a policy tool well suited to environmental concerns.[217] In particular, the cross-compliance requirements under the European Union's Common Agricultural Policy (CAP) is highlighted as an example of this.[218] Attaching environmental conditions for the receipt of direct payments by EU farmers (such as 'Greening Payments' or cross-compliance with the Union's Nitrates Directive) offers an example of the way in which the Green Box exemption has allowed states to give attention to the agricultural environmental protection domestically in a way that is compatible with the rules of the global agricultural trade regime.[219] Similar environmental conditions could be attached to existing or new decoupled or direct payments for livestock production, such as the European Union requiring measures to improve emissions from enteric fermentation for CAP payments to be made to farmers.[220]

Additionally, when considering livestock emissions as a specific environmental problem, decoupled payments may be environmentally preferable to production-based subsidies under the Amber Box. No production is required to receive direct payments as payment is not paired with levels of production. This has the benefit of making production responsive to market conditions, as opposed to farmers producing certain agricultural goods based on the existence of specific subsidies.[221] The volume of emissions-intensive goods produced, such as beef, therefore should not be linked to the amount of money a farmer receives.[222] As a result, inflated

[217] Cardwell and Smith (n 9) 887.

[218] ibid.

[219] See more F Smith, 'Mind the Gap: "Greening" Direct Payments and the World Trade Organization', in *Research Handbook on EU Agriculture Law* (Edward Elgar, 2015) www.elgaronline.com/display/edcoll/9781781954614/9781781954614.00031.xml, accessed 29 August 2023.

[220] Interestingly, under the most recent CAP Reform period, a new component of the CAP was introduced – Eco-Schemes. In a document published by the Commission with guidance and potential Eco-Schemes, measures to address enteric fermentation were included as a potential Eco-Scheme. See 'Commission Publishes List of Potential Eco-Schemes' (European Commission, 2021) https://ec.europa.eu/info/news/commission-publishes-list-potential-eco-schemes-2021-jan-14_en, accessed 15 June 2021.

[221] Cardwell and Smith (n 9) 886.

[222] Agreement on Agriculture, Annex 2, para 6(e). However, there is still a level of financial support provided to the beef and milk sector in the EU, such as voluntary coupled support (in addition to CAP payments more broadly). For example, a 2014 study suggested that the removal of this coupled support for the cattle sector would have reduced production in the beef sector by 2.5 percent and in the dairy sector by 0.7 percent. See D Mottershead et al, 'Evaluation Study of the Impact of the CAP on Climate Change and Greenhouse Emissions' (EU Commission, 2019) https://ec.europa.eu/agriculture/sites/

production of these emissions-intensive goods should not occur, thereby avoiding an overproduction scenario similar to those that plagued the global agricultural market at the time of the Uruguay Round.

Although the previously discussed empirical literature suggested that agricultural trade liberalisation may cause an increase in GHG emissions, it is possible here to see why the removal of these production-based subsidies tackled the specific context of overproduction and global price distortion at the time. As studies that were undertaken many years after the introduction of the Amber Box restrictions have shown, agricultural trade liberalisation does cause environmental degradation and increase in emissions.[223] However, tackling (and preventing on an ongoing basis) the widely distorting overproduction dynamics in the EU and US agricultural markets did serve its historical purpose by limiting production to levels determined by market forces – though not necessarily for environmental motivations, but rather to reduce protectionism and its consequential socioeconomic impacts.

It is likely that agricultural trade liberalisation in this overproduction context produces diminishing environmental returns now that the most significant levels of market distortion have been rectified. However, given its role in preventing future overproduction, the Amber Box maintains its environmental benefits. The demand-driven environmental impacts of livestock production associated with overconsumption are still not addressed by the removal of production-based subsidies. As a result, while demand for goods such as beef or milk remains, there will be an incentive to increase production to satisfy this demand even in the absence of production-related subsidies. This runs the risk that the negative environmental impacts of liberalising the agricultural sector outlined in the aforementioned studies will occur. Nonetheless, the exemption of decoupled payments does not undermine the potential indirect environmental benefits of preventing coupled payments from being attached to emissions-intensive (or environmentally degrading) agricultural production.

It is also worth mentioning here that concerns have been raised about decoupled income support being used to 'mask' otherwise trade-distorting behaviour.[224] In particular, there are concerns that developed-country members are using decoupled income support and direct payments as a 'back door' for providing domestic support that is actually trade distorting.[225] For example, concerns had been raised

agriculture/files/evaluation/market-and-income-reports/2019/cap-and-climate-evaluation-report_en.pdf, accessed 31 May 2019.

[223] See the earlier agricultural trade liberalisation section of this chapter for more examples of studies.

[224] See eg 'Review and Clarification of Green Box Criteria' (Institute for Agriculture and Trade Policy 2005) G20 /DS/Greenbox. FINAL 02/06/05; Action Aid (n 60); Ronald and Tsai (n 214); D Diakosavvas, 'The Greening of the WTO Green Box: A Quantitative Appraisal of Agri-Environmental Policies in OECD Countries' (IATRC Symposium, Italy, 23–26 June 2003); Galperín and Miguez (n 60).

[225] Although the robustness of its methodology is not entirely clear, one report suggests that US$40bn of Green Box payments annually are likely to be trade-distorting and therefore break WTO rules: see Action Aid, Caritas, CIDSE, Oxfam (2005) (n 60).

that the environmental 'cross-compliance' required under the decoupled support exemption in the European Union was not monitored or assessed sufficiently to be effective,[226] and these measures applied to all farmers irrespective of whether they received decoupled income support.[227] The 'Greening Payments' of past CAP iterations have also continually been branded as insufficient in their climate mitigation ambition, despite the EU Commission's supposed increased 'greening' of CAP Reforms.[228]

Consequently, a two-sided tension arises between (1) ensuring Green Box measures have no or minimal trade-distorting effects to eradicate instances of 'masking' or 'box-switching' measures that actually have trade-distorting effects; and (2) recognising that decoupled payments discourage overproduction and its corresponding environmental degradation, as well as providing an avenue for environmental conditions to be attached to the receipt of direct support by farmers, such as cattle farmers. Although no revision of the Green Box is on the negotiation table, restricting the scope of decoupled payments to avoid 'box switching' may deter members from shifting their more environmentally unfriendly Amber Box subsidies into the generally more environmentally friendly Green Box. However, equally, 'box switching' can be unfair to developing countries' agricultural sectors and the aforementioned example of cross-compliance under the CAP demonstrates that there may be an unfair mismatch between the actual environmental action required by farmers and financial support provided by a WTO member.

Overall, the current utilisation of decoupled and direct payments for environmental protection purposes has contributed to some track record of addressing agri-environmental protection in the global agricultural trade regime (whether or not the levels of environmental protection are deemed as stringent or sufficient). Importantly, these routes provide an alternative to more environmentally harmful overproduction under the Amber Box, thereby preventing overproduction of emissions-intensive agricultural products, such as beef. This being said, issues with overconsumption are not tackled through decoupled payments, and issues with the trade-distorting impacts of decoupled and direct payments make the exemption contentious. As a result, whilst some agri-environmental protection can be secured from the decoupled income support and direct payment exemption, its utilisation in reality for environmental measures, such as in the CAP, has been questioned.

[226] See generally, European Court of Auditors, 'Making Cross-compliance More Effective and Achieving Simplification Remains Challenging' (European Court of Auditors, 2016) 26.

[227] EU Court of Auditors, 'Special Report: Common Agricultural Policy and Climate: Half of EU Climate Spending but Farm Emissions Are Not Decreasing' (EU Court of Auditors, 2021) Special Report 16, 31.

[228] See more, ibid; 'Guide to Eco-Schemes in the New CAP: Opportunities and Challenges for Managing Authorities' (2020) https://ieep.eu/publications/guide-to-eco-schemes-in-the-new-cap-opportunities-and-challenges-for-managing-authorities, accessed 15 June 2021.

Resource Retirement

Resource retirement programmes are Green Box exempt under paragraph 10 of Annex 2 of the AoA.[229] The resource retirement exemption privileges support which is 'conditional upon the retirement of land from marketable agricultural production for a minimum of three years (or, in the case of livestock, conditional on slaughter or definitive permanent disposal)'.[230] Although perhaps initially envisioned as a measure to tackle issues with overproduction at the time of the Uruguay Round, the exemption could also play a future role in WTO members securing agricultural environmental protection in a WTO-compatible way.

Agricultural production can cause resources, such as land, to become degraded over time – particularly if agricultural production is not practised sustainably.[231] Exempting payments made to retire land from agricultural production could enable the financing of a reduction of land being subjected to environmental degradation for livestock production purposes. In terms of GHG emissions, this may be beneficial as the land may be restored to a state with more CO_2-neutralising potential, or it may lead to emissions-intensive goods, such as cattle, being 'retired' from production on a specific plot of land if this is suitable for arable farming.[232]

This being said, this exemption has not yet been used for this purpose. Thus, its utilisation in a livestock production context is merely hypothetical. Even in a non-livestock context, this avenue for environmental protection is not readily utilised for this purpose in reality. For example, the aforementioned US Conservation Reserve Programme used to notify payments under the resource retirement exemption.[233] However, payments were subsequently switched to be notified under the aforementioned domestic environmental programme exemption instead.[234] As a result, although worthy of brief discussion here as a hypothetical route for swapping land from livestock to arable production, the resource retirement programme is not currently utilised for this purpose, or showing signs of being used for such in the future.

Blue Box Exemptions

Blue Box exemptions are another component of the AoA that was created with a view to tackling overproduction and agricultural surpluses in developed countries.

[229] Agreement on Agriculture (15 April 1994) LT/UR/A-1A/2, Annex 2, para 10.
[230] ibid Annex 2, para 10(b).
[231] Hence, the environmental rationale of programmes such as the 'land set-aside' programme that was in place in the European Union from 1988 to 2008. See more in LG Firbank et al, 'Managing Set-Aside Land for Wildlife' (Natural Environment Research Council, 1993) ITE Research Publication No 7 <https://nora.nerc.ac.uk/id/eprint/7648/1/Managing_set_aside.pdf> accessed 30 August 2023.
[232] See more on the discussion on the 'food choice' argument in the Introduction of this book to outline the rationale of making this land shift from livestock to arable farming and the more efficient food production and nutrition provision that may stem from this.
[233] Cardwell and Smith (n 9) 885.
[234] ibid.

Under Article 6(5) of the Agreement, direct payments under production-limiting programmes are exempt from reduction commitments.[235] This is because production limitation was deemed less trade-distorting than measures that encouraged production, due to its less depressing effect on global prices. In the past, is it has been reported that the European Union utilised this exemption for schemes that restrict agricultural production, such as requiring compulsory set-aside of arable land.[236] Although created for the purpose of tackling overproduction, this set-aside had recognised environmental benefits, such as the protection of biodiversity.[237]

Similar schemes aimed at limiting livestock production levels could hypothetically be exempted under this Blue Box exemption. However, EU schemes such as these were largely scrapped in the wake of food security concerns after the 2007–08 food crisis.[238] The European Union now requires farmers to comply with similar environmental conditions to receive the CAP's green direct payment (which is exempted instead under the Green Box of the AoA).[239] Alongside the Conservation Reserve Programme in the United States, this switch further demonstrates a trend to use the Green Box (and particularly the domestic environmental programme or direct payment) for WTO-compliant agri-environmental protection for WTO members.

For the sake of completeness, it was worth outlining the historical and hypothetical use of the Blue Box exemptions for WTO members pursuing agricultural environmental protection. However, currently, the Blue Box exemption is also not readily utilised for environmental protection and accordingly contributes to a general narrative that the use of agri-environmental provisions is not well established in the international agri-trade regime.

Summary

Overall, there is an opportunity for members to address agri-environmental protection in the global agri-trade regime, particularly through the existence of the Green Box exemptions. The Blue Box and Resource Retirement Programme under the Green Box also could provide routes for members' agri-environmental measures to be WTO-complaint, though their historic utilisation (or lack thereof) indicates their

[235] Agreement on Agriculture (15 April 1994) LT/UR/A-1A/2, Art 6(5).

[236] Commission Regulation (EEC) No 1272/88 of 29 April 1988 laying down detailed rules for applying the set-aside incentive scheme for arable land; Directorate General for Internal Policies, 'New Direct Payments Scheme: Targeting and Redistribution in the Future Cap' (2012) IP/B/AGRI/CEI/2011-097/E003/SC1, www.europarl.europa.eu/RegData/etudes/note/join/2012/474528/IPOL-AGRI_NT(2012)474528_EN.pdf, accessed 30 August 2023.

[237] Set aside in the EU context is different to land retirement as set-aside was able to be rotated and changed over time. Whilst originally designed to limit production, its purpose is to literally 'set aside' a proportion of each farm's land – also bringing with it environmental benefits such as biodiversity protection. Land retirement as part of resource retirement instead refers to the permanent retirement of land for agricultural purposes.

[238] See European Commission, CAP Health Check – Impact Assessment Note No 2 (2008).

[239] For more on the new CAP implementation period's coverage of biodiversity, see G Pe'er et al, 'How Can the European Common Agricultural Policy Help Halt Biodiversity Loss? Recommendations by Over 300 Experts [2022] *Conservation Letters*, https://doi.org/10.1111/conl.12901.

lack of utility for members seeking to introduce WTO-compliant agri-environmental measures domestically via this route. Instead, domestic environmental programmes and direct payment exemptions under the Green Box are where instances of members' agricultural environmental protection measures are mostly seen. Whilst not utilised to date in a way that is specific to the issue of agricultural emissions (livestock or otherwise), this provision and its historic utilisation do provide some basis from which livestock emissions mitigation measures could be adopted by members and exempted from the general liberalisation agenda of the AoA.

Although there are options for members to include potentially permissible domestic agri-environmental measures, trade liberalisation remains the default position within the global agricultural trade regime. The aforementioned domestic environmental programmes require a political willingness on the part of members to create these programmes, which is often lacking. Moreover, even when these programmes are created, their robustness or efficacy is not always guaranteed due to a lack of detail provided on how these programmes should be formed.

Additionally, while direct payments discourage overproduction and the use of potentially environmentally degrading subsidies under the Amber Box, environmental degradation linked to overconsumption is not addressed by the exemption. Debates on the trade-distorting impacts of Green Box payments and the inadequacy of current 'Greening Payments' can also undermine the extent to which agri-environmental protection can be fairly implemented by members utilising the exemption in reality. Overall, it can be said that there is an opportunity for agri-environmental counterbalances to the liberalisation provisions under the AoA to exist within the international agri-trade regime, though there is potential for agri-environmental protection to be bolstered by the WTO members beyond current levels. Again, this may reflect the WTO's position as a facilitator of its members' original free-trade mandate rather than as a body that can impose a non-negotiated, non-trade agenda, such as environmental protection.

Climate-Focused Agri-environmental Protection under the Agreement on Agriculture

General Climate Change Mitigation under the WTO

The agri-environmental options mentioned above can be used domestically to pursue agricultural-emissions-focused programmes by WTO members. However, it is worth considering to what extent climate change as an issue has been considered within the broader international agri-trade regime to date. Over the past decade climate change awareness has rocketed and the WTO has not been isolated from increased attempts to integrate climate considerations into policy-making. Whilst climate change is not referred to in the AoA, a report on trade and climate change was published in 2009 by the WTO and the UNEP. This demonstrated awareness of the intersection of trade and climate change.[240] At the time, this intersection had not been investigated by the two institutions, but the report established the empirical impacts of trade on the climate and vice versa (both ecologically and economically). Overall, the report found that trade and climate change can be mutually supportive, in that trade can support the growth of the green economy – though opening trade is largely deemed to increase overall GHG emissions.[241] Additionally (and in concurrence with previous conclusions put forward in this chapter), it found that national climate change strategies can exist within the WTO rules but that this largely depends on their design and very specific conditions for implementation to avoid clashes with other trade-liberalisation principles embodied in the GATT.

Specific References to Agricultural Emissions under the WTO

In terms of the links between agriculture, trade and climate change, publications by the WTO and UNEP Secretariats highlight the importance of the interrelationship – largely for food security purposes. For example, the aforementioned original WTO–UNEP report on trade and climate change frequently emphasises that global agricultural trade will be invaluable in preserving global food security in developing regions that have agricultural systems vulnerable to climate change.[242] Due to the global comparative advantages that exist for different agricultural goods, the reports state the importance of global agricultural trade as a 'cushion' to climate change's impact on food security, such as decreased yields from increased drought and weather pattern changes of climate change that are experienced in developing regions in particular.[243] Moreover, it is reported that reducing trade barriers (such as trade-restricting subsidies) will enable the full potential of this 'cushioning' effect on food security.[244]

By contrast, only one study (the aforementioned study by Verburg et al[245]) is referred to by the Secretariats in the report in relation to the impact of agricultural trade *on* climate change – rather than in response to it.[246] Moreover, it was recognised that the actual ability of global agricultural trade to 'cushion' food insecurity

[240] Abaza et al (n 94), see Foreword for more on the collaboration between the WTO and UNEP on this work.

[241] ibid, eg Part II of the Report on Trade and Climate Change: Theory and Evidence.

[242] ibid, eg 19.

[243] ibid 20.

[244] ibid, referring to C Rosenzweig et al, 'Climate Change and World Food Supply' (Environmental Change Unit, 1993) and T Hertel and T Randhir, 'Trade Liberalisation as a Vehicle for Adapting to Global Warming' (2000) 29(2) *Agriculture and Resource Economic Review* 1–14.

[245] Verburg et al (n 71).

[246] Though the EU–Mercosur association agreement was also highlighted as leading to an increase in global CO_2 emissions of about 0.15 percent as a result of the full liberalisation of agriculture and of manufactured goods. See Abaza et al (n 94) 58.

in developing countries will depend on these countries' purchasing power to buy food imports, particularly if global food scarcity is reflected in increased prices for global agricultural commodities.[247] Nonetheless, the Secretariats highlighted avenues under the WTO Agreements that could offer useful opportunities to improve the sustainability of the global agricultural sector, including the aforementioned Green Box under the AoA, or the potential of labelling schemes under the Technical Barriers to Trade Agreement 1994 that have not been discussed in this chapter.[248] Potential national measures to reduce livestock emissions were also referred to, albeit largely focused on supply-side technical fixes, such as changing livestock feeding methods or adopting energy-saving practices (and any trade-distorting policies that encourage this), rather than demand-side drivers relating to livestock consumption.[249]

Although the AoA and its subsequent ministerial decisions do not explicitly include sustainable agriculture terminology[250] in their provisions, these reports demonstrate an effort to bring the two areas (climate change and agricultural trade) together to a small extent. Whilst the initial analysis in this chapter focuses on largely key legal documents in the agri-trade regime, other sites of agri-trade governance are relevant to mention here albeit briefly. For example, the WTO Secretariat monitors notifications[251] from members and conducts a survey annually to identify those that relate to the environment.[252] This survey has found that the share of notifications related to the environment almost doubled to 15 percent of total notifications in 2016, up from 8 percent in 1997.[253] It is not clear exactly how many of these relate to climate change (or agricultural emissions more specifically), but nonetheless shows efforts to further bring together trade and environment within the WTO regime.

Additionally, information collected on notifications often serves as a 'springboard' for thematic discussions in WTO Committees, such as the Committee on Trade and Environment.[254] Twice a year, government representatives meet in the Committee on Trade and Environment to discuss issues relating to trade and environment (such as carbon footprint schemes) to share domestic experiences, discuss experiences and better understand the mutual supportiveness of trade and environment policies.[255]

[247] ibid 62. See more in WR Cline, 'Global Warming and Agriculture: Impact Estimates by Country' (Peterson Institute for International Economics, 2007).

[248] See more L Ankersmit and J Lawrence, 'The Future of Environmental Labelling: *US – Tuna II* and the Scope of the TBT' (2012) 39 *Legal Issues of Economic Integration* 127.

[249] Abaza et al (n 94) 88.

[250] As opposed to more general references to sustainable development or the environment, such as the preamble to the WTO Agreement, of which the AoA forms a part, makes.

[251] Or in other words, when members are required to inform other members of trade-related measures, such as technical regulations, licensing procedures, subsidies or agricultural trade policies – through the submission of this information to the WTO Secretariat.

[252] WTO (n 251) 57.

[253] ibid.

[254] ibid 57.

[255] ibid 56.

These meetings are often intended to be practical and technical in nature, to provide government officials with information and experience to design domestic measures that are efficient, coherent and fit for purpose.[256] As a result, the WTO Secretariat argues that it is 'strengthening coherence between trade, environmental and other policies' around the world – though to extent this covers agricultural emissions is an unknown.[257] Generally, the limits of the trade regime as a vehicle for climate action have been repeatedly highlighted by the Secretariats.[258]

Overall, the impact of agricultural trade liberalisation (as imbued by the AoA) on the environment is still found to be largely negative – despite these other soft governance attempts facilitated by the WTO Secretariat and members. There are avenues, such as those highlighted above, for WTO-compliant programmes and work to be established to improve the sustainability of trade in agricultural products, such as livestock. Global agricultural trade in theory could help dampen the impact of climate change on food security, though this overlooks the current purchasing power and political economy of developing countries in the global agricultural market.[259] Ultimately, as noted earlier, introducing explicit livestock emissions programmes remains subject to the motivation of individual members, and even then, a high threshold exists when balancing these exemptions against trade liberalisation's dominance within the broader regime. The extent to which this can counter the historical path dependence of global agricultural trade and shift towards non-trade concerns is unclear, particularly given the original trade-liberalisation mandate of WTO Agreements and their limited work path on agri-climate issues to date.

Food Security

Environmental protection, such as livestock emissions reduction, is not the only 'non-trade' interest that is relevant when looking at the agri-trade regime and its relationship with the cattle sector. Beyond the abovementioned (and contested) potential role of global agricultural trade in cushioning agricultural vulnerability to climate change, further specific food security provisions are also included within

[256] ibid.

[257] ibid. Other highlighted work by the Secretariat includes the WTO's role in the UN Forum on Sustainability Standards (UNFSS) along with the UN Conference on Trade and Development, the FAO, the International Trade Centre and the UN Industrial Development Organization. The UNFSS is a platform for coordinated work on voluntary sustainability standards and aims to help 'producers, traders, consumers, standard-setters, certification bodies, non-governmental organizations and researchers' convene and share best practices on topics relating to voluntary sustainability standards.

[258] WTO, Doha Ministerial Declaration, WT/MIN(01)/DEC/I, 20 November 2001; WTO, *Making Trade Work for the Environment, Prosperity and Resilience* (WTO, 2018) www.wto-ilibrary.org/environment/making-trade-work-for-the-environment-prosperity-and-resilience_f14f8c90-en, accessed 5 August 2020, 43-8.

[259] See more K Pawlak and M Kołodziejczak, 'The Role of Agriculture in Ensuring Food Security in Developing Countries: Considerations in the Context of the Problem of Sustainable Food Production' (2020) 12 *Sustainability* 5488, see part 2.

the AoA. These provisions, depending on their scope and implementation, can have the potential to contribute to agriculture-driven environmental degradation. This is because as demand for food increases (as it is predicted to do so as global populations grow[260]), an intensification and increase in agricultural production may be pursued leading to increased natural resource usage.[261] Unconditionally increasing production does not address any of the distributive nuances of food security issues, such as the structural coexistence of regions of overconsumption alongside areas of food insecurity.[262] As a result, it is necessary to analyse these food security provisions under the AoA and their scope for increasing environmental degradation, such as livestock emissions.

Following the food crisis of 2007–08 and increasing concerns about the climate vulnerability of agricultural systems in certain world regions, there is arguably a greater focus on food security within the international agri-trade regime than previously, particularly for developing countries.[263] A socioeconomic focus on food security in developing countries was highlighted in the Doha Declaration itself, where special and differential treatment for developing countries was agreed to enable them to 'take account of their development needs, including food security and rural development'.[264] Although food insecurity is clearly a vital non-trade concern to be tackled, the environmental impacts of pursuing this goal need to be minimised.

The general reduction of protectionism pursued by the AoA does provide food security benefits, particularly for developing countries.[265] In particular, it prevents the 'dumping' of cheap agricultural imports into their domestic agricultural markets, thereby providing space for domestic agricultural markets to develop and become more self-sufficient (or generally to economically prosper, allowing for an increase in economic growth and consequently standards of living, including access to safe, nutritious and affordable food).[266] This being said, specific food-security-related measures have also been created under the AoA, demonstrating

[260] Food demand is expected to increase anywhere between 59 and 98 percent by 2050: see 'Global Demand for Food Is Rising. Can We Meet It?' (2016) https://hbr.org/2016/04/global-demand-for-food-is-rising-can-we-meet-it, accessed 8 March 2021.

[261] See, for example, as the global population increases, food crop production increases are predicted to need to increase from 25 to 75 percent above current levels by 2050. See more eg MC Hunter et al, 'Agriculture in 2050: Recalibrating Targets for Sustainable Intensification' (2017) 67(4) *BioScience* 386.

[262] See the Introduction of this book for more on the juxtaposition between global hunger and overconsumption across different countries and regions.

[263] See generally Cardwell and Smith (n 9).

[264] WTO, Doha Ministerial Declaration, WT/MIN(01)/DEC/I, 20 November 2001, para 13.

[265] For more on a practical example of the European Union's agricultural protectionism on developing countries, see, again, Action Aid (n 60).

[266] For more on the issue of 'dumping', see S Murphy, B Lilliston and M Lake, 'WTO Agreement on Agriculture: A Decade of Dumping' (2005) https://agris.fao.org/agris-search/search.do?recordID=GB2013201277, accessed 24 July 2020; Institute for Agriculture & Trade Policy 'The Costs of Agricultural Export Dumping for Farmers and Rural Communities' (IATP, 2019), https://www.iatp.org/documents/costs-agricultural-export-dumping-farmers-and-rural-communities, accessed 3 March 2021; D Green and M Griffith, 'Dumping on the Poor: The Common Agricultural Policy, the WTO and International Development' (IATP, 2002) www.eldis.org/document/A19957, accessed 3 March 2021.

the existence of tailored standalone food security provisions under the international agri-trade regime. Two categories of measures identified are outlined in light of this: (1) food security 'safety nets'; and (2) agricultural productivity improvements. Additionally, the extent to which these measures promote food security at the expense of other environmental goals, such as emissions mitigation, is highlighted.

Food Security 'Safety Nets'

There are a number of 'safety nets' in place to protect food security under the AoA. For example, in the 2008 Revised Draft Modalities for Agriculture, it was proposed that members can select 'Special Products' based on guiding indicators on the criteria on food security, livelihood security and rural development.[267] These 'Special Products' are not subject to the full imposition of tariff-reduction requirements.[268] Consequently, developing countries are not required to open up their domestic markets for these goods to competition from imported goods as quickly as developed countries. The illustrative list of indicators that guide developing countries in selecting their 'Special Products' is heavily based upon food-security and welfare considerations.[269] For example, a 'Special Product' must be a staple food or part of the basic food basket of the developing country.[270] Additionally, the 'Special Product' must also account for a significant proportion of the total food expenditure of households in a particular region or nationally.[271]

Multiple food-security 'safety nets' are also present under the Green Box exemption, often explicitly referring to the concept of food security. For example, public stockholding programmes are exempt from Domestic Support reduction commitments provided that 'the volume accumulation of such stocks shall correspond to predetermined targets related solely to food security'.[272] Public stockholding programmes in developing countries also (on an interim basis) could not be legally challenged if a country's breached its agreed limits for trade-distorting domestic support as of 2013.[273] Domestic food aid can also be eligible for exemption if based on 'clearly defined criteria related to nutritional objectives'.[274] Income insurance and income 'safety-net' programmes are also categorised as a Green Box Exemption.[275] Lastly, payments for relief from natural disasters are even exempted

[267] WTO, Revised Draft Modalities for Agriculture, TN/AG/W/4/Rev.4, 6 December 2008, paras 129–31.
[268] Cardwell and Smith (n 9) 879.
[269] WTO (n 269) Annex F.
[270] ibid Annex F, para 1.
[271] ibid Annex F, para 10.
[272] Agreement on Agriculture (15 April 1994) LT/UR/A-1A/2, Annex 2, para 3.
[273] WTO, 'Public Stockholding for Food Security Purposes Ministerial Decision of 7 December 2013' WT/MIN(13)/38, para 2.
[274] Agreement on Agriculture (15 April 1994) LT/UR/A-1A/2, Annex 2, para 4.
[275] ibid Annex 2, para 7.

under the Green Box, thus protecting food security in member nations when agricultural production is under natural threats.[276]

These measures can be classed as food security 'safety nets' because they do not promote blanket increases in production to respond to food insecurity. Instead, thresholds of food insecurity are required before these measures are engaged. Moreover, these thresholds are often directly linked to indicators that are tailored to the different dimensions of food security, such as nutritional objectives, smallholder farmer livelihoods or core dietary components.[277]

At this point, it is also necessary to draw a distinction between core staple crops, such as cereals, and 'luxury' dietary components that are more emissions-intensive, such as beef. The 2007–08 food crisis was deemed a crisis because of rocketing cereal prices, and key cereal crops such as maize, rice and wheat are the most important items in the human diet, accounting for an estimated 42.5 percent of the world's food calorie supply.[278] This understanding of what is considered a 'core' component of food security is reflected in Members' choices of 'Special Products'. For example, three of the four members that have selected a 'Special Product' since the establishment of the AoA selected rice as a staple food. As a result, food-security provisions under the AoA do not necessarily compromise the goals of emissions mitigation in the case of livestock production. This is because the sectoral protection provided by these 'safety nets' does not artificially maintain the production of non-core dietary components, such as beef. For the most part, developing-country food security benefits from the 'safety nets' in place under the AoA without significantly increasing agricultural emissions from livestock or other emissions-intensive, non-essential crops.

Agricultural Productivity Improvements

Some food-security-related measures under the AoA could have adverse effects on the environment. For example, inputs to improve agricultural productivity are often exempted as 'Developmental Measures' under the AoA. Agricultural investment and input subsidies in particular are exempted from restrictions for developing countries under Article 6(2) AoA.[279] Improving the resilience and efficiency of agricultural production in developing countries is beneficial

[276] ibid para 8.

[277] Such as 'Special Products'.

[278] See more on the 2007–08 food crisis here: DG Environment Service, 'Causes of the 2007–2008 Global Food Crisis Identified' (2011) https://ec.europa.eu/environment/integration/research/newsalert/pdf/225na1_en.pdf, accessed 3 March 2021; T Reeves et al, 'Cereals and Us: Time to Renew an Ancient Bond', Save and Grow in practice: maize, rice, wheat (2014) http://www.fao.org/in-action/inpho/crop-compendium/cereals-grains/en/, accessed 3 March 2021.

[279] Agreement on Agriculture (15 April 1994) LT/UR/A-1A/2, Art 6(2).

for a number of reasons, including increasing overall production and reducing production externalities.[280]

However, inputs to improve agricultural productivity can have adverse effects of increasing the environmental impacts if intensive farming techniques are promoted to improve efficiency.[281] Unless effective environmental safeguards are also promoted in the course of this shift, the environmental impacts of more intensive production may be experienced. Agricultural research and extension and advisory services (which are exempt from restrictions under paragraph 2 of Annex 2) may play a role in promoting the uptake of these safeguards and ensuring the food-security gains of investment are not undermined by environmental losses.[282] However, for goods such as beef, the mere scaling up of production, even with safeguards, may cause an increase in climate impacts because cattle rearing is resource intensive: as cows are natural emitters of methane and substantial land is needed to grow their feed.[283]

In general, investments in agricultural productivity can be key to protecting food security, particularly in developing countries facing increasing food insecurity and agricultural system vulnerability.[284] However, a tension exists between improving the productivity and efficiency of key agricultural commodities and avoiding the scaling up of emissions (and resource) intensive agricultural commodities, such as beef. Meat production in itself is often seen as inefficient when trying to address food security.[285] This is particularly the case if arable land that could be used for growing staple crops for human consumption is being used to grow crops for livestock consumption.[286] As a result, the most efficient extraction of nutritional value

[280] Smallholder farmers are often those most vulnerable to climate change or external shocks; see eg JF Morton, 'The Impact of Climate Change on Smallholder and Subsistence Agriculture' (2007) 104 *Proceedings of the National Academy of Sciences of the United States of America* 19680.

[281] See more on this discussion of the trade-offs between the intensification of agricultural production and environmental degradation in the Introduction of this book. An example could be increasing the number of livestock per hectare to reduce grazing land required. However, this causes a trade-off in needing to supplement with feed (which has its own land-use impacts), and more intensive nitrate application to land from manure. See also H Menzi et al, Impacts of Intensive Livestock Production and Manure Management on the Environment' in Steinfeld H et al (eds) *Livestock in a Changing Landscape* (Island Press, 2010) 144–45.

[282] Agreement on Agriculture (15 April 1994) LT/UR/A-1A/2, para 2 Annex 2.

[283] Again, see Menzi et al (n 83).

[284] See more generally in D Hallam, 'International Investment in Developing Country Agriculture – Issues and Challenges' (2011) 3 *Food Security* 91; Q Li and A Mihalache-O'Keef, 'Modernization vs Dependency: Effects of Foreign Direct Investment on Food Security in Less Developed Countries' (2011) 55(1) *International Studies Quarterly* 71–93; MW Rosegrant, 'Global Food Security: Challenges and Policies' (2003) 302 *Science* 1917.

[285] See the Introduction of this book for more discussion of empirical studies on this and the food choice argument generally.

[286] See eg ES Cassidy et al, 'Redefining Agricultural Yields: From Tonnes to People Nourished per Hectare' (2013) 8 *Environmental Research Letters* 034015; KF Davis et al, 'Meeting Future Food Demand with Current Agricultural Resources' (2016) 39 *Global Environmental Change* 125; HHE Van Zanten et al, 'Defining a Land Boundary for Sustainable Livestock Consumption' (2018) 24 *Global Change Biology* 4185; P Alexander et al, 'Human Appropriation of Land for Food: The Role of Diet' (2016) 41 *Global Environmental Change* 88.

from a plot of land is not achieved. Even with agricultural investments into environmental efficiency, livestock will maintain a baseline level of protein conversion inefficiency[287] if reared on arable land due to its resource-intensive nature.[288]

If used to improve the environmental efficiency of staple crops for human consumption, these measures could have significant beneficial impacts on food security and environmental efficiency. However, if these investments are targeted towards cattle rearing (or even for livestock feed) and environmental efficiency trade-offs are not properly addressed, the environmental impact of such investments may not be as positive. As with all of these measures, the choice of sector for agricultural investment input is down to the individual WTO members. Consequently, a level of political will to address livestock emissions is needed to utilise the potential (and avoid the potential negative impacts) of using agricultural investments.

Overall, the majority of food security provisions under the AoA will not affect the environmental footprint of the international livestock sector as the measures are only engaged when a certain level of food insecurity is present. Nonetheless, a potential clash in food security and environmental goals may exist if agricultural productivity inputs are improperly targeted towards livestock production rather than other essential agricultural products, such as cereals. Whether this clash is actualised depends on individual Members' mandates, though it is worth being aware of this tension within the international agri-trade regime.

Conclusion

Overall, the prevailing dominance of an agricultural trade liberalisation mandate is identified under the AoA. The AoA was created with the aim of establishing a 'fair and market-oriented agricultural trade system', and is formed largely around measures designed to reduce barriers to global agricultural trade. When the Appellate Body has had to decide between free-trade-oriented principles and exceptions for environmental protection under the GATT, there is a high (but not impossible) threshold of policy design and consideration required to be GATT compliant. It is possible for members to create GATT-compliant domestic agri-environmental protection measures under the AoA through Green Box exemptions such as domestic environmental programmes.

However, as the WTO acts as a facilitator rather than a norm-setter, introducing these measures is down to individual members' willingness to 'opt in' to creating rigorous domestic environmental programmes and so forth. As a

[287] See ch 2 for more on protein conversion efficiencies generally.

[288] See the Introduction of this book for more discussion on the relative protein conversion efficiency rates of different types of agricultural goods, such as legumes, meat and milk.

result, agri-environmental measures are not embedded as agricultural-trade-liberalisation norms under the WTO regime. Some hints towards the increasing recognition of the role of trade in agricultural goods on the climate can be identified through the joint work of the WTO and UNEP on the environment and trade. However, generally, mitigation measures need to be pursued through 'box-exempt' routes under the AoA, again making it contingent on member willingness and subject to the same balancing act against free-trade-oriented principles underpinning the WTO regime.

Food security 'non-trade' interests are also protected under the AoA, with specific measures functioning as 'safety nets' for food-security issues for core and commonly non-livestock agricultural commodities. However, with regards to agricultural productivity input provisions under the AoA, a tension can exist between (1) improving productivity and efficiency of key agricultural commodities, and (2) encouraging significant scaling up or intensification of high-emitting and land-inefficient agricultural commodities, such as beef. As a result, caution must be exercised in relation to these provisions, as they may have negative food security and climate impacts by encouraging the scaling up of livestock production, particularly on arable land.

Throughout this analysis of the international agri-trade regime, it is worth noting that agricultural *production* is the target of the AoA. As a result, its provisions cannot easily address or target issues with consumption that exist with livestock goods, but rather provide a baseline of protection from issues with overproduction stemming from market distortions. Overall, there is potential for livestock emissions reduction to be pursued under the AoA. However, in terms of the current reality of exemption use and the default trade liberalisation position of the AoA, agricultural trade liberalisation norms still dominate the international agri-trade regime. Only through members' motivation can specific WTO-compliant domestic measures be made to address the emissions impact of their international trade in livestock products and feed.

However, considering the comparative strength of the WTO's rules-based system with other weaker international legal regimes analysed in this book, in addition to the more palatable alignment of the AoA's liberalisation mandate with members' economic interests, understandably concern exists regarding whether the international agri-trade regime acts as a roadblock to livestock emissions mitigation – as will be explored subsequently in the concluding chapter.

6

Conclusion: Reconciling Climate Justice in the International Legal Order for Climate Change and Cattle

A vast amount of material, spanning several legal regimes, has been covered in this book to address the gap that exists in environmental legal literature surrounding livestock emissions. From the analysis undertaken, it is evident that the international legal order is intrinsically intertwined with the livestock sector and its stakeholders' interests – whether that be to the benefit or detriment of climate-change mitigation goals. This conclusion seeks to identify key insights from the analysis to delineate common themes and tensions across the regimes analysed, before highlighting what this reveals about how to govern cattle and other livestock emissions mitigation more effectively and fairly on the international level.

The structure of the conclusion is as follows. Firstly, the main broad approaches within the international legal order for the cattle sector identified in the text are outlined in three main categories: mitigation, food security and other intersecting interests, such as agricultural industry interests. Then, the common themes and tensions arising from the analysis are delineated. Common themes include (1) agriculture being a neglected sector with regard to climate-change mitigation, (2) a preference to address livestock emissions through adaptation and food-security measures rather than mitigation, and (3) regimes being in a period of transition where public health–climate links are being utilised to further livestock emissions mitigation. One key tension is identified, namely the one that exists between agricultural interests (in terms of economic interests and farmer livelihood interests) and livestock emissions reduction.

The last part of this conclusion highlights one key takeaway of the text, focusing on affluence as the 'evasive' problem in reducing cattle emissions. The importance of this key insight in terms of tackling future livestock emissions trajectories is explained, particularly in relation to the climate-justice dimensions of climate mitigation. The responsibility of both affluent countries and affluent groups within poorer countries to reduce excessive consumption of beef and dairy is emphasised in light of the established principle of Common but Differentiated Responsibilities and Respective Capabilities (CBDRRC) in light of different national circumstances. From this, a better understanding of responsibility attribution between wealthier and poorer actors can be derived for livestock emissions mitigation.

Given the contribution of this book in highlighting this issue and the urgency and importance of taking fair and sustainable action to tackle livestock emissions, some potential solutions are provided, drawing on existing work addressing overconsumption of livestock goods by wealthier actors. Lastly, a summary of the broader contribution of this book's conclusions for addressing affluence's role in environmental (and even broader social) issues is given.

Categorisation of Approaches in the International Legal Order for Cattle

These categories were briefly presented in the Introduction to provide context to the rest of the book. However, following the book's analysis of different institutional regimes across the international legal order for cattle and climate change, it is now possible to outline the main categories of approaches that institutions take towards livestock governance in more detail. Three main categories can be identified, namely: (1) food security approaches; (2) mitigation approaches; and (3) approaches focusing on other intersecting interests. The distinction between these approaches was not always entirely clear-cut or existing in isolation, though they are broadly categorised in this way to help gain a macro-level synthesis of different approaches towards livestock governance and its climate impact within the international legal order.

Food security approaches presented livestock governance in terms of food security and adaptation. For example, food security approaches were identified from the FAO's work path on livestock. Here, livestock products were seen as a source of nutrients that are able to improve poverty levels, food security and nutrition in vulnerable populations, such as women in developing countries with scarce food supply. Moreover, under the international climate regime, livestock emissions reduction was presented as a way to make livestock production more efficient, maintaining and increasing food supply in light of a growing global population and to adapt to agricultural system vulnerability to climate change. Although food security and adaptation are naturally key goals for sustainable development, these approaches saw livestock as a sector *affected* by climate change, rather than necessarily as a driver of emissions or a sector where radical emission reductions are required to tackle the climate crisis.

Mitigation approaches, by contrast, *did* present the livestock sector as one where radical emissions reduction are required to tackle the climate crisis. They recognised that the livestock sector contributes considerably to global GHG emissions and elevates the importance of livestock emissions reduction beyond simply a co-benefit of adaptation or improving food security. These frames often recognised that mitigation needs to go beyond supply-side technical solutions and recognises the role of consumption habits in driving the sector. For example, a mitigation approach was identified from other aspects of the work of the FAO, most strongly when integrated with public health concerns. This included the promotion of mitigation solutions, such as dietary change, that target actors whose consumption of large quantities of beef and dairy products contribute to levels of GHG emissions. Similar recognition of the role of diet in addressing livestock emissions was seen in the international climate-change regime at COP27 through the creation of informal initiatives such as I-CAN. In this sense, this identified mitigation approach recognises the livestock sector's role as a contributor to climate change more fully.

Lastly, there were other approaches to livestock identified that reflected 'other intersecting interests' within the livestock sector. These approaches were not adaptation, food security or mitigation focused, but rather reflected broader stakeholder interests that relate to livestock production. For example, under the international agri-trade regime, an agricultural trade liberalisation mandate was identified as underpinning international trade in livestock products. This approach largely reflects a promotion of agricultural industry interests, such as aiding the growth of the agricultural sector through international trade. Similar protection of the agricultural industry was seen in Bolsonaro's approach to forest governance in Brazil which involved watering down environmental protections and administration during his term.

Farmer livelihood protection was similarly seen as another 'intersecting interest' in livestock governance. For the author's purposes, agricultural-sector interests more often refer to the interests of larger-scale agri-business, whereas farmer livelihood protection focuses on smaller-scale or vulnerable farmer protection – such as sustenance farmers protected under the FAO's Pro-Poor Livestock Initiative. These other 'intersecting interests' were important to delineate and identify because action stemming from these approaches can have a direct impact on livestock emissions mitigation due to having the same target of governance (namely, agricultural goods).

Figure 6 The three main categorisations of approaches of livestock governance identified in the international legal order for the cattle sector and climate change

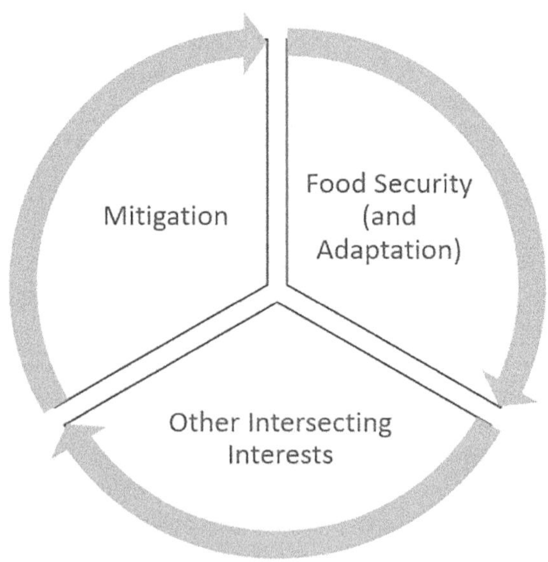

These categorisations provide an initial breakdown of the international legal order's range of approaches towards livestock governance. Beyond this, it was possible to identify further common themes and tensions in livestock governance across the international legal order for climate change and cattle – demonstrating some of the prevailing narratives, biases and priorities in agri-climate governance internationally ahead of outlining the key takeaways from the book's analysis.

Common Themes and Tensions in Livestock Governance in the International Legal Order for Climate Change and Cattle

As stated above, this section seeks to provide a synthesised overview of where similarities and differences exist in the range of approaches towards livestock production across the international legal order for cattle and climate change. Firstly, common themes that emerged across the different regimes' approaches to livestock governance are identified and discussed. These include (1) agriculture being a neglected sector with regards to climate change mitigation, (2) a preference to address livestock emissions through adaptation and food-security approaches rather than mitigation, and (3) many regimes being in a period of transition where public health–climate links are being utilised to further livestock emissions mitigation. A key tension between agricultural interests (in terms of economic interests and farmer livelihood interests) and livestock emissions reduction is then also identified.

Common Themes Across the International Legal Order for Cattle and Climate Change

Agriculture as a Neglected Sector for Climate-Change Mitigation

As was demonstrated in the Introduction of this book, much of the scientific literature on the environmental impacts of the agricultural sector is relatively recent. Similarly, other related areas of literature, such as agri-environmental economics, have only been in circulation since the 1990s and only became more comprehensive as traction for agri-environmental issues grew in the late 2000s. More generally, due to the quasi-public status of agriculture and food, agriculture has also frequently been granted 'exceptional status' from other legal regulation.[1] As a

[1] See agri-trade chapter and the 'exceptional status' of agriculture in the general trade liberalisation agenda of the WTO and GATT 1947.

result, agriculture and climate change can generally be seen as relatively new issues on the radar of environmental law and governance. Insight across the chapters' analysis perhaps reflects the area's novelty: agriculture was often found to be a 'neglected sector' for climate-change mitigation.

For example, within key legal documents in the International Climate Regime, references to the agricultural sector and its impact *on increasing* atmospheric concentrations of GHGs are historically and currently lacking.[2] Food production references in the climate-change treaties could even be interpreted as a perceived trade-off with agricultural emissions mitigation within the international climate regime.[3]

When looking at International Forest Regime, it was shown that REDD+ (which seeks to reduce forest-related emissions in developing countries) members have poor agricultural forest emissions coverage in their national plans. While Brazil did include the agricultural sector in its REDD+, much of its forest protection has been undermined by the Bolsonaro administration. This diluted agriculture-focused mitigation under REDD+ due to its lack of durability[4] in the face of shifts in domestic environmental policy. More generally, while synergies between forest protection and climate-change mitigation generally have been developed through programmes such as REDD+, these synergies have not been as actively utilised for the agricultural sector. This is despite other forest-related sectors, such as the timber sector, being more readily addressed for its environmental impacts by policymakers in programmes such as the European Union's FLEGT+ Action Plan and Timber Regulation.

Generally, mitigation for the agricultural sector was neglected or bypassed. The following section highlights how this evasiveness translated across the international legal order for cattle and climate change into a preference to largely refer to livestock emissions through language of adaptation and food-security goals, rather than as livestock being viewed as a *driver* of climate change.

A Preference to Address Livestock Emissions Through the Lens of Adaptation and Food Security

Where agricultural emissions mitigation coverage did exist across the analysed legal regimes, this was more often framed in terms of synergies with adaptation or food security whereby emissions reductions in the livestock sector could enable increases in global demand for livestock goods to be met more efficiently. For example, in the international climate regime chapter, references to livestock

[2] See also the first chapter, and also Alexander Zahar, 'Agricultural Exceptionalism in the Climate Change Treaties' (2023) 12 *Transnational Environmental Law* 42.

[3] See eg Art 2 UNFCCC.

[4] See more in the previous chapter and in AJ Jordan and B Moore, *Durable by Design?: Policy Feedback in a Changing Climate* (Cambridge University Press, 2020) www.cambridge.org/core/books/durable-by-design/635638C9209435D8C8491EB3EC288081, accessed 16 August 2021.

emissions were largely included only to the extent they can also improve food security. This preference was also identified in the first round of NDCs submitted to the Paris Agreement. For example, from analysis of the first NDCs submitted, it was identified that parties to the Agreement were 3.5 times more likely to have concrete actions for climate-change adaptation in their NDCs than for climate change mitigation[5] – further demonstrating the preference of actors to present the livestock sector as one that is affected by climate change, rather than as a driver of climate change. Similarly, developments following negotiations at Sharm El Sheikh at COP27 still largely presented any emissions mitigation in the livestock sector as an adaptation issue for food security – avoiding references to 'full food systems language' rather than recognising that there is a need for fuller structural changes in the sector to address the climate crisis.[6]

Naturally, food security and any adaptation needed in the agriculture sector to protect this are vital to human development needs, particularly in developing countries. However, a significant point to highlight about this preference to frame livestock production as a food security or adaptation issue is that it was often found to limit the scope of actors undertaking policies that can reduce livestock emissions. As a result, the burden for mitigation action was found to fall more often on less efficient producers of beef and dairy, often in developing countries such as those in South America or sub-Saharan Africa. Moreover, it was often found that nations that consume high levels of meat and dairy (which often are wealthier, though produce livestock more environmentally efficiently) were not including their own livestock sectors within the scope of their climate commitments.

For example, no developed country party referred to livestock in their first NDC, though this did improve slightly in later iterations of national climate plans.[7] Many FAO initiatives in the past (such as the Pro-Poor Livestock Initiative) target only developing-country actors. Although financed through developed country contributions, REDD+ largely places the onus of forest management on developing countries to address deforestation and forest degradation. Consequently, while the need to reduce developing-country agricultural emissions is an important piece of the mitigation puzzle, agricultural emissions were less often framed as an issue that wealthy, developed countries can also play a role in remedying through their consumption patterns. This is despite the significant role consumption of these goods in developed regions has and continues plays in driving livestock emissions.

[5] R Strohmaier et al, 'The Agriculture Sectors in the Intended Nationally Determined Contributions – Analysis' (FAO, 2016) Environment and Natural Resources Working Paper No. 62.

[6] See more Carbon Brief Staff, 'COP27: Key Outcomes for Food, Forests, Land and Nature at the UN Climate Talks in Egypt', *Carbon Brief*, 24 November 2022, www.carbonbrief.org/cop27-key-outcomes-for-food-forests-land-and-nature-at-the-un-climate-talks-in-egypt/, accessed 10 January 2023.

[7] See eg WWF, 'Unlocking and Scaling Climate Solutions in Food Systems: An Assessment of Nationally Determined Contributions.' (2022) https://wwfint.awsassets.panda.org/downloads/unlocking_and_scaling_climate_solutions_in_food_systems___wwf_analysis_of_ndcs_2022.pdf, accessed 10 January 2023.

The issue with this focus will be more fully addressed later in the conclusion of this chapter. However, for now, it is worth provisionally noting the fairness of this distribution of responsibility and the limitations this places on emissions-reduction pathways for the future if the significant role of wealthy, developed country consumers in driving livestock emissions is not sufficiently recognised in current mitigation solutions. Nonetheless, the following section highlights an incipient change in this narrative that has been identified from the analysis undertaken.

Transitional Period and Utilised Synergies with Public Health Goals

As mentioned above, approaches to livestock emissions mitigation appear to be in a state of transition, whereby underlying structural issues underpinning livestock emissions are becoming increasingly acknowledged in livestock governance (particularly when considered in combination with public health concerns). More specifically, *consumers* of livestock products rather than solely *producers* of livestock products are being recognised as responsible for undertaking climate action to tackle emissions from the sector.

One example of this included in the analysis of the International Agri-Trade Regime was the European Union's new due-diligence regulation proposal that sought to improve the sustainability of forest and ecosystem risk commodities supply chains in the EU Single Market in a WTO-compliant way.[8] Here, the European Union is actively addressing its role as a consumer of embodied environmental harm in its imports and is attempting to leverage its market power to encourage shifts in practice in third countries. However, generally, this recognition and transition in approach was most commonly seen when it was linked with public health goals.[9] As was established at many points throughout the text, excessive consumption of certain livestock goods can have a number of public health impacts, particularly on levels of non-communicable disease, incidents of colorectal cancer and obesity. As a consequence, addressing high consumption levels of these goods can be beneficial for both public health and climate goals. Across the regimes analysed, evidence of a fuller food systems approach to livestock governance was beginning to emerge in relation to this.

Increasing references to the role of a 'healthy, sustainable global diet' were found across a number of legal regimes in the international legal order for climate

[8] See more in the previous chapter and in G Marín Durán and J Scott, 'Regulating Trade in Forest-Risk Commodities: Two Cheers for the European Union' [2022] *Journal of Environmental Law* eqac002.

[9] Although, the EU Due Diligence Proposal arguably feeds into the EU's broader Farm to Fork Strategy which also contains relevant dietary and health considerations. See para 10 of Regulation (EU) 2023/1115 of the european parliament and of the Council of 31 May 2023 on the making available on the Union market and the export from the Union of certain commodities and products associated with deforestation and forest degradation and repealing Regulation (EU) No 995/2010, L150/206.

change and cattle. For example, in the International Climate Change Regime, while the new formal decision on agriculture at COP27 in Sharm El Sheikh was largely food security-focused, new informal initiatives, such as the I-CAN initiative, emerged out of COP meetings that seek to address issues such as diet and nutrition alongside the Paris Agreement's climate goals.[10] During formal COP27 negotiations, discussions of whole food system approaches (which consider the role of diet) were raised,[11] and increasing references to diet are being included in successive NDC submission rounds.[12] The FAO's expert role in agri-climate governance on the international level was also found to bolster the recognition of issues such as dietary choice in driving agricultural emissions through their high-profile work on 'healthy, sustainable diets'. While the KJWA mandate has come to an end, discussions of 'unbalanced diets' formed part of KJWA Workshop discussions,[13] and further work has been completed by the FAO to similar ends, such as analysing national dietary guidelines in light of sustainability and health standards.[14]

Again, it must be emphasized that many of these policies are not fully fledged or concrete legal obligations for the sector. Nonetheless, their potential should not be ignored, as they begin to confront the historically evasive approach to the agricultural sector in climate-change mitigation plans and extend livestock mitigation to beyond simply a co-benefit to adaptation or food security. This synergy is undoubtedly gaining traction in agri-climate policy-making and can continue to be utilised to secure agricultural emissions mitigation without compromising food security in poorer or vulnerable populations. Most importantly, this synergy has the potential to carve a greater role for affluent, high-consuming actors in livestock emissions mitigation in a more politically palatable way.[15]

The importance of this is more fully outlined in the second part of this chapter. But, identifying these common themes across the different regimes in the international legal order for climate change and cattle was an important part of the macro-level analysis that this book sought to undertake. Delving further into common tensions that have also arisen offers the potential to 'unblock' tensions across these regimes to better integrate agricultural and climate goals in the future. As a consequence, the subsequent section focuses

[10] Decision 3.CP/27, Sharm El-Sheikh Joint Work on Implementation of Climate Action on Agriculture and Food Security Decision 3.CP/27, FCCC/CP/2022/10/Add.1.

[11] Carbon Brief Staff (n 6).

[12] WWF (n 7).

[13] See more in the agricultural regime chapter and in FAO, *Koronivia Joint Work on Agriculture – Summary of Workshop on Topic 2(d) : Improved Nutrient Use and Manure Management towards Sustainable and Resilient Agricultural Systems* (FAO, 2020) www.fao.org/documents/card/en/c/ca8802en, accessed 7 December 2021.

[14] C Gonzalez Fischer and T Garnett, *Plates, Pyramids, Planet: Developments in National Healthy and Sustainable Dietary Guidelines: A State of Play Assessment* (FAO, 2016) www.fao.org/documents/card/en/c/d8dfeaf1-f859-4191-954f-e8e1388cd0b7/, accessed 7 October 2020.

[15] In that states can make domestic gains and cost savings in public health, rather than being motivated solely by climate considerations – which, as we have seen, is not always a top political priority, particularly in leadership with an anti-climate sentiment.

on the key tension identified from the book's analysis, before highlighting the key takeaways of the book in light of this.

Tensions between Agricultural Interests and Agricultural Emissions Reduction

A key tension between agricultural interests and agricultural emissions reduction was identified with respect to two main stakeholder interests: (1) agricultural industry interests (such as large agri-businesses), and (2) farmer livelihoods (often on a smaller smallholder scale).

Under the AoA, a tension between agricultural industry interests and livestock emissions mitigation was revealed as this was found to have a default agricultural trade liberalisation mandate that is likely to cause detrimental environmental impacts. By comparison, options for WTO members to pursue domestic environmental protection measures, such as agricultural emissions mitigation, are not mandatory. For example, the Article XX 'environmental' exceptions under the GATT require significant political will from WTO members to formulate carefully designed national agri-climate measures that are WTO compliant. In a similar vein, environmental-protection-focused provisions of the AoA, such as domestic environmental programmes, are only 'opt-in' and not rigorously defined under the AoA, making their impact on cattle emissions 'weaker' than that perhaps of the AoA's default agricultural trade liberalisation mandate. As a result, it can be said that the default agricultural trade interests, rather than non-trade interests, dominate in the agri-trade regime.

Some synergies between agri-trade liberalisation measures and climate-change mitigation were also found to exist. For example, trade-liberalisation-driven measures to reduce overproduction may have provided environmental as well as economic benefits in the past. This is because the overproduction of agricultural goods can cause both detrimental economic (because excess production drives down global prices) and environmental (because excessive natural resources are used) consequences. As a result, the AoA's encouragement of decoupled payments historically may have discouraged overproduction of agricultural goods and simultaneously prevented emissions through reduced livestock production levels.

However, this potential reduction was not intended as a climate change mitigation strategy, but rather an economic one. As a result, it was found that the limits of this synergy have been utilised now the number of production-increasing measures has been reduced since the introduction of the AoA. Following from this, the strong agricultural trade liberalisation mandate imbued by the AoA and its highly legalised mechanisms still results in tensions with weaker environmental-focused provisions under the Agreement. Moreover, the AoA's rules and penalty-based system can be seen as particularly dominant across the regimes analysed, especially when compared to the softer coverage of livestock emissions reduction from other institutions, such as the FAO's information dissemination work. As a result, this tension between agri-trade interests and broader environmental regimes can also be identified between the different regimes analysed within the international legal order for cattle and climate change, not just within the international agri-trade regime.

Cattle farmer livelihood protection is the other main form of 'agricultural interest' that was identified during the course of the book's analysis. A tension was again found between cattle farmer livelihood protection and livestock emissions mitigation if policies were not carefully formulated and targeting the correct actors at an appropriate scale when providing farmer livelihood support.

For example, strong farmer livelihood protection was identified under the FAO's work path that focuses on livestock's role in supporting less wealthy farmers and vulnerable populations, particularly in developing countries. Similarly, much of the international climate regime's work on livestock highlighted the particular importance of the livestock sector for smallholder farmers' livelihoods, such as the new Sharm El Sheikh decision on agriculture.[16] Targeting this support towards solely smaller-scale and poorer sustenance farmers was found to have valuable food-security and socioeconomic benefits that should not be discouraged, especially where the scale of livestock production is less polluting than larger industrial agricultural systems. However, a tension may arise between livestock emissions mitigation and cattle farmer livelihood support if all types of farms are supported and sheltered from the costs of necessary mitigation requirements, rather than only providing support or exemption for smaller-scale farms.

Unfortunately, this differentiation does not always occur in practice to the extent necessary. As a result, tensions with livestock emissions mitigation can occur if support is blanketly provided in wealthier countries where food security is not significantly threatened and issues with *overconsumption* of livestock goods exist. On top of this, as highlighted in the International Agri-Trade Regime chapter, the agricultural sectors in many developed regions, such as the European Union and the United States, have historically (and at times, ongoingly) been labelled as highly protectionist and damaging to developing countries' agricultural sectors. Failing to differentiate between different types of farms when providing farmer livelihood support can further evade developing-country responsibility for their livestock sectors, with risks of path dependency continuing the harm these agricultural economies have historically caused to global agricultural markets.

In global negotiating contexts, such as COP meetings under the international climate regime, these interests are difficult to balance when all global parties are required to agree on the wording of any decision texts. For example, at COP27,

[16] Sharm El-Sheikh Joint Work on Implementation of Climate Action on Agriculture and Food Security Decision (n 10).

we saw the watering down of ambitious language in the Sharm El Sheikh Joint Work Decision that would have required greater restructuring of industrial-scale agriculture and food systems.[17] More generally beyond this, agricultural industry lobbyists are often found in great numbers in these negotiating arenas (both representing industry and as national delegates), leading to a blurring of political interests driving inaction on livestock emissions.[18] Whilst small-scale and sustenance farmers have valid reasons for requiring exemption from and support during full-scale food-system restructuring, agricultural lobbyists can piggyback off this sentiment to evade their own climate responsibility – ultimately causing a tension with livestock emissions mitigation goals.

Affluence as the Evasive Problem in Reducing Cattle Emissions

From the common themes and tensions identified above, one normative aspect of the analysis stands out as a key issue that needs to be understood and addressed to realise just and sustainable livestock solutions. Namely, that affluence (and the high consumption of livestock goods that correlates with it) is an evasive problem in the international legal order's approach to climate change and cattle emissions. Arguably, this is beginning to shift somewhat, as demonstrated in the previous discussion of the emergence of the concept of 'healthy, sustainable diets'.[19] Nonetheless, affluence is frequently sidelined in discussions on agricultural emissions mitigation, and instead replaced with discussions of food security and the importance of protecting small-scale, poor livestock farmers. These are not unimportant objectives but focusing predominantly on these issues distracts from the main issue at hand from a fairness perspective: wealthy people consume too many livestock products.

Properly addressing affluence as a dominant driver in livestock emissions is particularly important for two reasons: (1) current approaches that neglect affluence as a driver are out of sync with a key international climate law principle, CBDRRC in light of different national circumstances; and (2) the need to address the growing wealthy global middle class that will drive the future agricultural emissions trajectory through increased meat consumption.

In this section, firstly, the concept of CBDRRC will be introduced and a discussion of why current livestock approaches do not respect this principle is provided. Then a reconceptualisation of our understanding of the CBDRRC in the livestock

[17] See eg Carbon Brief Staff (n 6).

[18] See more in 'Power, Access & Influence: Which Food Organisations Participated at COP27?' (Food Research Collaboration, 2022) https://foodresearch.org.uk/blogs/power-access-influence-which-food-organisations-participated-at-cop27/, accessed 22 June 2023.

[19] For example, see this terminology being used by the FAO in the agricultural regime chapter and in Gonzalez Fischer and Garnett (n 14).

sector to better include the responsibility of wealthy actors for livestock emissions will be outlined. Lastly, tentative suggestions for future livestock solutions and addressing affluence in global issues are highlighted.

The Principle of CBDRRC and Livestock Emissions

Throughout the analysis undertaken in this book, a strong distinction between developed-country consumption and developing-country production was found to exist with regards to livestock emissions. In a number of emerging livestock mitigation approaches, a strong 'wealthy' versus 'poor' distinction between actors was present to ensure mitigation burdens, such as implementing dietary change, were imposed on the appropriate actors. These approaches sought to increase recognition of the responsibility for wealthy actors to address their high levels of consumption, whilst simultaneously preventing negative food security or livelihood impacts for less wealthy or vulnerable populations. However, as this section will show, most current laws and policies are still out of sync with the principle of CBDRRC, and if this principle was better respected in livestock solutions, it could help provide fairer and more effective livestock mitigation in the future.

The rest of this section summarises the development of the principle of CBDRRC and what each of its constituent elements entails for burden sharing in climate-change mitigation broadly. How institutional approaches surrounding the issue of livestock emissions currently 'misallocate' these burdens will also be highlighted. Lastly, potential pathways and solutions to be investigated in the future to more fairly allocate the burden of livestock emissions mitigation are identified.

The Development of the Principle of CBDRRC

CBDRRC is a central principle in international climate change law that has helped to sculpt the 'differentiation' of obligations and expectations of developed and developing countries in a fair way.[20] In short, states have common responsibilities in securing climate change mitigation, but these are differentiated depending on a multitude of factors.

The principle of CBDRRC finds its grounding in Principle 7 of the Rio Declaration, which reads: 'States shall cooperate in a spirit of global partnership to conserve, protect and restore the health and integrity of the Earth's ecosystem.'[21]

[20] For more on 'differentiation' generally, see L Rajamani, *Differential Treatment in International Environmental Law* (Oxford University Press, 2006) https://oxford-universitypressscholarship-com.eui.idm.oclc.org/view/10.1093/acprof:oso/9780199280704.001.0001/acprof-9780199280704, accessed 11 November 2020; L Rajamani et al, 'National "Fair Shares" in Reducing Greenhouse Gas Emissions within the Principled Framework of International Environmental Law' (2021) 21 *Climate Policy* 983.

[21] Art 7 Rio Declaration 1992.

Rajamani explains how the principle came to be included in the UNFCCC (another significant outcome of the Rio Conference), thereby providing the basis for burden sharing (or differentiation) under the climate-change regime.[22]

The principle was used to underpin the 'contentious' binary annex differentiation between developed and developing countries under the Kyoto Protocol,[23] though when it came to negotiating the Paris Agreement it was agreed that any reference to CBDRRC would also include the phrase 'in light of different national circumstances'.[24] This phrase was introduced to add an element of 'dynamic differentiation' to climate responsibility under the Paris Agreement, allowing states the flexibility to qualify their mitigation contribution in light of their national circumstances, such as levels of poverty or economic development.[25] Moreover, it offered a way for levels of responsibilities of different states to 'evolve' over time as their national circumstances change – rather than being bound by crude categorisations of development and state responsibility for mitigation.[26]

As a result, the principle of CBDRRC is now constituted of three main elements that form the basis for determining burden sharing between actors for mitigation, namely: (1) common but differentiated responsibilities; (2) respective capabilities; and (3) national circumstances. Each of these elements will be outlined further below, before then discussing the current misallocation of responsibility for livestock emissions mitigation in light of these elements.

Common but Differentiated Responsibilities

Common responsibility describes the 'shared obligation' of two or more states towards the protection of the atmosphere.[27] While the extent and legal nature of each state's responsibility may differ, it is understood that a common legal responsibility to cooperate in preventing damage to the atmosphere exists.[28] Differentiated responsibility, by contrast, seeks to ensure equity between differing levels of state

[22] For more on the development of the CBDRRC principle, see generally L Rajamani, 'Ambition and Differentiation in the 2015 Paris Agreement: Interpretative Possibilities and Underlying Politics Shorter Articles and Notes' (2016) 65 *ICLQ* 493.

[23] ibid 507.

[24] ibid 508.

[25] See more in C Voigt and F Ferreira, 'Dynamic Differentiation: The Principles of CBDR-RC, Progression and Highest Possible Ambition in the Paris Agreement' (2016) 5 *Transnational Environmental Law* 285.

[26] ibid 294. Boyte also refers to this as 'graduation' out of development categories. See R Boyte, 'Common but Differentiated Responsibilities: Adjusting the Developing/Developed Dichotomy in International Environmental Law' (2010) 14 *New Zealand Journal of Environmental Law* 6.2.

[27] Rajamani (n 18) 508.

[28] P Sands et al, *Principles of International Environmental Law* (Cambridge University Press, 2018) www-cambridge-org.eui.idm.oclc.org/highereducation/books/principles-of-international-environmental-law/B32CA39427B24F1947BDC5F884CCADC0 accessed 28 November 2021, 245.

responsibility in addressing climate change.[29] As Voigt and Ferreira highlight, 'differentiation is expected to bridge the gap between the formal equality of states under international law and the deep inequalities in wealth, power and responsibility that divide them'.[30]

In practical terms, it refers to differential environmental standards being set for states on the basis of a multitude of factors, including the future economic development of developing countries and historical contributions to climate change.[31] The historical contribution of developed countries towards current levels of emissions, in addition to their increased financial and technical capacity, is particularly emphasised by the principle to ensure developed states are 'leading the way' for climate-change mitigation.[32] This also links to consideration of the 'respective capabilities' of states in the CBDRRC principle, discussed further below.

Respective Capabilities

The 'respective capabilities' of states are also considered when determining the extent to which they dedicate resources to tackling climate change. The climate change policies of states should not 'adversely affect the present and future development potential of developing countries' and thus levels of climate responsibility are required to 'reflect the environmental and development context to which they apply'.[33] Here, special priority is often given to developing countries (especially the least developed and environmentally vulnerable) which may not have the financial or technical resources of their developed country counterparts.[34] A state's 'respective capability' to contribute to climate change mitigation has typically been established on the basis of indicators such as national income, human assets (such as health, nutrition or education) and economic vulnerability.[35]

At the same time, Rajamani highlights that if a developing country's 'relevant differences [to developed countries] cease to exist' – both in terms of emissions levels and capacity – their contribution to collective climate action should adapt to this.[36] As an increasing number of developing countries industrialise and their pressure on the global environment and domestic capabilities increases, an

[29] Explanation of this principle focuses on climate change mitigation (though discusses adaptation). It is worth noting that the CBDRRC principle also applies to climate change policy-making beyond mitigation, such as adaptation or finance. ibid 244.

[30] Voigt and Ferreira (n 21) 286.

[31] Sands et al (n 28) 245.

[32] Boyte (n 26) 69.

[33] See the Art 30 1974 Charter of Economic Rights and Duties of States reference in Sands et al (n 28) 246.

[34] Voigt and Ferreira (n 25) eg 287.

[35] See discussion of criteria for designation of 'Least Developed Country' status at 6.4 in Boyte (n 32).

[36] Rajamani (n 16) 162.

expectation that they will assume greater climate responsibilities exists.[37] This is where the addition of the phrase 'in light of different national circumstances' to the CBDRRC principle in the lead-up to Paris is particularly relevant.

In Light of Different National Circumstances

As mentioned above, the addition of the phrase 'in light of different national circumstances' to the principle in the CBDDRC led to a change in the way the principle is applied in international climate change law. As Voigt and Ferreria highlight, the qualifier 'in the light of different national circumstances' introduces a 'dynamic and flexible element to interpreting both responsibilities and capabilities'.[38] It allows for a much more tailored and 'complex' approach to climate responsibility, broadening the parameters for differentiation with a wider array of criteria – such as past, current and projected emissions, financial and technical capabilities, human capacity, population size, other demographic criteria, abatement costs, opportunity costs, skills, etc.[39] The dynamic component of this element also allows for the 'upward adjustment' of states' efforts, because as national circumstances evolve, so does the formulation of the common but differentiated responsibility of states.[40] In this sense, the addition of the phrase 'in light of different national circumstances' represents a strong departure from binary differentiation seen in previous climate treaties, requiring instead a strongly contextualised and fluid formulation of both climate responsibilities and capabilities.

The following section seeks to outline how the responsibility for livestock emissions reduction is currently misallocated with respect to these different elements. Additionally, it discusses how the CBDRRC principle can be utilised to formulate fairer climate solutions for livestock emissions reduction, particularly in relation to ensuring affluence is not neglected as a driver of livestock emissions.

The Current Misallocation of Responsibility for Livestock Emissions Reduction under the CBDRRC Principle

The principle of CBDRRC can shed light on the current misallocation of responsibility for reducing emissions from the agricultural sector. As mentioned previously, a divide between wealthier and poorer states or groups in relation to their agricultural emissions reduction strategies (or lack thereof) was found across the legal regimes analysed. Although developed countries are supposed to be 'leading the way' for

[37] Voigt and Ferreira (n 25) 287.
[38] ibid 294.
[39] ibid.
[40] ibid 303.

climate change mitigation under the CBDRRC principle, it was found that this has largely not been the case for livestock emissions. The rest of this section addresses each of the elements of the CBDRRC principle and why climate responsibility is currently misallocated in relation to this, particularly in relation to affluent actors.

Common but Differentiated Responsibilities

Although the livestock production of developed countries is often more environmentally efficient, 'imported emissions' that are embodied in livestock imports still remain high and affluent consumption patterns underpin rapidly rising livestock emissions trajectories for the future. Despite this, agricultural emissions have been more commonly framed in terms of food security or adaptation, leading to technical fixes being promoted as livestock climate solutions, rather than solutions targeting developed countries' consumption. As a result, responsibility was often laid at the door of developing countries rather than developed countries, and wealthier actors have often failed to include livestock emissions in their mitigation coverage.

This is incompatible with the concept of 'common but differentiated responsibilities' as developed countries are not contributing adequately to the 'common' goal of addressing climate change while their lack of action persists. In particular, developed countries are supposed to 'lead the way', even where climate responsibilities are differentiated between different state parties. Whilst developing countries continue to face the brunt of agricultural emission reduction pressure under international climate policy-making, the principle of CBDRRC is not respected in relation to livestock emissions mitigation. Although a nascent move towards 'better' agricultural emissions mitigation was identified in developed regions, such as considering the role of 'healthy sustainable diets' as a mitigation strategy, these commitments are currently weak. They must be solidified and furthered to ensure developed-country responsibility is sufficiently ambitious and equitable under the CBDRRC principle.

Respective Capabilities

In a similar vein, food security or socioeconomic concerns, such as adaptation to climate change, may be viewed as key examples of factors that limit developing countries' capabilities to contribute to livestock emissions reductions. Yet currently it is developing countries, not developed countries, that continue to lead the way in agricultural emissions mitigation. This is despite developed countries' (generally) lower levels of climate vulnerability and higher levels of food security and greater technical and financial capacity that would enable them to undertake livestock emissions mitigation. Consequently, the relative inaction of developed-country actors on livestock emissions reduction can be seen as inconsistent with the principle of CBDRRC.

In Light of Different National Circumstances

Lastly, this inconsistency is further exacerbated when additional national circumstances of developed countries are considered. For example, in relation to livestock consumption, the highest consumers of meat are wealthier nations, with the average European and North American consuming almost 80 and over 110 kg of meat per year, respectively.[41] By contrast, regions such as sub-Saharan Africa, or India and China have lower consumption of these goods per capita, in addition to lower human development indicators in general. Whilst the less efficient nature of developing-country livestock production is a potential national circumstance that could be taken into consideration when differentiating between levels of climate responsibility for livestock solutions, the fact that developed countries fail to address their high levels of consumption ignores a fundamental 'national circumstance' that is driving their contribution to global livestock emissions.

High consumption of livestock goods among the wealthy elite in non-developed countries could also be considered as a relevant national circumstance for developing countries to consider in order to formulate more ambitious livestock emissions mitigation strategies. However, this will be discussed in the subsequent section that outlines how livestock emissions reduction should be understood and conceptualised under the CBDRRC principle to secure better responsibility attribution for livestock emissions mitigation between different types of actors.

Reconceptualising Current Understanding of the CBDRRC Principle for the Livestock Sector

This section seeks to reconceptualise the current understanding and consideration of the CBDRRC principle for livestock emissions mitigation to ensure fairer responsibility attribution for its costs. It is argued that this can be achieved in three ways: (1) recognising the emissions contribution of livestock systems beyond those in less efficient developing countries; (2) partially reconceptualising the principle of CBDRRC to include consumption and the mitigation responsibility stemming from it for more affluent actors; and (3) to use the phrase 'in light of national circumstances' to begin to derive responsibility for wealthy consumers in developing countries for livestock emissions and avoid any 'hiding behind the poor' in terms of agricultural sector mitigation.[42]

[41] See more in H Ritchie and M Roser, 'Meat and Dairy Production' [2017] *Our World in Data* https://ourworldindata.org/meat-production, accessed 11 September 2020.

[42] For the original use of this terminology, see S Chakravarty and MV Ramana, 'The Hiding Behind the Poor Debate: A Synthetic Overview' in *Handbook of Climate Change and India* (Routledge, 2014) www.taylorfrancis.com/books/9780203153284, accessed 3 November 2020.

Recognising the Emissions Contribution of Efficient Livestock Systems

Currently, livestock emissions are framed as a problem stemming from less efficient livestock production in developing countries, rather than developed countries where production may be more efficient, or emissions for the sector have stagnated. To take better account of the principle of CBDRRC, the role of these more efficient livestock production systems should also be recognised as playing a role in contributing to livestock emissions.[43] This in turn would ensure that developed countries make the most ambitious possible contribution towards the common global responsibility for the sector's mitigation. Whilst having more efficient production per unit of livestock product, there are still mitigation contributions that can be made by developed-country actors, such as improvements in internal agri-environmental policy. Moreover, there are steps that can be taken by developed countries in relation to their high levels of consumption (to be discussed further below).

Through recognising the role of developed-country production in also driving global livestock emissions, the CBDRRC principle is better reflected in climate solutions. Particularly given the stronger capabilities of developed countries to implement livestock emissions reduction strategies with less significant trade-offs to human development, ambitious action should be undertaken to ensure they are 'leading the way' and contributing towards collective action for agricultural emissions mitigation.

Reconceptualising CBDRRC to Include Consumption

Beyond this, this book argues for a partial reconceptualisation of the principle of CBDRRC to include responsibility for consumption as well as production. Currently, the UNFCCC system allocates responsibility on a production-based basis.[44] If consumption was recognised as a driver of emissions (or at least a relevant 'national circumstance' to be considered in climate responsibility) the scope of those needing to contribute towards livestock emissions reduction becomes wide enough to include high-consuming developed countries.[45]

[43] For more on the efficiency of production, see the introduction to climate change and the cattle sector chapter of this book.

[44] For more on the possibility of utilising empirical-consumption-based accounting methods under the climate regime, see M Grasso, 'The Political Feasibility of Consumption-Based Carbon Accounting' (2016) 21 *New Political Economy* 401; Dario Caro et al, 'Mapping the International Flows of GHG Emissions within a More Feasible Consumption-Based Framework' (2017) 147 *Journal of Cleaner Production* 142.

[45] For arguments surrounding of whether, and if so when, it is appropriate for the European Union to include extraterritorial GHG emissions within the scope of its climate change laws thereby using its market power to extend the geographical reach of its mitigation efforts generally, see J Scott, 'The

If the political choice is made to recognise the role of consumption in driving livestock emissions, developed countries will be seen to have responsibility in addressing the emissions stemming from their consumption of livestock goods. Thus, countries such as EU Member States that import forest and ecosystem risk agricultural goods from high-risk deforestation areas in South America will also be seen to have additional responsibility for tackling livestock emissions that are largely driven by their consumption levels.[46] Through this reframing of responsibility in the livestock sector, reduction efforts can be more fairly attributed between developing and developed countries, with developed countries significantly increasing their efforts in line with the real agricultural emissions impact from their consumption.

Following this reconceptualisation, livestock emissions mitigation responsibility for developed countries can stretch beyond technical efficiency improvements in internal agricultural policy to include actions such as technology transfer and financial assistance to developing agricultural sectors from which developed countries are importing their agricultural goods. Moreover, solutions, such as dietary change (with or without making reference to synergies with public health goals), can be pursued to help reduce emissions stemming from their consumption.

Recognising the Role of Affluent Consumers in Developing Countries

Lastly, the CBDRRC principle should be understood in a way that also recognises the responsibility of significant groups of affluent, high-consuming people who live in states that are comparatively poor overall. Through the phrase 'in light of different national circumstances', a political choice to recognise wealth amongst the 'consumer elite' or the 'super affluent'[47] as a relevant factor in determining respective levels of climate responsibility and mitigation capabilities can be made. Through this, the wealthiest classes who are consuming the highest levels of meat in industrialising countries can also be targeted by livestock emissions mitigation and, thus, wealthy 'consumer elites' are unable to 'hide behind the poor' in their state.[48]

The global middle class is set to be the most significant driver of meat consumption in the coming years and capturing this 'consumer elite' enables a pathway for

Geographical Scope of the EU's Climate Responsibilities' (2015) 17 *Cambridge Yearbook of European Legal Studies* 92.

[46] See this exact argument again in Marín Durán and Scott (n 7) 257–61.

[47] This terminology is coined from E Houzer and I Scoones, *Are Livestock Always Bad for the Planet? Rethinking the Protein Transition and Climate Change Debates* (PASTRES, 2021). See also similar discussion of the demographic, instead coined as the 'super-affluent', in T Wiedmann et al, 'Scientists' Warning on Affluence' (2020) 11 *Nature Communications* 3107.

[48] For critical discussion on this, again see Chakravarty and Ramana (n 42).

the trajectory of livestock emissions to be sufficiently addressed, whilst not disadvantaging more vulnerable groups who rely upon livestock for their well-being or livelihood. Of course, wealthy nations should be leading the way in livestock emissions reductions and not be allowed to remain complicit in their respective levels of inaction, but through this reconceptualization of the CBDRRC principle future emissions trajectories for the sector could also be fairly addressed.

This conclusion only provides the initial outline of this perspective on the issue of cattle emissions, and how this might aid finding equitable and ambitious livestock emissions mitigation solutions. Any policies will have to take into account the nuances of different demographics within a national context. For example, a meat tax in high-consuming jurisdictions may be one way to reduce consumption of high-emitting dietary components such as meat.[49] However, such taxes are often contentious to due distributional concerns of the tax burden on poorer households.[50] This has the potential to not sit comfortably with broader principles of environmental justice,[51] and policies targeting wealthier actors must seek to avoid unintended negative consequences for poor or vulnerable groups, such as pregnant women or children and those living in poverty.

These takeaways begin to open the door towards understanding climate justice[52] issues in relation to the agricultural sector, in addition to addressing the future emissions trajectory of the sector. Whilst this book is diagnostic in the main and its analysis has made the issue of affluence and livestock emissions more visible, the following section seeks to provide tentative suggestions for future areas of study to address affluence in the agricultural sector to achieve a fairer and more ambitious livestock emissions mitigation. Comment is then provided on the broader importance of this book's conclusion for other environmental (or even certain social) issues.

Tentative Suggestions for the Future to Build on Existing Work Being Done

Numerous options exist to better account for the role of affluent actors in driving the predicted growth in livestock emissions. As mentioned above, the main purpose of this conclusion was to reconceptualise the understanding of CBDRRC

[49] See more in M Springmann et al, 'Health-Motivated Taxes on Red and Processed Meat: A Modelling Study on Optimal Tax Levels and Associated Health Impacts' (2018) 13 *PLoS ONE* e0204139.

[50] See discussion in F Funke et al, 'Toward Optimal Meat Pricing: Is It Time to Tax Meat Consumption?' (2022) 16 *Review of Environmental Economics and Policy* 219.

[51] Which, under Gonzalez's definition, includes elements of social injustice because environmental degradation is 'inextricably intertwined with deeper structural ills, such as poverty and racism'. See C Gonzalez, 'Environmental Justice, Human Rights, and the Global South' (2015) 13 *Santa Clara Journal of International Law* 151.

[52] See particularly part IV in J Dehm for a critical discussion of climate justice in the literature and international climate regime, 'Carbon Colonialism or Climate Justice: Interrogating the International Climate Regime from a TWAIL Perspective' (2016) 33 *Windsor Yearbook of Access to Justice* 129.

for livestock emissions mitigation to encourage greater responsibility for affluent actors, rather than suggest a definitive list of potential emissions solutions. The range of options in the livestock emissions toolkit can be wide-ranging, from undoing legally embedded market distortions or removing protectionist agricultural subsidies to the introduction of a meat tax, as previously discussed.[53] In fact, what this toolkit looks like will largely depend on the 'national circumstances' referred to in the breakdown of CBDRRC above. The most important aspect of this conclusion is then to broaden the current conceptualisation of *who* is responsible for taking agri-climate action, given the evasive role of wealthy actors previously in agri-climate governance.

Nevertheless, there are some interesting examples of work being done in this vein that are worthy of further monitoring and assessment to further develop just livestock emissions solutions in the future. For example, on the international level, informal initiatives such as I-CAN are emerging from the COP processes to address sustainability and nutrition. Whilst language surrounding full food system approaches was shied away from at COP27 in the Sharm El Sheikh Joint Work decision, there are still global parties that want agri-climate responsibilities to include broader demand-side measures to address the full emissions picture of livestock production. Work by the FAO (and the surrounding technical communities) should be continued to help shed further light and awareness on the issue of livestock emissions internationally, and the role of high-consuming actors in driving the sector's climate impact. For example, exercises completed by the FAO on national agri-environmental policies, such as their NDC[54] and national food-based dietary guidelines analysis,[55] should be continued to provide a basis for critical appraisal of different countries' actions on livestock emissions.

Examples of unilateral actions addressing livestock consumption in affluent countries are also already emerging and can provide useful exemplars for global parties' legal and policy toolkits for addressing livestock emissions more fully. For example, the EU Commission's new Due Diligence Regulation for forest and ecosystem risks commodities is an innovative example of a policy that seeks to address the sustainability of its agricultural supply chains collaboratively in a way that could be deemed WTO compliant.[56] The Due Diligence Regulation can be seen as an example of a policy that should be monitored for its effectiveness and leaned upon for understanding the future legal possibilities for addressing livestock emissions that different countries and actors could use to address the impact of their consumption habits beyond their borders in the absence of international standards being agreed.

[53] For more on these potential solutions, see R Williams, 'Law and Policy Can Support Sustainable Diets' (2023) 4 *Nature Communications Earth & Environment* 375.

[54] Strohmaier et al (n 5).

[55] Gonzalez Fischer and Garnett (n 14).

[56] See more in the previous chapter, and in Marín Durán and Scott (n 46).

Recognising Affluence Beyond Livestock Emissions Mitigation

Beyond agriculture, by reconceptualising the CBDRRC principle to reconsider livestock emissions, comparable GHG emissions driven by the global elite can be approached from a similar lens. A recent UN report suggests that the richest 1 percent of the global population emits more than twice the amount of emissions than the poorest 50 percent.[57] Moreover, it reports that rich countries have higher consumption-based emissions than territorial-based emissions.[58] As a result, the role of addressing consumption by wealthier actors to achieve just responses to the climate crisis is not unique to the livestock or agricultural sector example, and can be utilised across different sectors and climate issues – perhaps even in justifying the responsibility of actors beyond the state, such as corporations.[59]

Beyond climate change, this issue of affluence underpins a multitude of other environmental issues. The relevance of the CBDRRC principle, and differentiated responsibilities more broadly, has been seen as relevant across a host of other international environmental law instruments and regimes, such as the Convention on Biodiversity, the UN Convention of Combating Desertification and the Montreal Protocol.[60] Other environmental issues currently or yet to be addressed on the international level can benefit from this expanded conceptualisation of CBDRRC to include affluence-driven consumption. For example, the new Plastics Treaty (which may be in force as soon as 2025) will probably have a need for differentiated responsibilities among global parties.[61] Almost half of all plastic waste is reported to be generated in OECD countries.[62] It is also reported that most rich countries are net exporters of plastic waste, even sparking China to ban the import of most types of plastics waste in 2017.[63] Utilising this broader conceptualisation of CBDRRC can help to shed valuable light on dynamics of responsibility among global parties in negotiations such as this and future environmental issues yet to be accounted for the international level – whether that be fast fashion, aviation or even cryptocurrency.

[57] See XXV, Executive Summary in *Emissions Gap Report 2020* (United Nations, 2021).

[58] ibid XV, Executive Summary.

[59] For more on this concept, see P Castro, 'Common But Differentiated Responsibilities Beyond the Nation State: How Is Differential Treatment Addressed in Transnational Climate Governance Initiatives?' (2016) 5 *Transnational Environmental Law* 379.

[60] P Pauw et al (eds), *Different Perspectives on Differentiated Responsibilities: A State-of-the-Art Review of the Notion of Common but Differentiated Responsibilities in International Negotiations* (Deutsche Institut für Entwicklungspolitik 2014) 30–48.

[61] E Bryce, 'First Steps Agreed on Plastics Treaty after Breakthrough at Paris Talks', *The Guardian*, 6 June 2023, www.theguardian.com/environment/2023/jun/06/first-steps-agreed-on-plastics-treaty-after-breakthrough-at-paris-talks, accessed 8 September 2023.

[62] See OECD, *Global Plastics Outlook: Economic Drivers, Environmental Impacts and Policy Options* (OECD, 2022) www.oecd-ilibrary.org/environment/global-plastics-outlook_de747aef-en, accessed 8 September 2023.

[63] H Ritchie, 'Ocean Plastics: How Much Do Rich Countries Contribute by Shipping Their Waste Overseas?' [2022] *Our World in Data*, https://ourworldindata.org/plastic-waste-trade, accessed 8 September 2023.

As the global middle class grows in size with economic growth, developed countries will need to be leading the way in addressing the climate impacts of their consumption to ensure environmental justice is at the forefront of environmental responses.

More broadly, equity[64] considerations are becoming more and more important in international law in times of geopolitical insecurity. The economic impact of the COVID-19 pandemic and the Russia-Ukraine war are particularly felt by developing countries. Most countries have suffered economic losses during these times, but inequality in global economic power has increasingly worsened for developing countries – placing strain on economic development, food, energy supply and increasing the incidence of humanitarian crises. For example, levels of affluence (or a lack thereof) determined much of the vaccine and personal protective equipment supply inequality experienced during the COVID-19 pandemic (coincidentally with livestock production also being cited as one of zoonotic disease's main drivers more generally[65]).[66] The new 'Pandemic Treaty' can learn from international climate law's experience and operationalisation of provisions underpinned by equity concerns, such as the principle of CBDRRC and this book's takeaways on the role of affluence and the role it should form within it.[67] Greater focus in international law on the consideration of affluence can help to ensure proper levels of support are provided to developing regions and responsibility evasion by the wealthy is not by-passed in international legal responses to issues being faced in current global society.

Conclusion

Overall, this conclusion provided a summary of the vast material covered in this book and the key findings derived from its analysis. Both important common themes and a main common tension were identified from the book to provide a broad, macro-level analysis of the common issues arising in relation to the international governance of the cattle sector and climate change.

Having regard for the key takeaways outlined, the book concludes that a fairer solution to tackling livestock emissions should be found in the future. It argued that affluence is often a 'evasive' factor in taking steps to reduce cattle emissions. This means that developed countries, and even wealthier groups within developing countries, do not contribute their fair share towards agricultural emissions

[64] For more on the meaning of equity in international law, see Sands et al (n 24) 126–27.

[65] Seeeg J Brice, The Relation between Different Zoonotic Pandemics and the Livestock Sector (Committee on the Environment, Public Health, and Food Safety, Policy Department of Economic, Scientific and Quality of Life Policies, 2021).

[66] See more on this at the WHO, UNDP, and Oxford COVID-19 Government Response Tracker's Vaccine Equity Tracker, accessible here: https://data.undp.org/vaccine-equity/.

[67] For examples of discussion of the principle of CBDRRC in the context of the new Pandemic treaty, see S Switzer et al, 'Equity in Global Health Law – Policy Brief' (Scottish Council for Global Affairs, ESRC IAA Policy Impact Fund, 2023).

mitigation. This normative finding is important when considering what steps should be taken to bend the future livestock emissions trajectory curve downwards compared to business-as-usual. It is also important to ensure respect for a key principle of international climate law, namely the principle of CBDRRC.

On the basis of this finding, a better understanding of climate responsibility attribution between wealthier and poorer actors was outlined for the agricultural sector. It is hoped that this analysis, in addition to these brief suggestions for further research, could help identify future pathways towards a more effective and fairer framework for reducing emissions from beef and dairy (and even beyond).

BIBLIOGRAPHY

Books

Abidin H, *The Protection of Indigenous Peoples and Reduction for Forest Carbon Emissions: The REDD+ Regime and International Law* (Brill Nijhoff, 2015)
Adams CJ, *The Sexual Politics of Meat: A Feminist-Vegetarian Critical Theory* (Continuum, 1990)
Ansell C, *What's the Beef? The Contested Governance of European Food Safety* (MIT Press, 2006)
Ayres I and Braithwaite J, *Responsive Regulation: Transcending the Deregulation Debate* (Oxford University Press, 1992)
Fiddes, N, *Meat: A Natural Symbol* (Routledge, 1991).
International Agency for Research on Cancer, *Red Meat and Processed Meat* (WHO, 2018)
Jordan AJ and Moore B, *Durable by Design? Policy Feedback in a Changing Climate* (Cambridge University Press, 2020)
Kemmerer L, *Animals and World Religions* (Oxford University Press, 2012)
Natarajan U and Dehm J, *Locating Nature: Making and Unmaking International Law* (Cambridge University Press, 2022)
O'Broin, S et al, *70 Years of FAO (1945–2015)* (FAO, 2015).
Oppenlander, R, *Food Choice and Sustainability: Eating Less Meat, and Taking Baby Steps Won't Work* (Langdon Street Press, 2013)
Perren, R, *Taste, Trade and Technology* (Ashgate, 2006).
Pollack MA and Dunoff JL, *Interdisciplinary Perspectives on International Law and International Relations* (Cambridge University Press, 2013)
Rajamani, L, *Differential Treatment in International Environmental Law* (Oxford University Press, 2006)
Sands P et al, *Principles of International Environmental Law* (Cambridge University Press, 2018)
Smil, V, *Should We Eat Meat?* (Wiley Blackwell, 2013)
Valenze D, *Milk: A Local and Global History* (Yale University Press, 2011)
Wallbott L and Recio E, *Practicing Human Rights across Scale: Indigenous Peoples' Affectedness and Recognition in REDD+ Governance* (Routledge, 2020)
Warren, W, *Meat Makes People Powerful* (University of Iowa Press, 2018).

Book Chapters

Chakravarty S and Ramana MV, 'The Hiding Behind the Poor Debate: A Synthetic Overview' in *Handbook of Climate Change and India* (Routledge, 2014)
Charnovitz S, 'Judicial Independence in the World Trade Organization' in *The Path of World Trade Law in the 21st Century* (World Scientific, 2014)
Christianen, J, 'Four Stages of Social Movements', in *Sociology Reference Guide: Theories of Social Movements*, 2nd edn (Salem Press 2016)
Di Pietro Paolo L, 'From the Cancun Adaptation Framework to the Paris Agreement' in M del Pilar Bueno Rubial and L Siegele, (eds), *Negotiating Climate Change Adaptation: The Common Position of the Group of 77 and China* (Springer, 2020)
Eickhout B et al, 'The Impact of Environmental and Climate Constraints on Global Food Supply' in TW Hertel, SK Rose and RSJ Tol (eds), *Economic Analysis of Land Use in Global Climate Change Policy* (Routledge, 2009)

Fraser D, 'Animal Welfare and the Intensification of Animal Production' in P Thompson (ed), *The Ethics of Intensification*, vol 16 (Springer, 2008)

Galperín C and Miguez I, 'Green Box Subsidies and Trade-Distorting Support: Is There a Cumulative Impact?' in R Melendez-Ortiz et al (eds) *Agricultural Subsidies in the WTO Green Box* (Cambridge University Press, 2009)

Ghaleigh NS, 'Science and Climate Change Law – The Role of the IPCC in International Decision-Making' in C Carlarne et al (eds), *The Oxford Handbook of International Climate Change Law* (Oxford University Press, 2016)

Goossaert V, 'The Beef Taboo and the Sacrificial Structure of Late Imperial Chinese Society' in R Sterckx (ed), *Of Tripod and Palate: Food, Politics, and Religion in Traditional China* (Palgrave Macmillan, 2005)

Grossman GM and Krueger AB, 'Environmental Impacts of a North American Free Trade Agreement' in PM Garber (ed), *The US–Mexico Free Trade Agreement* (MIT Press, 1993)

Kissinger G, 'Linking Forests and Food Production in the REDD+ Context' in M Behnassi, O O Pollmann and G Kissinger, (eds), *Sustainable Food Security in the Era of Local and Global Environmental Change* (Springer, 2013)

McLaren S, 'Sustainable Diets: Eating Within Planetary Boundaries' in *New Zealand Land & Food Annual 2017* (Massey University Press, 2017) 131

Menzi H et al, 'Impacts of Intensive Livestock Production and Manure Management on the Environment' in H Steinfeld et al (eds) *Livestock in a Changing Landscape* (Island Press, 2010)

Ronald S and Tsai C, 'The Environmental Impact of Green Box Subsidies: Exploring the Linkages' in R Melendez-Ortiz, C Bellmann and J Hepburn (eds), *Agricultural Subsidies in the WTO Green Box* (Cambridge University Press, 2009).

Smith, F, 'Mind the Gap: "Greening" Direct Payments and the World Trade Organization' in *Research Handbook on EU Agriculture Law* (Edward Elgar, 2015).

Solomon S and Intergovernmental Panel on Climate Change and Intergovernmental Panel on Climate Change (eds), '2.10.2 Direct Global Warming Potentials' in *Climate Change 2007: The Physical Science Basis: Contribution of Working Group I to the Fourth Assessment Report of the Intergovernmental Panel on Climate Change* (Cambridge University Press, 2007)

Young MA, 'Introduction: The Productive Friction between Regimes' in MA Young (ed), *Regime Interaction in International Law* (Cambridge University Press, 2011)

Journal Articles

Abbott K, 'The Transnational Regime Complex for Climate Change' (2011) 20 *Environment and Planning C: Government and Policy* 571.

Abbott KW, 'Orchestrating Experimentation in Non-State Environmental Commitments' (2017) 26 *Environmental Politics* 738

Abbott KW and Snidal D, 'Hard and Soft Law in International Governance' (2000) 54 *International Organization* 421

Ackerman F and Heinzerling L, 'Pricing the Priceless: Cost–Benefit Analysis of Environmental Protection' (2002) 150 *University of Pennsylvania Law Review* 1553

Alexander P et al, 'Human Appropriation of Land for Food: The Role of Diet' (2016) 41 *Global Environmental Change* 88

Alexander P et al, 'Losses, Inefficiencies and Waste in the Global Food System' (2017) 153 *Agricultural Systems* 190

Anderson K, 'Agricultural Trade Liberalisation and the Environment: A Global Perspective' (1992) 15 *World Economy* 153

Araújo SMVG de, 'Environmental Policy in the Bolsonaro Government: The Response of Environmentalists in the Legislative Arena' (2020) 14 *Brazilian Political Science Review* e0005

Asselt H van, 'Managing the Fragmentation of International Environmental Law: Forests at the Intersection of the Climate and Biodiversity Regimes' (2012) 44 *International Law and Politics* 1205
Balogh JM and Jámbor A, 'The Environmental Impacts of Agricultural Trade: A Systematic Literature Review' (2020) 12 *Sustainability* 1152
Bandopadhyay A, 'The Colonial Legacy of Forest Policies in India' (2010) 38(1) *Social Scientist* 53
Barnard N, Levin S and Trapp C, 'Meat Consumption as a Risk Factor for Type 2 Diabetes' (2014) 6 *Nutrients* 897
Barnard ND et al, 'A Low-Fat Vegan Diet and a Conventional Diabetes Diet in the Treatment of Type 2 Diabetes: A Randomized, Controlled, 74-Wk Clinical Trial 1234' (2009) 89 *American Journal of Clinical Nutrition* 1588S
Barnard ND et al, 'A Low-Fat Vegan Diet Elicits Greater Macronutrient Changes, but Is Comparable in Adherence and Acceptability, Compared with a More Conventional Diabetes Diet among Individuals with Type 2 Diabetes' (2009) 109 *Journal of the American Dietetic Association* 263
Barnes A, 'Overweight versus Obese: Different Risk and Different Management' (2015) 42 *Texas Heart Institute Journal* 237
Batista E et al, 'Large-Scale Pasture Restoration May Not Be the Best Option to Reduce Greenhouse Gas Emissions in Brazil' (2019) 14 *Environmental Research Letters* 125009
Benartzi S et al, 'Should Governments Invest More in Nudging?' (2017) 28 *Psychological Science* 1041
Benford RD and Snow DA, 'Framing Processes and Social Movements: An Overview and Assessment' (2000) 26 *Annual Review of Sociology* 611
Berners-Lee M et al, 'Current Global Food Production Is Sufficient to Meet Human Nutritional Needs in 2050 Provided There Is Radical Societal Adaptation' (2018) 6 *Elementa* 52
Bloomfield MJ, 'Is Forest Certification a Hegemonic Force? The FSC and its Challengers' (2012) 21 *Journal of Environment & Development* 391
Timmer M, 'CO_2 Emissions Production-Based Accounting vs Consumption: Insights from the WIOD Databases' (2020) 23 *Review of International Economics* 575
Bondi SA and Lieuw K, 'Excessive Cow's Milk Consumption and Iron Deficiency in Toddlers: Two Unusual Presentations and Review' (2009) 1 *Infant, Child, & Adolescent Nutrition* 133
Bouvard V et al, 'Carcinogenicity of Consumption of Red and Processed Meat' (2015) 16 *Lancet Oncology* 1599
Boyte R, 'Common but Differentiated Responsibilities: Adjusting the Developing/Developed Dichotomy in International Environmental Law' (2010) 14 *New Zealand Journal of Environmental Law* 63
Bu M et al, 'Corporate Social Responsibility and the Pollution Haven Hypothesis: Evidence from Multinationals' Investment Decision in China' (2013) 20 *Asia-Pacific Journal of Accounting & Economics* 85
Bulut U, Ucler G and Inglesi-Lotz R, 'Does the Pollution Haven Hypothesis Prevail in Turkey? Empirical Evidence from Nonlinear Smooth Transition Models' (2021) 28 *Environmental Science and Pollution Research* 38563
Bustamante M et al, 'Estimating Greenhouse Gas Emissions from Cattle Raising in Brazil' (2012) 115 *Climatic Change* 559
Buttar H et al, 'Prevention of Cardiovascular Diseases: Role of Exercise, Dietary Interventions, Obesity and Smoking Cessation' (2005) 10(4) *Experimental Clinical Cardiology* 229
Cabello J and Gilbertson T, 'A Colonial Mechanism to Enclose Lands: A Critical Review of Two REDD+-Focused Special Issues' (2012) *Ephemera Theory & Politics in Organization* 162
Caney S, 'Two Kinds of Climate Justice: Avoiding Harm and Sharing Burdens: Two Kinds of Climate Justice' (2014) 22 *Journal of Political Philosophy* 125
Capper JL, 'Is the Grass Always Greener? Comparing the Environmental Impact of Conventional, Natural and Grass-Fed Beef Production Systems' (2012) 2 *Animals* 127
Cardwell M and Smith F, 'Renegotiation of the WTO Agreement on Agriculture: Accommodating the New Big Issues' (2013) 62 *ICLQ* 865
Caro D et al, 'Mapping the International Flows of GHG Emissions within a More Feasible Consumption-Based Framework' (2017) 147 *Journal of Cleaner Production* 142

Cassidy ES et al, 'Redefining Agricultural Yields: From Tonnes to People Nourished per Hectare' (2013) 8 *Environmental Research Letters* 034015

Castro P, 'Common But Differentiated Responsibilities Beyond the Nation State: How Is Differential Treatment Addressed in Transnational Climate Governance Initiatives?' (2016) 5 *Transnational Environmental Law* 379

Ceddia MG, Gunter U and Corriveau-Bourque A, 'Land Tenure and Agricultural Expansion in Latin America: The Role of Indigenous Peoples' and Local Communities' Forest Rights' (2015) 35 *Global Environmental Change* 316

Chai W et al, 'Dietary Red and Processed Meat Intake and Markers of Adiposity and Inflammation: The Multiethnic Cohort Study' (2017) 36 *Journal of the American College of Nutrition* 378

Chan JM et al, 'Dairy Products, Calcium, and Prostate Cancer Risk in the Physicians' Health Study' (2001) 74 *American Journal of Clinical Nutrition* 549

Chand R, 'The Global Food Crisis: Causes, Severity and Outlook' (2008) 43(26) *Economic and Political Weekly* 115

Chaudhary A and Krishna V, 'Country-Specific Sustainable Diets Using Optimization Algorithm' (2019) 53 *Environmental Science & Technology* 7694

Chazdon RL et al, 'When Is a Forest a Forest? Forest Concepts and Definitions in the Era of Forest and Landscape Restoration' (2016) 45 *Ambio* 538

Clémençon R, 'The Two Sides of the Paris Climate Agreement: Dismal Failure or Historic Breakthrough?' (2016) 25 *Journal of Environment & Development* 3

Colchester M, 'Do Commodity Certification Systems Uphold Indigenous Peoples' Rights? Lessons from the Roundtable on Sustainable Palm Oil and Forest Stewardship Council' (2016) 21 *Policy Matters*

Cole M and Elliott R, 'Determining the Trade-Environment Composition Effect: The Role of Capital, Labor and Environmental Regulations' (2003) 46 *Journal of Environmental Economics and Management* 363

Colli F, 'The EU–Mercosur Agreement: Towards Integrated Climate Policy?' (2019) 57 *European Policy Brief* 5

Collins YA, 'Colonial Residue: REDD+, Territorialisation and the Racialized Subject in Guyana and Suriname' (2019) 106 *Geoforum* 38

Condon BJ, 'Climate Change and Unresolved Issues in WTO Law' (2009) 12 *Journal of International Economic Law* 895

Copeland BR and Taylor MS, 'Trade, Growth and the Environment' (2004) 46 *Journal of Economic Literature* 7

Corbera E, Estrada M and Brown K, 'Reducing Greenhouse Gas Emissions from Deforestation and Forest Degradation in Developing Countries: Revisiting the Assumptions' (2010) 100 *Climatic Change* 355

Cottrell MP and Trubek D, 'Law as Problem Solving: Standards, Networks, Experimentation and Deliberation in Global Space' (2012) 21 *Transnational Law and Contemporary Problems* 359

Davis KF et al, 'Meeting Future Food Demand with Current Agricultural Resources' (2016) 39 *Global Environmental Change* 125

De Búrca G, Keohane RO and Sabel C, 'Global Experimentalist Governance' (2014) 44 *British Journal of Political Science* 477

Defries R et al, 'Deforestation Driven by Urban Population Growth and Agricultural Trade in the Twenty-First Century' (2010) 3 *Nature Geoscience* 178

Dehm J, 'Carbon Colonialism or Climate Justice: Interrogating the International Climate Regime from a TWAIL Perspective' (2016) 33 *Windsor Yearbook of Access to Justice* 129

Destek MA and Okumus I, 'Does Pollution Haven Hypothesis Hold in Newly Industrialized Countries? Evidence from Ecological Footprint' (2019) 26 *Environmental Science and Pollution Research* 23689

Devi SM et al, 'An Outline of Meat Consumption in the Indian Population – A Pilot Review' (2014) 34 *Korean Journal for Food Science of Animal Resources* 507

Dingwerth K, 'North–South Parity in Global Governance: The Affirmative Procedures of the Forest Stewardship Council' (2008) 14 *Global Governance* 53

Dinu M et al, 'Vegetarian, Vegan Diets and Multiple Health Outcomes: A Systematic Review with Meta-Analysis of Observational Studies' (2017) 57 *Critical Reviews in Food Science and Nutrition* 3640
Downs GW and Jones MA, 'Reputation, Compliance, and International Law' (2002) 31 *Journal of Legal Studies* S95
Drabo A, 'Climate Change Mitigation and Agricultural Development Models: Primary Commodity Exports or Local Consumption Production?' (2017) 137 *Ecological Economics* 110
Dupuits E and Cronkleton P, 'Indigenous Tenure Security and Local Participation in Climate Mitigation Programs: Exploring the Institutional Gaps of REDD+ Implementation in the Peruvian Amazon' (2020) 30 *Environmental Policy and Governance* 209
Eckersley R, 'The Big Chill: The WTO and Multilateral Environmental Agreements' (2004) 4 *Global Environmental Politics* 24
Escobar H, 'Amazon Fires Clearly Linked to Deforestation, Scientists Say' (2019) 365 *Science* 853
Feskanich D, Willett WC and Colditz GA, 'Calcium, Vitamin D, Milk Consumption, and Hip Fractures: A Prospective Study among Postmenopausal Women' (2003) 77 *American Journal of Clinical Nutrition* 504
Firbank L and et al, 'Managing Set-Aside Land for Wildlife' (ITE Research Publication No 7, Natural Environment Research Council, 1993)
Flachsbarth I et al, 'The Role of Latin America's Land and Water Resources for Global Food Security: Environmental Trade-offs of Future Food Production Pathways' (2015) 10 *PLoS ONE* e0116733
Frank S et al, 'Reducing Greenhouse Gas Emissions in Agriculture without Compromising Food Security?' (2017) 12 *Environmental Research Letters* 105004
Frankel J and Rose A, 'Is Trade Good or Bad for the Environment? Sorting Out the Causality' (2005) 87 *Review of Economics and Statistics* 85
Franzen A and Mader S, 'Consumption-Based versus Production-Based Accounting of CO_2 Emissions: Is There Evidence for Carbon Leakage?' (2018) 84 *Environmental Science & Policy* 34
Funke F et al, 'Toward Optimal Meat Pricing: Is it Time to Tax Meat Consumption?' (2022) 16 *Review of Environmental Economics and Policy* 219
Garrelts H and Flitner M, 'Governance Issues in the Ecosystem Approach: What Lessons from the Forest Stewardship Council?' (2011) 130 *European Journal of Forest Research* 395
Gatti LV et al, 'Amazonia as a Carbon Source Linked to Deforestation and Climate Change' (2021) 595 *Nature* 388
Gibbs HK et al, 'Brazil's Soy Moratorium' (2015) 347 *Science* 377
Giessen L, 'Reviewing the Main Characteristics of the International Forest Regime Complex and Partial Explanations for its Fragmentation' (2013) 15 *International Forestry Review* 60
Godden L and Tehan M, 'REDD+: Climate Justice and Indigenous and Local Community Rights in an Era of Climate Disruption' (2016) 34 *Journal of Energy & Natural Resources Law* 95
Godfray HCJ et al, 'Meat Consumption, Health, and the Environment' (2018) 361 *Science* eaam5324
Golub AA et al, 'Global Climate Policy Impacts on Livestock, Land Use, Livelihoods, and Food Security' (2013) 110 *Proceedings of the National Academy of Sciences of the United States of America* 20894
Gonzalez C, 'Bridging the North–South Divide: International Environmental Law in the Anthropocene' (2015) 32 *Pace Environmental Law Review* 29
Gonzalez C, 'Environmental Justice, Human Rights, and the Global South' (2015) 13 *Santa Clara Journal of International Law* 151
Goodman J and Roberts E, 'Is the United Nations' REDD Scheme Conservation Colonialism by Default?' (2010) 5 *International Journal of Water* 419
Grasso M, 'The Political Feasibility of Consumption-Based Carbon Accounting' (2016) 21 *New Political Economy* 401
Grossi G et al, 'Livestock and Climate Change: Impact of Livestock on Climate and Mitigation Strategies' (2019) 9 *Animal Frontiers* 69
Guthrie J, Mancino L and Lin C-TJ, 'Nudging Consumers toward Better Food Choices: Policy Approaches to Changing Food Consumption Behaviors' (2015) 32 *Psychology & Marketing* 501
Guzel AE and Okumus İ, 'Revisiting the Pollution Haven Hypothesis in ASEAN-5 Countries: New Insights from Panel Data Analysis' (2020) 27 *Environmental Science and Pollution Research* 18157

Hale T and Roger C, 'Orchestration and Transnational Climate Governance' (2013) 9(1) *Review of International Organisations* 59

Hallam D, 'International Investment in Developing Country Agriculture – Issues and Challenges' (2011) 3 *Food Security* 91

Han M et al, 'Agricultural CH_4 and N_2O Emissions of Major Economies: Consumption- vs Production-Based Perspectives' (2019) 210 *Journal of Cleaner Production* 276

Hanley-Cook GT et al, 'EAT–Lancet Diet Score Requires Minimum Intake Values to Predict Higher Micronutrient Adequacy of Diets in Rural Women of Reproductive Age from Five Low- and Middle-Income Countries' (2021) 126 *British Journal of Nutrition* 92

Harwatt H, 'Including Animal to Plant Protein Shifts in Climate Change Mitigation Policy: A Proposed Three-Step Strategy' (2019) 19 *Climate Policy* 533

Hausen H zur and Villiers E-M de, 'Dairy Cattle Serum and Milk Factors Contributing to the Risk of Colon and Breast Cancers' (2015) 137 *International Journal of Cancer* 959

Havlik P et al, 'Climate Change Mitigation through Livestock System Transitions' (2014) 111(10) *Proceedings of the National Academy of Sciences of the United States of America* 3709

Hayek MN and Garrett RD, 'Nationwide Shift to Grass-Fed Beef Requires Larger Cattle Population' (2018) 13 *Environmental Research Letters* 084005

Heilmayr R et al, 'Brazil's Amazon Soy Moratorium Reduced Deforestation' (2020) 1 *Nature Food* 801

Hett W, 'US Corn and Soybean Subsidies: WTO Litigation and Sustainable Protections' (2008) 17 *Transnational Law & Contemporary Problems* 775

Hirvonen K et al, 'Affordability of the EAT–Lancet Reference Diet: A Global Analysis' (2020) 8 *Lancet Global Health* e59

Hoffman AJ, 'Talking Past Each Other? Cultural Framing of Skeptical and Convinced Logics in the Climate Change Debate' (2011) 24(1) *Organisation & Environment* 3

Huang WM, Lee GWM and Wu CC, 'GHG Emissions, GDP Growth and the Kyoto Protocol: A Revisit of Environmental Kuznets Curve Hypothesis' (2008) 36 *Energy Policy* 239

Hulme M and Mahony M, 'Climate Change: What Do We Know about the IPCC?' (2010) 34(5) *Progress in Physical Geography: Earth and Environment* 705

Hyland JJ et al, 'The Role of Meat in Strategies to Achieve a Sustainable Diet Lower in Greenhouse Gas Emissions: A Review' (2017) 132 *Meat Science* 189

Joy MK et al, 'The Grey Water Footprint of Milk Due to Nitrate Leaching from Dairy Farms in Canterbury, New Zealand' (2022) 29 *Australasian Journal of Environmental Management* 177

Kahleova H et al, 'A Plant-Based Diet in Overweight Individuals in a 16-Week Randomized Clinical Trial: Metabolic Benefits of Plant Protein' (2018) 8 *Nutrition & Diabetes* 1

Karpoff J and Lott and J, 'The Reputational Penalties for Environmental Violations: Empirical Evidence' (2005) 48(2) *Journal of Law and Economics* 653

Keohane RO and Victor DG, 'The Regime Complex for Climate Change' (2011) 9 *Perspectives on Politics* 7

Kim JA, 'Regime Interplay: The Case of Biodiversity and Climate Change' (2004) 14 *Global Environmental Change* 315

Klinsky S and Dowlatabadi H, 'Conceptualizations of Justice in Climate Policy' (2009) *Climate Policy* 22

Kroenke CH et al, 'High- and Low-Fat Dairy Intake, Recurrence, and Mortality After Breast Cancer Diagnosis' (2013) 105 *Journal of the National Cancer Institute* 616

Kuznets S, 'Economic Growth and Income Inequality' (1955) 45 *American Economic Review* 1

Lang A and Scott J, 'The Hidden World of WTO Governance' (2009) 20 *European Journal of International Law* 575

Lang ATF, 'Reflecting on "Linkage": Cognitive and Institutional Change in the International Trading System' (2007) 70 *Modern Law Review* 523

Lapola DM 'UNESP et al, 'Pervasive Transition of the Brazilian Land-Use System' (2014) *Nature Climate Change* 27

Larsson SC and Wolk A, 'Meat Consumption and Risk of Colorectal Cancer: A Meta-analysis of Prospective Studies' (2006) 119 *International Journal of Cancer* 2657

Lee DJ and Zhang J, 'Efficiency, Equity, and Environmental Implications of Trade Liberalization: A Computable General Equilibrium Analysis' (2009) 18 *Journal of International Trade & Economic Development* 347
Lesnikowski A et al, 'What Does the Paris Agreement Mean for Adaptation?' (2017) 17 *Climate Policy* 825
Li Q and Mihalache-O'Keef A, 'Modernization vs Dependency: Effects of Foreign Direct Investment on Food Security in Less Developed Countries' (2011) *International Studies Quarterly* 55(1)
Lopez R, 'The Environment as a Factor of Production: The Effects of Economic Growth and Trade Liberalization' (1994) 27 *Journal of Environmental Economics and Management* 163
Managi S, 'Trade Liberalization and the Environment: Carbon Dioxide for 1960–1999' (2004) 17 *Economics Bulletin* 1
Mann JI, 'Optimizing the Plant-Based Diet' (2000) 9 *Asia Pacific Journal of Clinical Nutrition* S60
Marín Durán G and Scott J, 'Regulating Trade in Forest-Risk Commodities: Two Cheers for the European Union' (2022) *Journal of Environmental Law* eqac002
Marteau TM et al, 'Judging Nudging: Can Nudging Improve Population Health?' (2011) 342 *British Medical Journal* d228
McEvoy CT, Temple N and Woodside JV, 'Vegetarian Diets, Low-Meat Diets and Health: A Review' (2012) 15 *Public Health Nutrition* 2287
McMacken M and Shah S, 'A Plant-Based Diet for the Prevention and Treatment of Type 2 Diabetes' (2017) 14 *Journal of Geriatric Cardiology* 342
Medina G, 'Where Are Governments Leading Their Agricultural Sectors? Comparative Lessons from Agri-environmental Measures Promoted in the US, Europe and Brazil' (2019) 27 *Estudos Sociedade e Agricultura* 5
Micha R, Michas G and Mozaffarian D, 'Unprocessed Red and Processed Meats and Risk of Coronary Artery Disease and Type 2 Diabetes – An Updated Review of the Evidence' (2012) 14 *Current Atherosclerosis Reports* 515
Michaëlsson K et al, 'Milk Intake and Risk of Mortality and Fractures in Women and Men: Cohort Studies' (2014) 349 *BMJ* g6015
Montonen J et al, 'Consumption of Red Meat and Whole-Grain Bread in Relation to Biomarkers of Obesity, Inflammation, Glucose Metabolism and Oxidative Stress' (2013) 52 *European Journal of Nutrition* 337
Moog S, Spicer A and Böhm S, 'The Politics of Multi-stakeholder Initiatives: The Crisis of the Forest Stewardship Council' (2015) 128 *Journal of Business Ethics* 469
Moomaw WR and Unruh GC, 'Are Environmental Kuznets Curves Misleading Us? The Case of CO_2 Emissions' (1997) 2 *Environment and Development Economics* 451
Morton JF, 'The Impact of Climate Change on Smallholder and Subsistence Agriculture' (2007) 104 *Proceedings of the National Academy of Sciences of the United States of America* 19680
Moutinho P, Guerra R and Azevedo-Ramos C, 'Achieving Zero Deforestation in the Brazilian Amazon: What Is Missing?' (2016) 4 *Elementa* 000125
Movassagh EZ et al, 'Tracking Dietary Patterns over 20 Years from Childhood through Adolescence into Young Adulthood: The Saskatchewan Pediatric Bone Mineral Accrual Study' (2017) 9(9) *Nutrients* 990
Myers N and Tucker R, 'Deforestation in Central America: Spanish Legacy and North American Consumers' (1987) 11(1) *Environmental Review* 55
Ngangjoh-Hodu Y, 'Relationship of GATT Article XX Exceptions to Other WTO Agreements' (2011) 80 *Nordic Journal of International Law* 219
Overdevest C and Zeitlin J, 'Assembling an Experimentalist Regime: Transnational Governance Interactions in the Forest Sector: Assembling an Experimentalist Regime' (2014) 8 *Regulation & Governance* 22
Pan A et al, 'Red Meat Consumption and Risk of Type 2 Diabetes: 3 Cohorts of US Adults and an Updated Meta-Analysis' (2011) 94 *American Journal of Clinical Nutrition* 1088
Parry M, Rosenzweig C and Livermore M, 'Climate Change, Global Food Supply and Risk of Hunger' (2005) 360 *Philosophical Transactions of the Royal Society B: Biological Sciences* 2125

Pattberg P, 'The Forest Stewardship Council: Risk and Potential of Private Forest Governance' (2005) 14 *Journal of Environment & Development* 356
Pernet, CA and Forclaz AR, 'Revisiting the Food and Agriculture Organization (FAO): International Histories of Agriculture, Nutrition, and Development' (2018) *International History Review* 41(2)
Pimentel D et al, 'Water Resources: Agricultural and Environmental Issues' (2004) 54 *BioScience* 909
Popp A, Lotze-Campen H and Bodirsky B, 'Food Consumption, Diet Shifts and Associated Non-CO_2 Greenhouse Gases from Agricultural Production' (2010) 20 *Global Environmental Change* 451
Qi L et al, 'Genetic Predisposition, Western Dietary Pattern, and the Risk of Type 2 Diabetes in Men123' (2009) 89 *American Journal of Clinical Nutrition* 1453
Rae AN and Strutt A, 'Livestock Production and the Environment: Some Impacts of Growth and Trade Liberalisation' (2001) 35 *New Zealand Economic Papers* 176
Rajamani L and Bodanksy D, 'Balancing International Prescriptiveness with National Discretion' (2019) *ICLQ* 68
Rajamani L, 'Ambition and Differentiation in the 2015 Paris Agreement: Interpretative Possibilities and Underlying Politics Shorter Articles and Notes' (2016) 65 *ICLQ* 493
Rajamani, L 'National "Fair Shares" in Reducing Greenhouse Gas Emissions within the Principled Framework of International Environmental Law' (2021) 21 *Climate Policy* 983
Rajamani, L 'The 2015 Paris Agreement: Interplay Between Hard, Soft and Non-obligations' (2016) 28 *Journal of Environmental Law* 22
Rasul G and Sharma B, 'The Nexus Approach to Water–Energy–Food Security: An Option for Adaptation to Climate Change' (2016) 16 *Climate Policy* 682
Rayner S, 'Uncomfortable Knowledge: The Social Construction of Ignorance in Science and Environmental Policy Discourses' (2012) 41 *Economy and Society* 107
Regan D, 'The Meaning of "Necessary" in GATT Article XX and GATS Artile XIV: The Myth' (2007) 6 *World Trade Review* 347
Revell B, 'Meat and Milk Consumption 2050: The Potential for Demand-Side Solutions to Greenhouse Gas Emissions Reduction' (2015) 14 *EuroChoices* 4
Rizzo NS et al, 'Nutrient Profiles of Vegetarian and Non Vegetarian Dietary Patterns' (2013) 113 *Journal of the Academy of Nutrition and Dietetics* 1610
Roberts CK et al, 'Effect of a Diet and Exercise Intervention on Oxidative Stress, Inflammation and Monocyte Adhesion in Diabetic Men' (2006) 73 *Diabetes Research and Clinical Practice* 249
Rodrigues M, 'Will Brazil's President Lula Keep His Climate Promises?' (2023) 613 *Nature* 420
Rodrigues R de AR et al, 'The Actions of the Brazilian Agricultural Sector in the Context of Climate Change Negotiations' (2019) 10 *Sustentabilidade em Debate* 28
Rodrigues, M, 'How Is Brazil's President Lula Doing on Climate? Experts Rate His Performance' (2023) 620 *Nature* 10.1038/d41586-023-02511-x
Rodríguez Fernández-Blanco C, Burns SL and Giessen L, 'Mapping the Fragmentation of the International Forest Regime Complex: Institutional Elements, Conflicts and Synergies' (2019) 19 *International Environmental Agreements: Politics, Law and Economics* 187
Romero C et al, 'Evaluation of the Impacts of Forest Stewardship Council (FSC) Certification of Natural Forest Management in the Tropics: A Rigorous Approach to Assessment of a Complex Conservation Intervention' (2017) 19 *International Forestry Review* 36.
Röös E et al, 'Greedy or Needy? Land Use and Climate Impacts of Food in 2050 under Different Livestock Futures' (2017) 47 *Global Environmental Change* 1
Rosegrant MW, 'Global Food Security: Challenges and Policies' (2003) 302 *Science* 1917
Sabel C, O'Donnell R and O'Connell L, 'Self Organization under Deliberate Direction: Irish Dairy and the Possibilities of a New Climate Change Regime' [Forthcoming] *Regulation and Governance*
Savaresi A, 'The Paris Agreement: A New Beginning?' (2016) 34 *Journal of Energy & Natural Resources Law* 16
Schepers D, 'Challenges to Legitimacy at the Forest Stewardship Council' (2010) 92 *Journal of Business Ethics* 279
Schmitz C, 'Agricultural Trade and Tropical Deforestation: Interactions and Related Policy Options' (2015) 15 *Regional Environmental Change* 1757

Schmitz C et al, 'Trading More Food: Implications for Land Use, Greenhouse Gas Emissions, and the Food System' (2012) 22 *Global Environmental Change* 189

Scott J, 'The Geographical Scope of the EU's Climate Responsibilities' (2015) 17 *Cambridge Yearbook of European Legal Studies* 92F

Shaffer G and Ginsburg T, 'The Empirical Turn in International Legal Scholarship' (2012) 106 *American Journal of International Law* 1

Shafik N, 'Economic Development and Environmental Quality: An Econometric Analysis' (1994) 46 *Oxford Economic Papers* 757

Sharma SK et al, 'Demystifying Blue Box Support to Agriculture Under the WTO: Implications for Developing Countries' (2021) 22 *South Asia Economic Journal* 161

Shen J et al, 'Does Migration of Pollution-Intensive Industries Impact Environmental Efficiency? Evidence Supporting "Pollution Haven Hypothesis"' (2019) 242 *Journal of Environmental Management* 142

Shimshack JP and Ward MB, 'Regulator Reputation, Enforcement, and Environmental Compliance' (2005) 50 *Journal of Environmental Economics and Management* 519

Shindell DT et al, 'Improved Attribution of Climate Forcing to Emissions' (2009) 326 *Science* 716

Siri-Tarino PW et al, 'Meta-analysis of Prospective Cohort Studies Evaluating the Association of Saturated Fat with Cardiovascular Disease' (2010) 91 *American Journal of Clinical* Nutrition 535

Smith F, 'Regulating Agriculture in the WTO' (2011) 7 *International Journal of Law in Context* 233

Smith P, Haberl H, Popp A et al. 'How Much Land-Based Greenhouse Gas Mitigation Can Be Achieved without Compromising Food Security and Environmental Goals' (2013) *Global Change Biology* 19

Smith P, Martino D, Cai Z et al 'Greenhouse Gas Mitigation in Agriculture' (2008) 363 *Philosophical Transactions of the Royal Society of London B: Biological Sciences* doi.org/10.1098/rstb.2007.2184

Solarin S et al, 'Investigating the Pollution Haven Hypothesis in Ghana: An Empirical Investigation' (2017) 124 *Energy* 706

Soto Golcher C and Visseren-Hamakers IJ, 'Framing and Integration in the Global Forest, Agriculture and Climate Change Nexus' (2018) 36 *Environment and Planning C: Politics and Space* 1415

Soto Golcher C, Arts B and Visseren-Hamakers I, 'Seeing the Forest, Missing the Field: Forests and Agriculture in Global Climate Change Policy' (2018) 77 *Land Use Policy* 627

Springmann M et al, 'Health-Motivated Taxes on Red and Processed Meat: A Modelling Study on Optimal Tax Levels and Associated Health Impacts' (2018) 13 *PLoS ONE* e0204139

Springmann M, et al, 'The Healthiness and Sustainability of National and Global Food Based Dietary Guidelines: Modelling Study' (2020) *British Medical Journal* 370

Stehfest E et al, 'Climate Benefits of Changing Diet' (2009) 95 *Climatic Change* 83

Switzer S, 'A Contract Theory Approach to Special and Differential Treatment and the WTO' (2017) 16 *Journal of International Trade Law and Policy* 126

Sykes AO, 'Regulatory Protectionism and the Law of International Trade' (1999) 66 *University of Chicago Law Review* 1

Torras M and Boyce J, 'Income, Inequality and Pollution' (1998) 25 *Ecological Economics* 147

van der Veen M, 'When Is Food a Luxury?' (2003) 34 *World Archaeology* 405

van Meijl H et al, 'The Impact of Different Policy Environments on Agricultural Land Use in Europe' (2006) 114 *European Agriculture Ecosystems Environment* 21

Van Zanten HHE et al, 'Defining a Land Boundary for Sustainable Livestock Consumption' (2018) 24 *Global Change Biology* 4185

Vasileiadou E, Heimeriks G and Petersen AC, 'Exploring the Impact of the IPCC Assessment Reports on Science' (2011) 14 *Environmental Science & Policy* 1052

Verburg R et al, 'The Effect of Agricultural Trade Liberalisation on Land-Use Related Greenhouse Gas Emissions' (2009) *Global Environmental Change* 13

Verschuuren J, 'The Paris Agreement on Climate Change: Agriculture and Food Security Mini-Symposium on the Paris Agreement on Climate Change' (2016) 7 *European Journal of Risk Regulation* 54

Villagrán-García EF et al, 'Introduction of Pasteurized/Raw Cow's Milk During the Second Semester of Life as a Risk Factor of Type 1 Diabetes Mellitus in School Children and Adolescents' (2015) 32 *Nutricion Hospitalaria* 634

Voigt C and Ferreira F, 'Dynamic Differentiation: The Principles of CBDR-RC, Progression and Highest Possible Ambition in the Paris Agreement' (2016) 5 *Transnational Environmental Law* 285
Voigt C and Ferreira F, 'The Warsaw Framework for REDD+: Implications for National Implementation and Access to Results-Based Finance' (2015) 9 *Carbon & Climate Law Review* 113
Vranken L et al, 'Curbing Global Meat Consumption: Emerging Evidence of a Second Nutrition Transition' (2014) 39 *Environmental Science & Policy* 95
Wheeler T and von Braun J, 'Climate Change Impacts on Global Food Security' (2013) 341 *Science* 508
Wiedmann T et al, 'Scientists' Warning on Affluence' (2020) 11 *Nature Communications* 3107
Willett W et al, 'Food in the Anthropocene: The EAT–Lancet Commission on Healthy Diets from Sustainable Food Systems' (2019) 393 *The Lancet* 447
Wollenberg E et al, 'Reducing Emissions from Agriculture to Meet the 2 °C Target' (2016) 22 *Global Change Biology* 3859
Zahar A, 'Agricultural Exceptionalism in the Climate Change Treaties' (2023) 12 *Transnational Environmental Law* 42
Zeitlin J and Overdevest C, 'Experimentalist Interactions: Joining Up the Transnational Timber Legality Regime' (2021) 15 *Regulation & Governance* 686.
Zhang B et al, 'Consumption-Based Accounting of Global Anthropogenic CH_4 Emissions' (2018) 6 *Earth's Future* 1349
Zheng D and Shi M, 'Multiple Environmental Policies and Pollution Haven Hypothesis: Evidence from China's Polluting Industries' (2017) 141 *Journal of Cleaner Production* 295

Reports and Policy Papers

Abaza H et al, *Trade and Climate Change: A Report by the United Nations Environment Programme and the World Trade Organization* (WTO-UNEP, 2009)
Argentina, 'Nationally Determined Contribution – Argentina' (Government of Argentina, 2021) https://unfccc.int/sites/default/files/NDC/2022-05/Traduccio%CC%81n%20NDC_Argentina.pdf
Barth E et al, 'Risk Management Evaluation for Concentrated Animal Feeding Operations' (Office of Research & Development, 2004) EPA/600/R-04/042
Benton TG et al, *Food System Impacts on Biodiversity Loss* (Chatham House, 2021)
Brazil Ministry of Environment, 'National Strategy for Reducing Emissions from Deforestation and Forest Degradation, and the Role of Conservation of Forest Carbon Stocks, Sustainable Management of Forests and Enhancement of Forest Carbon Stocks' (Brazilian Government, 2016) https://redd.unfccc.int/files/brazil_national_redd__strategy.pdf
Brazil Ministry of Foreign Affairs and Ministry of Science, Technology, Innovations and Communications, 'Brazil's Third Biennial Report to the UNFCCC' (Brazilian Government, 2019)
Brice J, The Relation between Different Zoonotic Pandemics and the Livestock Sector (Policy Department of Economic, Scientific and Quality of Life Policies, 2021)
Bruinsma J and FAO, *World Agriculture: Towards 2015/2030 : An FAO Study* (FAO, 2017)
Buto O et al, *Climate Finance in the Agriculture and Land Use Sector – Global and Regional Trends between 2000 and 2018* (FAO, 2021)
CAP Health Check – Impact Assessment Note No 2 (2008)
Cappellini OR, *Dairy Development in Argentina* (FAO, 2011)
Caroline Chaumont TCS, *Towards Zero Hunger and Sustainability* (FAO, 2017) http://www.fao.org/documents/card/en/c/fa6a801c-5bd4-4522-a2ff-bfbef1e56529/
Charlton A, *The Collapse of the Doha Trade Round* (Centrepiece, 2006)
Chiriacò MV et al, *Koronivia Joint Work on Agriculture: Analysis of Submissions* (FAO, 2018)
Climate Action Network International Ad Hoc Legal Working Group, 'COP Decisions: Binding or Not?' (CAN International, 2009)
Colchester M, *Do Commodity Certification Systems Uphold Indigenous Peoples' Rights? Lessons from the Roundtable on Sustainable Palm Oil and Forest Stewardship Council* (IUCN, 2016)

Costa Rica, 'Contribución Nacionalmente Determinada de Costa Rica 2020' (Costa Rica, 2020)
Council of the EU, 'Submission to the UNFCCC on behalf of the European Union and its Member States on the update of the nationally determined contribution of the European Union and its Member States' [2023] 14222/1/20
Counsell S and Loraas KT, *Trading in Credibility: The Myth and Reality of the Forest Stewardship Council* (Rainforest Foundation, 2002)
Daniel B, 'Paris Agreement' (UN Audiovisual Library of International Law, 2015)
Diakosavvas D, 'The Greening of the WTO Green Box: A Quantitative Appraisal of Agri-environmental Policies in OECD Countries' (IATRC Symposium, Italy, 23–26 June 2003)
EUCourt of Auditors, 'Making Cross-compliance More Effective and Achieving Simplification Remains Challenging' (EU Court of Auditors, 2016)
EU Court of Auditors, 'Special Report: Common Agricultural Policy and Climate: Half of EU Climate Spending but Farm Emissions Are Not Decreasing' (EU Court of Auditors, 2021) Special Report 16
European Commission, 'List of Potential Agricultural Practices that Eco-Schemes Could Support' (European Commission, 2021)
FAO, *The State of Food and Agriculture* (FAO, 2009)
FAO, *The Technology of Traditional Milk Products in Developing Countries* (FAO, 1990)
FAO and UNEP, *The State of the World's Forests 2020: Forests, Biodiversity and People* (FAO and UNEP, 2020)
FAO Animal Production and Health Division, *Farmer Field Schools for Small-Scale Livestock Producers: A Guide for Decision Makers on Improving Livelihood* (FAO, 2018)
FAO Legal and Ethics Office, 'International Regulatory Co-operation and International Organisations: The Case of the Food and Agriculture Organization of the United Nations (FAO)' (OECD/FAO, 2016)
FAO Regional Office for Asia and the Pacific, 'Dairy Asia: Towards Sustainability' (FAO, 2014)
FAO Regional Office for Asia and the Pacific, 'Smallholder Dairy Development: Lessons Learned in Asia' (FAO, 2009)
FAO, 'Africa Sustainable Livestock 2050: Technical Meeting and Regional Launch, Addis Ababa, Ethiopia, 21–23 February 2017' (FAO, 2017)
FAO, *Dairy Development for the Resource Poor Part 1: A Comparison of Dairy Policies and Development in South Asia and East Africa* (FAO, 2008)
FAO, *Dairy Development for the Resource Poor Part 2: Kenya and Ethiopia Dairy Development Case Studies* (FAO, 2008)
FAO, *Dairy Development for the Resource Poor Part 3: Pakistan and India Dairy Development Case Studies* (FAO, 2008)
FAO, *Dairy Development Programs in Andhra Pradesh, India: Impacts and Risks for Small-Scale Dairy Farms* (FAO, 2006)
FAO, *Developing Countries and the Global Dairy Sector Part II: Country Case Studies* (FAO, 2006)
FAO, *Developing Sustainable Value Chains for Small-Scale Livestock Producers* (FAO, 2019)
FAO, *Environmental Performance of Feed Additives in Livestock Supply Chains. Guidelines for Assessment: Version 1* (FAO, 2020)
FAO, *Environmental Performance of Pig Supply Chains: Guidelines for Assessment (Version 1): Livestock Environmental Assessment and Performance Partnership* (FAO, 2018)
FAO, *FAO Success Stories on Climate-Smart Agriculture* (FAO, undated)
FAO, *FAO's Work with Small Island Developing States* (FAO, 2019)
FAO, *Five Practical Actions towards Low-Carbon Livestock* (FAO, 2019)
FAO, *From Reference Levels to Results Reporting: REDD+ under the United Nations Framework Convention on Climate Change* (FAO 2020)
FAO, 'Greenhouse Gas Emissions from Agrifood Systems' (FAOSTAT Analytical Brief 50, FAO, 2022)
FAO, 'Koronivia Joint Work on Agriculture – Summary of Workshop on Topic 2(f): Socio-economic and Food Security Dimensions of Climate Change in the Agricultural Sector' (FAO, 2021)

FAO, 'Koronivia Joint Work on Agriculture – Summary of Workshop on Topic 2(c) : Improved Soil Carbon, Soil Health and Soil Fertility under Grassland and Cropland as Well as Integrated Systems, Including Water Management' (FAO, 2020)

FAO, 'Koronivia Joint Work on Agriculture – Summary of Workshop on Topic 2(d) : Improved Nutrient Use and Manure Management towards Sustainable and Resilient Agricultural Systems' (FAO, 2020)

FAO, 'Koronivia Joint Work on Agriculture Analysis of Submissions on Topic 2(d)' (FAO, 2020)

FAO, *Livestock Solutions for Climate Change* (FAO, 2017)

FAO, *Reducing Emissions Intensity and Improving Natural Resources Management through Livestock in Natural Grasslands in Uruguay* (FAO, 2020)

FAO, *Strategic Framework 2010–2019* (FAO, 2009)

FAO, *The Role of Agriculture in the Development of the Least Developed Countries and their Integration into the World Economy* (FAO, 2002)

FAO, *The Economics of Milk Production in Cajamarca, Peru, with Particular Emphasis on Small-Scale Producers* (FAO, 2006)

FAO, *The Economics of Milk Production in Chiang Mai, Thailand, with Particular Emphasis on Small-Scale Producers* (FAO, 2005)

FAO, *The Economics of Milk Production in Hanoi, Vietnam, with Particular Emphasis on Small-Scale Producers* (FAO, 2006)

FAO, *Ukraine: Improving Milk Supply in Northern Ukraine : Technical Assistance to Ukraine's Dairy Sector* (FAO, 2013)

FAO, *World Livestock: Transforming the Livestock Sector through the Sustainable Development Goals* (FAO, 2018)

FAO, Animal Production and Health Division, *Shaping the Future of Livestock; Sustainably, Responsibly, Efficiently* (FAO, 2018)

FAO, Global Dairy Platform, IFCN Dairy Research Network, *Dairy's Impact on Reducing Global Hunger* (FAO, 2020)

FAO and CCAC, *Options for Low Emission Development in the Bangladesh Dairy Sector* (FAO, 2020)

FAO and CCAC, *Options for Low Emission Development in the Sri Lanka Dairy Sector* (FAO, 2017)

FAO and CCAC, *Options for Low-Emission Development in the Kenya Dairy Sector* (FAO, 2017)

FAO, IFAD, UNICEF, EFP and WHO, *The State of Food Security and Nutrition in the World 2023* (FAO, 2023)

Filho BS et al, *Challenges for Low-Carbon Agriculture and Forest Conservation in Brazil* (Inter-American Development Bank, 2012)

Fischer G, Shah MM and van Velthuizen HT, 'Climate Change and Agricultural Vulnerability' (International Institute for Applied Systems Analysis, 2002)

G20 Parties, 'Review and Clarification of Green Box Criteria' (Institute for Agriculture and Trade Policy, 2005)

Gerber PJ et al, *Tackling Climate Change through Livestock: A Global Assessment of Emissions and Mitigation Opportunities* (FAO, 2013)

Global Agenda for Sustainable Livestock, *Towards Sustainable Livestock* (GASL, 2014)

Goldman E et al, *Estimating the Role of Seven Commodities in Agriculture-Linked Deforestation: Oil Palm, Soy, Cattle, Wood Fiber, Cocoa, Coffee, and Rubber* (WRI, 2020)

Gonzalez Fischer C and Garnett T, *Plates, Pyramids, Planet: Developments in National Healthy and Sustainable Dietary Guidelines: A State of Play Assessment* (FAO, 2016)

Green D and Griffith M, *Dumping on the Poor: The Common Agricultural Policy, the WTO and International Development* (CAFOD, 2005)

Greenpeace, *Eating Up the Amazon* (Greenpeace, 2006)

Halderman M and Nelson M, 'EU Policy Making: Reform of the CAP and EU Trade in Beef and Dairy with Developing Countries' (Working Paper No 18, Pro Poor Livestock Policy Initiative, undated)

Hallaert J-J, 'Special Agricultural Safeguards: Virtual Benefits and Real Costs – Lessons for the Doha Round' (IMF Working Paper WP.05/131, 2005)

Havlík P et al, 'Climate Change Impacts and Mitigation in the Developing World: An Integrated Assessment of the Agriculture and Forestry Sectors' (World Bank, 2015) 7477

Healy S et al, 'An Overview of the Negotiations on Agriculture' in *The implications of the Uruguay Round Agreement on Agriculture for Developing Countries: A Training Manual* (FAO, 1998)

Hoekman B and Mavroidis PC, 'Burning Down the House? The Appellate Body in the Centre of the WTO Crisis' (Colombia Law School Faculty Publications, 2019)

Houzer, E, and Scoones I, *Are Livestock Always Bad for the Planet? Rethinking the Protein Transition and Climate Change Debates* (PASTRES, 2021).

Hristov AN, *Mitigation of Greenhouse Gas Emissions in Livestock Production – A Review of Technical Options for Non-CO2 Emissions* (FAO, 2013)

IMF Staff, 'Global Trade Liberalization and Developing Countries' (IMF Issues Brief, IMF, 2001)

Independent High-Level Expert Group on Climate Finance, 'Finance for Climate Action: Scaling Up Investment for Climate and Development (IHELG, 2022).

IPCC, 'Summary for Policymaker' in TF Stocket et al, *Climate Change 2013: The Physical Science Basis. Contribution of Working Group I to the Fifth Assessment Report of the Intergovernmental Panel on Climate Change* (Cambridge University Press, 2013).

Jevinger R, *Growing the Good: The Case for Low-Carbon Transition in the Food Sector* (Changing Markets Foundation, Mighty Earth, Compassion in World Farming, 2018)

Kalfagianni A and Duyck, S, *The Evolving Role of Agriculture in Climate Change Negotiations: Progress and Players* (CCAFS, 2015)

Margulis S, *Causes of Deforestation of the Brazilian Amazon* (World Bank, 2004)

Marin Duran G and Scott J, 'Reducing the European Union's Global Deforestation Footprint through Trade Regulation' (EUI Working Paper, European University Institute, 2021) https://cadmus.eui.eu/handle/1814/73189

Mary B (ed), 'Agricultural Policy Reform in the WTO – The Road Ahead' (Agricultural Economic Report No 802, Market and Trade Economics Division, Economic Research Service, US Department of Agriculture, 2001)

Mbow C et al, 'Food Security' in PR Shukla et al, *Climate Change and Land: An IPCC Special Report on Climate Change, Desertification, Land Degradation, Sustainable Land Management, Food Security, and Greenhouse Gas Fluxes in Terrestrial Ecosystems* (IPCC, 2019)

McCarney GR and Adamowicz WL, 'The Effects of Trade Liberalization on the Environment: An Empirical Study' (Annual Meeting, Canadian Agricultural Economics Society, 2005).

Meredith S, *Guide to Eco-Schemes in the New CAP: Opportunities and Challenges for Managing Authorities* (IEEP, 2020)

Mitra S and Josling T, 'Agricultural Export Restrictions: Welfare Implications and Trade Disciplines' (IPC Position Paper, International Food and Agricultural Trade Policy Council, 2009)

Mottershead D et al, 'Evaluation Study of the Impact of the CAP on Climate Change and Greenhouse Emissions' (EU Commission, 2019)

Mukhtar A, *Policy Space for Sustainable Agriculture in the World Trade Organization Agreement on Agriculture* (FAO, 2020)

Muller A and Bautze L, *Agriculture and Deforestation: The EU Common Agricultural Policy, Soy, and Forest Destruction: Proposals for Reform* (Fern, 2017)

Müller C, 'Brazil and the Amazon Rainforest: Deforestation, Biodiversity and Cooperation with the EU and International Forums' (Policy Department for Economic, Scientific and Quality of Life Policies, European Parliament, 2020)

Muriuki HG, *Dairy Development in Kenya* (FAO, 2011)

Murphy S, Lilliston B and Lake M, *WTO Agreement on Agriculture: A Decade of Dumping* (Institute of Agriculture and Trade Policy, 2005) 4

OECD, *The Uruguay Round Agreement on Agriculture: An Evaluation of Its Implementation in OECD Countries* (OECD, 2001)

OECD, *Global Plastics Outlook: Economic Drivers, Environmental Impacts and Policy Options* (OECD, 2022)

Oliveira Pires M et al, *Implementing Prevention and Control Policies for Reducing Deforestation* (International Partnership on Mitigation and MRV, undated)

Pauw P and Mbeva K, *Self-differentiation of countries' Responsibilities: Addressing Climate Change through Intended Nationally Determined Contributions* (Deutsches Institut für Entwicklungspolitik, 2016).

Pauw P et al (eds), *Different Perspectives on Differentiated Responsibilities: A State-of-the-Art Review of the Notion of Common but Differentiated Responsibilities in International Negotiations* (Deutsches Institut für Entwicklungspolitik, 2014)

Pauwelyn J, 'US Federal Climate Policy and Competitiveness Concerns: The Limits and Options of International Trade Law' (NI WP 07(02), Nicholas Institute Working Paper, 2007)

Pica-Ciamarra U et al, *Livestock Sector Policies and Programmes in Developing Countries A Menu for Practitioners* (Pro-Poor Livestock Policy Initiative, 2010)

Pica-Ciamarra U et al, *Livestock Assets, Livestock Income and Rural Households* (FAO, 2011)

Randrup C, 'Evaluating the Effects of Colonialism on Deforestation in Madagascar: A Social and Environmental History' (Thesis, Oberlin College, 2010) Honors Papers 390, https://digitalcommons.oberlin.edu/honors/390

Reeves T et al, *Save and Grow in Practice: Maize, Rice, Wheat* (FAO, 2016)

Runge C et al, 'Liberal Agricultural Trade as a Public Good: Free Trade vs Free Riding under GATT' (University of Minnesota Staff Paper Series, 1987)

Runge CF, *Environmental Effects of Trade in the Agricultural Sector; A Case Study* (Center for International Food and Agricultural Policy, 1992)

Schneider F, 'Statement by GASL on the EAT-Lancet Commission Report' (Global Agenda for Sustainable Livestock, 2019)

Steinfeld H et al, *Livestock's Long Shadow: Environmental Issues and Options* (FAO, 2006)

Strohmaier R et al, 'The Agriculture Sectors in the Intended Nationally Determined Contributions – Analysis' (Environment and Natural Resources Working Paper No 62, FAO 2016)

Stuart L and Riechert T, *Green but Not Clean: Why a Comprehensive Review of Green Box Subsidies Is Necessary* (Action Aid, Caritas, CIDSE, Oxfam 2005)

Study Group of the International Law Commission, 'Fragmentation of International Law: Difficulties Arising from the Diversification and Expansion of International Law' (A/CN.4/L.682, ILC, 2006)

Switzer S and et al, 'Equity in Global Health Law – Policy Brief' (Scottish Council for Global Affairs, ESRC IAA Policy Impact Fund 2023)

Taher SM, *Dairy Development in Morocco* (FAO, 2011)

UN, *Inequality – Bridging the Divide* (United Nations, undated)

UNEP, *Emissions Gap Report 2020* (United Nations, 2021)

UNFCCC Adaptation Committee, *25 Years of Adaptation under the UNFCCC* (UNFCCC, 2019)

UNFCCC Secretariat, 'Socioeconomic and Food Security Dimensions of Climate Change in the Agricultural Sector Workshop Report by the Secretariat: Workshop Report' (FCCC/SB/2021/2, UN, 2021)

USDA Foreign Agricultural Service, *Dairy: World Markets and Trade* (USDA, 2018)

USDA Foreign Agricultural Service, *Livestock and Poultry: World Markets and Trade* (USDA, 2018)

von Grebmer, K et al, *2019 Global Hunger Index: the Challenge of Hunger and Climate Change* (Global Hunger Index, 2019)

Wageningen University et al, 'Research for Agri Committee – The EU Cattle Sector: Challenges and Opportunities – Milk and Meat' (European Parliament, 2017)

Wellesley L, Happer C and Froggatt A, *Changing Climate, Changing Diets: Pathways to Lower Meat Consumption* (Chatham House, 2015)

World Bank, *World Development Report 1992: Development and the Environment* (World Bank, 1992)

World Health Organization, *Initiative on Climate Action and Nutrition (I-CAN)* (WHO, 2022)

World Trade Organization, *Making Trade Work for the Environment, Prosperity and Resilience* (WTO, 2018)

WWF, *Unlocking and Scaling Climate Solutions in Food Systems: An Assessment of Nationally Determined Contributions* (WWF, 2022)

Websites and Online Sources

About FAO, http://www.fao.org/about/en/

AQUASTAT, www.fao.org/land-water/databases-and-software/aquastat/en/

COWSPIRACY: The Sustainability Secret, www.cowspiracy.com

FAOSTAT, http://www.fao.org/faostat/en/#home/

FAST Initiativ,' http://example.com/index.htm

FSC-Certified Wood and Products Fetch Higher Prices, https://fsc.org/en/newsfeed/fsc-certified-wood-and-products-fetch-higher-prices

Global Livestock Environmental Assessment Model (GLEAM), http://www.fao.org/gleam/en/

High Level Conference, www.fao.org/foodclimate/hlc-home/en/

Paris Agreement – Status of Ratification, https://unfccc.int/process/the-paris-agreement/status-of-ratification

SDG Indicators Data Portal, http://www.fao.org/sdg-progress-report/en/

The 10 FSC Principles, www.fsc-uk.org:443/en-uk/about-fsc/what-is-fsc/fsc-principles

WTO Trade and Environment – WTO and the Challenge of Climate Change, www.wto.org/english/tratop_e/envir_e/climate_challenge_e.htm

CCA Coalition, 'Global Methane Pledge', www.ccacoalition.org/sites/default/files/resources//Global%20Methane%20Pledge.pdf

Conniff R, 'Greenwashed Timber: How Sustainable Forest Certification Has Failed' (*Yale E360*, 2018) https://e360.yale.edu/features/greenwashed-timber-how-sustainable-forest-certification-has-failed

FAO 'Climate-Smart Agriculture Sourcebook', www.fao.org/climate-smart-agriculture-sourcebook/en/

FAO, 'GLEAM in Practice', http://www.fao.org/gleam/in-practice/en/

Gallagher S, 'The EAT Lancet Diet: New Findings' (Friedman School of Nutrition Science and Policy, 2019) https://nutrition.tufts.edu/news/eat-lancet-diet-new-findings

Hansen-Kuhn K and Murphy S 'The Costs of Agricultural Export Dumping for Farmers and Rural Communities' (IATP, 2019) www.iatp.org/documents/costs-agricultural-export-dumping-farmers-and-rural-communities

Lang C, 'Norway's Support for REDD: The New Colonialism and the Failure of Democracy' (REDD-Monitor, 2019) https://redd-monitor.org/2019/01/08/norways-support-for-redd-the-new-colonialism-and-the-failure-of-democracy/

Newton J, 'Change on the Horizon for the Conservation Reserve Program?' (American Farm Bureau Federation, undated) www.fb.org/market-intel/usda-resumes-conservation-reserve-program-enrollment

Office of the Spokesperson, 'Global Methane Pledge: From Moment to Momentum – United States Department of State' (Global Methane Pledge, 2022) www.state.gov/global-methane-pledge-from-moment-to-momentum/

Ritchie H and Roser M, 'Meat and Dairy Production' (Our World in Data, 2017) https://ourworldindata.org/meat-production

Ritchie, H 'Ocean Plastics: How Much Do Rich Countries Contribute by Shipping Their Waste Overseas?' (Our World in Data, 2022) https://ourworldindata.org/plastic-waste-trade

So A 'Power, Access & Influence: Which Food Organisations Participated at COP27?' (Food Research Collaboration, 2022) https://foodresearch.org.uk/blogs/power-access-influence-which-food-organisations-participated-at-cop27/

Staff CB, 'COP27: Key Outcomes for Food, Forests, Land and Nature at the UN Climate Talks in Egypt', *Carbon Brief*, 24 November 2022, www.carbonbrief.org/cop27-key-outcomes-for-food-forests-land-and-nature-at-the-un-climate-talks-in-egypt/

Statista, 'Europe: Vegetarianism & Veganism among Young Adults 2021' (Statista, 2021) www.statista.com/statistics/768475/vegetarianism-and-veganism-among-young-adults-in-selected-european-countries/

UNFCCC, 'ETF Reference Manual for the Enhanced Transparency Framework under the Paris Agreement: Understanding the enhanced transparency framework and its linkages' (UNFCCC Secretariat, 2022) https://unfccc.int/sites/default/files/resource/ETFReferenceManual.pdf

Union of Concerned Scientists, 'The Importance of Brazil's Cerrado' (Union of Concerned Scientists, 2016) www.ucsusa.org/sites/default/files/attach/2016/11/cerrado-fact-sheet-ucs-october-2016.pdf

Wei H, 'It's the Year of the Ox, So Where's the Beef?', *#SixthTone*, 11 February 2021, www.sixthtone.com/news/1006796

WTO, 'Explanation of the Agreement – Domestic Support' (undated) www.wto.org/english/tratop_e/agric_e/ag_intro03_domestic_e.htm

WTO, 'Tenth WTO Ministerial Conference – Nairobi' (WTO Briefing Note, 2015) www.wto.org/english/thewto_e/minist_e/mc10_e/briefing_notes_e/brief_agriculture_e.htm

Wyatt S et al, 'Great Power Resource Competition in a Changing Climate New America's Natural Security Index' (New America, 2019) www.newamerica.org/resource-security/reports/great-power-resource-competition-changing-climate/

News Items

Associated Press, 'Brazil's Lula Lays out Plan to Halt Amazon Deforestation', *Politico*, 6 June 2023, www.politico.com/news/2023/06/06/brazils-lula-lays-out-plan-to-halt-amazon-deforestation-00100342

Bronstein H and Heath M, 'Argentina Cuts Soy Export Tax Rate in Bid to Boost FX Reserves', Reuters, 3 October 2020, https://uk.reuters.com/article/us-argentina-grains-taxes-idUKKBN26N03R

Bryce E, 'First Steps Agreed on Plastics Treaty after Breakthrough at Paris Talks', *The Guardian*, 2023, www.theguardian.com/environment/2023/jun/06/first-steps-agreed-on-plastics-treaty-after-breakthrough-at-paris-talks

Buxton A, 'COP27, World's Largest Climate Crisis Conference, Sparks Controversy After Serving Meat', *Plant Based News*, 12 November 2022) https://plantbasednews.org/news/environment/cop27-climate-crisis-conference-serving-meat/

Fahy, G and Baczynska G, 'EU Piles Pressure on Brazil over Amazon Fires', *Reuters*, 23 August 2019, https://uk.reuters.com/article/uk-eu-mercosur-ireland-idUKKCN1VD0PV

Fearnside, P, 'Will President Bolsonaro Withdraw Brazil from the Paris Agreement? (Commentary)', *Mongabay News*, 31 January 2019, https://news.mongabay.com/2019/01/commentary-will-president-bolsonaro-withdraw-brazil-from-the-paris-agreement/

Kuo L '"Operation Empty Plate": Xi Jinping Makes Food Waste his Next Target', *The Guardian*, 2020, www.theguardian.com/world/2020/aug/13/operation-empty-plate-xi-jinping-makes-food-waste-his-next-target

Marques K and Fernandes T 'Bolsonaro Requested Not to Hold Climate Summit in Brazil', *Folha*, 2018, www1.folha.uol.com.br/internacional/en/brazil/2018/11/bolsonaro-requested-not-to-hold-climate-summit-in-brazil.shtml

Paraguassu L, 'Brazil's Lula Unveils Plan to Stop Deforestation in Amazon by 2030', 5 June *Reuters*, 2023, www.reuters.com/world/americas/brazils-lula-launches-plan-stop-deforestation-amazon-by-2030-2023-06-05/

Phillips T, 'Amazon Deforestation Surges to 12-Year High under Bolsonaro', *The Guardian*, 1 December 2020, www.theguardian.com/environment/2020/dec/01/amazon-deforestation-surges-to-12-year-high-under-bolsonaro

Reuters Staff, 'Brazil Agriculture Minister Calls Amazon Soy Moratorium "Absurd"', *Reuters*, 13 November 2019, www.reuters.com/article/us-brazil-soy-moratorium-idUSKBN1XN2LM

Reuters Staff, 'Brazil Foreign Minister Says "There Is No Climate Change Catastrophe"', *Reuters*, 11 September 2019, https://uk.reuters.com/article/us-brazil-environment-araujo/brazil-foreign-minister-says-there-is-no-climate-change-catastrophe-idUKKCN1VW2S2

Rocha J, 'Bolsonaro Government Reveals Plan to Develop the "Unproductive Amazon"', *Mongabay Environmental News*, 28 January 2019 https://news.mongabay.com/2019/01/bolsonaro-government-reveals-plan-to-develop-the-unproductive-amazon/

Samora R, 'Brazil Farmers Push Traders to End Amazon Soy Moratorium', *Reuters*, 5 November 2019, https://uk.reuters.com/article/us-brazil-soybeans-moratorium-idUKKBN1XF2J6

Stone J, 'Emmanuel Macron Says He Will Block EU Trade Deal with Brazil over Amazon Forest Fires', *The Independent*, 23 August 2019, www.independent.co.uk/news/world/europe/macron-amazon-forest-fires-veto-mercosur-eu-trade-deal-brazil-a9076181.html

UN Climate Press Office 'COP27 Reaches Breakthrough Agreement on New "Loss and Damage" Fund for Vulnerable Countries' (UNFCCC, 2022) https://unfccc.int/news/cop27-reaches-breakthrough-agreement-on-new-loss-and-damage-fund-for-vulnerable-countries

INDEX

www.ingramcontent.com/pod-product-compliance
Ingram Content Group UK Ltd.
Pitfield, Milton Keynes, MK11 3LW, UK
UKHW020812290926
15470UKWH00003B/1103

9 781509 968589